CARE, COMMUNITIES AND CITIZENS

Care, Communities and Citizens

Marian Barnes

LONGMAN
London and New York

Addison Wesley Longman Limited,
Edinburgh Gate, Harlow,
Essex CM20 2JE, England
and Associated Companies throughout the world.

Published in the United States of America
by Addison Wesley Longman Inc., New York

© Addison Wesley Longman Limited 1997

The right of Marian Barnes to be identified as the author of this
Work has been asserted by her in accordance
with the Copyright, Designs and Patents Act 1988.

First published 1997

ISBN 0 582 25129X PPR

British Library Cataloguing-in-Publication Data

A catalogue record for this book is
available form the British Library

Library of Congress Cataloging-in-Publication Data

Barnes, Marian.
  Care, communities, and citizens / Marian Barnes.
    p. cm.
  Includes bibliographical references and index.
  ISBN 0-582-25129-X (ppr)
  1. Handicapped—Care—Government policy—Great Britain.
  2. Handicapped—Services for—Great Britain—Citizen participation.
  3. Aged—Care—Government policy—Great Britain. 4. Aged—Services
for—Great Britain—Citizen participation. 5. Community health
services—Great Britain. 6. Caregivers—Great Britain. 7. Great
Britain—Social policy. I. Title.
  HV1559.G7B37 1997
  362'.0425—dc20
                                            96-30249
                                                CIP

Set by 7 in 10/11 times
Produced through Longman Malaysia, TCP

CONTENTS

PREFACE

The subject of this book is community care. That apparently simple statement conceals substantial scope for dispute and confusion about what the content might actually be: ask a community nurse; a psychogeriatrician; a home care assistant; a disabled person; a social services planner; a Conservative politician or the parent of an adult son or daughter with learning difficulties 'what is community care?', and the responses are likely to demonstrate not only differences of content, but also considerable differences in attitude towards it.

Richard Titmuss was one of the earliest analysts to comment on the qualities with which the term was invested, at the same time as the ambiguity and uncertainty of its content:

> We are all familiar with the exotic hot-house climbing rose, 'The Welfare State', with its lovely hues of tender pink and blushing red, rampant and rampaging all over the place, often preventing people from 'standing on their own feet' in their own gardens. And what of the everlasting cottage-garden trailer 'Community Care'? Does it not conjure up a sense of warmth and human kindness, essentially personal and comforting, as loving as the wild flowers so enchantingly described by Lawrence in *Lady Chatterley's Lover*?
>
> (Titmuss, 1973, p. 104)

This book is about the way in which community care has come to be defined as a key social policy in the late twentieth century. The passage of the 1990 National Health Service and Community Care Act can be considered as a 'defining moment' in the acceptance of care within communities as the preferred way of meeting the needs of older people, those with mental health problems or learning difficulties, and of disabled people. However, in discussing the way in which that act defined 'community care' I demonstrate that this was a policy which was not and could not be implemented solely by means of action taken within the agencies of the welfare state. Since community care is as much about private lives as it is about public policy, the book is centrally concerned with the way in which the policy is experienced by those who use community care services and by members of their families who support them.

The social exclusion of many of those who are the 'objects' of community care policy is not solely a function of social policy, but also of public attitudes and of social organisation. Thus the book describes the way in which service users and carers have developed their own organisations to support each other, challenge their exclusion, exert influence over services provided from within the welfare state, and to become the 'subjects' of their own lives. The book is also about the new types of relationship which have been developing between users, carers and statutory services during the final two decades of the twentieth century, and considers the implications of these developments for future community care policy, how and by whom it might be delivered. I do not believe it is possible to reach an understanding of community care as either a policy or practice without also understanding the nature of 'community' and of 'care'. Martin Bulmer addressed both concepts in his book *The Social Basis of Community Care* (Bulmer, 1987). He warned in the preface to that book:

in significant respects, 'community care' policies rest upon fallacious common sense assumptions which are wrongly presented by policy-makers as sociological truths. As a result there is a vacuum at the heart of care policy which is likely to lead to ineffective or deteriorating provision of services, to the extent that care is transferred to 'the community'. Everyone interested in 'community care', whether as student, practitioner or citizen, needs to be aware that this vacuum is being created.

(*ibid*., p. ix)

Subsequent events suggest that Bulmer's warning was not heeded. As I demonstrate in Chapter 1, there is little evidence that the policy makers who shaped the legislation to define the financial and agency responsibilities through which community care was to be delivered in the UK, and the outcomes which the policy was intended to achieve, had considered the nature of communities in which and through which the policy was to be implemented. Scandals of neglect and violence considered to result from failures of the policy have been explained as resulting from people 'falling through the net' of services. Bulmer's cautionary notes about the possibility of 'interweaving' formal and informal care are highly pertinent in this respect. The holes in the net are usually considered to occur at those places where care and responsibilities transfer from one part of the system to another. But if such points of contact are not well understood, weaknesses at these points are inevitable.

In addressing questions about the current state and future develop-ment of community care in this book I am concerned not with the preoccupations of social administration – the organisational, financial and professional means through which social policy is delivered – but with sociological questions relating to how concepts of care and community are being interpreted through community care policy. In addressing these questions ten years after Bulmer, there is a vital additional perspective to draw on in such an analysis. The self-organisation of community care service users, and members of their family and friendship networks who have been constructed as their carers, has not only resulted in a new source of influence on the planning and management of services. They are also leading to a re-assessment of the meaning and significance of both 'care' and 'communities'. Some sections of the disability movement reject the centrality of care and assert instead the priority of citizenship rights. User groups themselves offer examples of 'communities of identity' acting as a source of support and care which their members have not found in communities of locality. Thus an important purpose of this book is to explore both the policy and conceptual developments indicated by the development of user movements.

At the same time as community care policy has moved centre stage within the health and social care arena, more general changes in the management of public services have created a different set of tensions within the relationship between those working in and those using community care services. Very broadly, the issue can be understood as a question of the relevance of a consumerist model of public service to community care. This is an issue which I and others have addressed elsewhere (e.g. Barnes and Prior, 1995; Wistow and Barnes, 1993) but which will, of necessity, reappear in the argument which I am developing in this book.

This book represents the culmination of work which I have been doing over a number of years, I draw heavily on research in which I have been involved, usually working with co-researchers and/or workers and service users involved in community care projects. My understanding of this subject area owes much to those with whom I have worked in a variety of capacities and I am glad to acknowledge their contribution to this. Some are acknowledged through being named in references, but many are anonymous interviewees or members of groups who have worked with me and with whom I have had discussions. I am no less grateful to them than to those who are named. I also draw on research conducted by others and hope that they will not be dismayed by the use to which I have put it. Once the results of our endeavours enter the public sphere we lose control over the direction they take. But we also hope that they will not simply rest unnoticed and I have referred to the ideas of others which have also enabled me to develop my understanding and thinking. The third major source of material for this book is that which comes directly from within user and carer movements. The development of this type of material is evidence of the way in which users and carers are contributing to the debate about community care beyond the negotiations taking place between advocates and professionals, and between user group representatives and officer members of planning groups. Its presence here is intended to reinforce my argument about the transformative potential of user and carer movements.

The structure of the book is as follows: Chapter 1 traces the development of community care policy from its post-war beginnings to the passage and implementation of the 1990 NHS and Community

Care Act. In Chapter 2, I consider the significance of the introduction of market principles for the recasting of people making use of health and social care services as 'consumers'. I also consider responses to such developments which have sought to offer alternative formulations of the role of citizens in determining the nature of services and how they should be provided. Chapter 3 discusses the growth of self-organisation among users of health and social care services and starts to consider how this relates to new understandings of both community and citizenship, and Chapter 4 discusses action from within welfare bureaucracies intended to enhance the influence of service users. In Chapters 5 and 6, I turn to the position of family carers. Chapter 5 discusses self-organisation among carers, while Chapter 6 considers the triangular relationship between family care providers, care receivers and statutory services. In the final two chapters, I take a broader view of community care policy and of the governance of public services to consider what implications these have for communities and citizens.

ACKNOWLEDGEMENTS

I am grateful to Mary Langan and Lorna Warren for helpful comments on a draft of this book; to David Prior, as ever the source of constructive criticism, useful ideas and more material sustenance; and to Jo Campling for her belief and support throughout. In the later stages of this work I have made reference to research funded by the ESRC as part of their 'Local Governance' programme, award no. L311253025.

CHAPTER 1

The origins of community care policy

In 1990 the Conservative Government in the UK passed the National Health Service and Community Care Act. The passage of this act followed a series of government-commissioned and other studies undertaken to investigate reasons for the slow and patchy implementation of the community care policy which had been evolving over the last 50 years. The Audit Commission report *Making a Reality of Community Care* (1986) noted that while the policy of successive national governments had been to promote and foster community care, services at a local level were still highly dependant on institutional and hospital-based resources. It reported slow and uneven progress in achieving a shift towards community-based services, and recommended organisational, staffing and funding changes intended to provide an impetus to change. The one option, the Audit Commission concluded, was 'to do nothing'.

Two years later Roy Griffiths submitted to the Secretary of State for Social Services a report addressing the following terms of reference: 'To review the way in which public funds are used to support community care policy and to advise me [the Secretary of State] on the options for action that would improve the use of these funds as a contribution to more effective community care' (Griffiths, 1988). One of the main (and surprising) conclusions of the Griffiths Report was that local authorities should have the lead responsibility for community care. This was surprising in view of the antipathy towards local government being shown by the national government of the time. At a time when national government was actively curbing the powers of local authorities, in particular their powers to raise and spend money, the government's adviser was not expected to come up with a proposal which would involve the transfer of financial resources *to* local authorities. More expected was Griffiths's view that publicly provided services should play a supportive role to the major care resource: 'families, friends, neighbours and other local people' (Griffiths, *ibid.*, para. 3.2). It may be that local government was considered to be in a better position than other agencies (such as health authorities) to use resources to support care being provided by families and friends.

The content of the 1990 Act itself was presaged in the White Paper *Caring for People* (Secretaries of State for Health, Social Security, Wales and Scotland, 1989) which built on these earlier reports and which set out how the government proposed to improve community care over the next decade and into the twenty-first century. The White Paper contained an explicit commitment to the policy of community care on the part of the government. It defined community care as:

> providing the services and support which people who are affected by problems of ageing, mental illness, mental handicap or physical or sensory disability need to be able to live as independently as possible in their own homes, or in 'homely' settings in the community.
>
> (*ibid.*, p. 3)

The White Paper set out a series of objectives to be achieved by the delivery of community care services; it defined the responsibilities of both the social and health services in implementing the policy; suggested ways in which high standards of care might be assured and made proposals about the way in which the policy would be resourced.

The 1990 NHS and Community Care Act itself was followed by a positive deluge of advice, guidance notes, task forces, and special projects aimed at both local authorities and health authorities, which sought to ensure that the intentions embodied in the legislation became a reality and that there was a real shift in the balance from institutional to community-based services. A road show of regional conferences took place in the spring of 1990 entitled *Care in the Community: Making it Happen* (Department of Health, 1990). These conferences involved policy makers, practitioners, academics and opinion formers and were designed to inspire and encourage those reluctant to commit to change. Later, the National Health Service Management Executive funded a management development programme which aimed to develop both knowledge and skills among those with key responsibilities for implementation (NHSTD, 1993), while a 'Community Care Task Force' visited different parts of the country to work with local managers and practitioners to help them implement changes. Alongside this supportive and developmental approach towards implementation, the Department of Health issued its usual circulars and letters containing guidance and targets for the achievement of specific tasks. Local authority social services departments and health authorities entered a phase of what felt to those employed within them like constant change: in organisation, in language, in guiding principles and in the nature of the work in which they were involved. One phrase which started to be heard, in a variety of forms, was: 'When community care starts . . .'.

For those who had been professionally involved in community-based social care services for many years, such a mode of speech must have been somewhat puzzling. Some commitment to the values of community care had been present within welfare policy since the foundation of the welfare state (Walker, 1994), and community care services had been developing within both the statutory and the voluntary sector throughout the post-war consensus period. Two White Papers which preceded *Caring for People* by between fifteen and twenty years, *Better Services for the Mentally Ill* (DHSS, 1975) and *Better Services for the Mentally Handicapped* (DHSS, 1971) had accepted that long stay hospitals were not the place for the majority of those with mental health problems, nor for those with learning difficulties. The Seebohm Report (1968), which led to the introduction of social services departments within local authorities, had a chapter on the topic of 'community', and the Barclay Report (1982) had further developed the notion of community social work.

While progress towards the closure of long-stay hospitals had been slow (Wistow and Barnes, 1995), local authority social services departments had been providing a range of services to support older people, disabled people and those with mental health problems or with learning disabilities living on their own or with families 'in the community'. Home helps, day centres, luncheon clubs, domiciliary occupational therapists and social workers were provided with the aim of meeting their 'social care' needs. Similarly, community nurses, physiotherapists, chiropodists and others were meeting health care needs 'in the community'. Since the establishment of the welfare state, welfare policies and services had recognised that there would be people who, through age or disability, needed assistance to live at home. The patchwork of legislation governing the provision of services had been matched by extremely variable quantity and quality of provision, but it would have been hard to find any local authority or health authority which did not provide some form of service likely to be defined by the term 'community care'. Within the voluntary sector, too, there had been substantial activity aimed at ensuring the availability of services for those in need of extra support. Voluntary organisations had been providers of services such as day centres and home visitors, as well as offering information and advice services and conducting campaigns on behalf of older people, disabled people, people with mental health problems or learning difficulties.

At the same time, and in spite of the claims of Conservative politicians that kinship obligations were being forgotten, the reality was that most 'community care' was being provided by families. The majority of older people were not being cared for in hospital or in residential homes, but in their own homes or in the homes of relatives. And while many disabled people were being inappropriately cared for in residential units, family care was the source of the bulk of the support for people with both physical and learning disabilities (Parker, 1990).

Community care was not introduced by statute in 1990. But what the 1990 Act did encapsulate was a shift in balance and boundaries. It codified a growing consensus among policy makers and service providers that the distinction beween those capable and those not capable of living an ordinary life within the community needed to be questioned. And, while there was no attempt to draw together the various pieces of legislation which directed or enabled the provision of community care services, it represented the first occasion on which community care *per se* had provided the central focus for welfare legislation. Significantly, it also attempted to set out the role of health services as well as local authority social services in the provision of community care. It was within the health service that the idea of community care was newly introduced to many service providers who had assumed that the needs of those with chronic health problems, with physical disabilities, mental impairments or mental health problems were primarily medical needs which should be met within a hospital environment (see Prior, 1993 for a discussion of this in relation to mental illness). For the health services, the policy emphasis on community care involved not only a reorganisation of service structures, but a re-definition of the nature of 'problems' which presented a challenge both to the knowledge base and to the authority of medical and other clinical professionals.

The 1990 Act was also passed at a time of much more widespread shifts in thinking and practice within public services. Eleven years of Tory government had resulted in profound changes within the management and governance of public services. The influence of neo-liberal political philosophies had led to a recasting of the definition of the purpose of public policy, placing an emphasis on individual responsibility and individual choice rather than on the responsibility of the state to ensure the well-being of its citizens. These philosophies were being played out in practice through changing boundaries between public and private sectors; attempts to curb the powers of professionals through an increase in the powers of managers; a reduction in the public accountability of public services resulting from a proliferation of appointed boards; the recasting of public service users as customers or consumers; and an emphasis on the responsibilities of active citizens to take charge of their own welfare and that of their families (e.g. Flynn, 1993; Pollitt, 1990). Neo-liberal philosophies were having an influence throughout the public sector. The National Health Service and local authority social services departments were subject to these broader shifts in thinking about public service management and governance, alongside the shifts taking place in policy regarding the appropriate ways of providing care and support for disabled people, older people, those with a learning difficulty and those experiencing mental distress.

Before looking at the significance of these broader shifts for the current state and future development of community care it is necessary to look more closely at community care as a policy and as a concept. Community care itself, as well its constituent concepts 'community' and 'care', is a disputed term, although this has not often been sufficiently acknowledged by those formulating policy. I will start with an exploration of the meanings of these concepts and consider how they have been applied in the course of the development of community care policy and practice.

Community

There is no one truth about what community is. The term community itself is used both empirically and normatively. It has been used to describe many different collectivities by those who have used it in the context of empirical research studies. In its normative capacity the term can encompass conflicting associations with both nostalgia and aspiration, as well as conformity and insularity (e.g. Bulmer, 1987; Mayo, 1994).

In its descriptive sense a distinction can be drawn between community in terms of locality, and community in terms of character-istics or interests. But closer examination of definitions based on locality reveal that description cannot be disentangled from normative assumptions. This is partly a matter of history. Community is a term which has been employed within the English language since the fourteenth century (Williams, 1976). Hence the contemporary use of the term is coloured by historical associations which have lost their meaning within present-day circumstances. The pre-industrial communities in which people lived were small-scale, often rural, and circumscribed many people's entire opportunity for social interaction. As urban development and industrialisation started to change the nature of the circumstances in which many people lived, the notion of community came to represent the Golden Age of an assumed past in which communal relationships based on personal ties served to bind people together for their mutual benefit.

Studies of community life provided a source of empirical research for sociologists working in the 1950s and 60s. Such studies were primarily located in working-class communities such as that of Bethnal Green in east London which was the base of the Institute of Community Studies. The work of Peter Townsend, Peter Wilmott and Michael Young brought anthropological research methods to the study of social issues within modern western societies and sought to understand the nature of the social and cultural ties which connected those living in physical proximity, usually in conditions of financial hardship. Peter Townsend's *The Family Life of Old People* (1963) was in this tradition and can be considered one of the earliest studies of 'community care' as experienced by older people and their families. Its starting point was one which would be familiar to contemporary policy makers: 'Concern about the growing number of old people springs partly from an assumption that many of them are isolated from their families and from the community' (Townsend, 1963, p. 13). The survey on which the book was based included analyses which feature in many later studies of family care: the frequency of contact between older people and different family members; the nature of the care or other support thought appropriate to be provided by different relatives; the stress resultant on caring for an ill or disabled relative; and the significance of contacts other than families for maintaining a sense of identity and connectedness in old age. Its conclusions were also familiar: that the extended family remained a highly significant social grouping and one which was a major source of care and support for older people. In this study and in many others of this era, community cannot effectively be distinguished from family for the purposes of analysing significant relationships.

A definition of community in terms of locality represents the most common usage of the term. Since local authority boundaries define responsibilities for, and thus the organisation of personal social services, locality is an important factor in determining statutory provision of community care services. Some analysts have sought to emphasise the locality definition and distance themselves from the normative associations of 'community' by employing alternative terms. This locality definition is explicit in Philip Abrams's work in which the term 'neighbourhood care' is employed to designate 'that part of the spectrum of community care that is associated with highly localised schemes, organisations, groups or projects which use local people to provide help or support for other people living near them' (Abrams *et al.*, 1989, p. 1). Adopting the term neighbourhood rather than community does not entirely remove the difficulty of arriving at a value-free definition, but it did enable Abrams and his colleagues to decide on a pragmatic solution in order to design research intended to explore neighbourhood care:

we chose to accept the term as a practical, common-sense construct, carrying an irreducible reference to some sort of bounded place of residence, and no more. For us the interesting research questions, therefore, are not about whether a given place of residence is or is not a neighbourhood, but about the sorts of social interaction and relationships which one might expect to find in one particular bounded place of residence as distinct from any other.

(*ibid.*, p. 14)

Bulmer (1987) also suggested an alternative concept in order to avoid the problematic nature of 'community' as a way of describing and understanding social relationships. He put forward the somewhat neglected notion of the 'primary group' as a concept which could include geographical propinquity, shared interests, or affect as the basis for interpersonal relationships:

A major benefit of shifting the emphasis from the study of 'community' to the study of the primary group – whether made up of neighbours, friends or kin – is that it gets away from the metaphysical problem of community. The study of neighbours, for example, indeed focuses upon the social relationships of geographical propinquity and certainly the term 'neighbour' needs careful definition – there are degrees of nearness and farness ... – but it does not involve the reification of a geographical or structural entity which has proved so problematic in the case of 'community'.

(*ibid.*, p. 39)

This notion of primary group makes explicit the assumption that kinship groups are central to an understanding of community as a source of care. That families are the major source of community care is empirically uncontroversial (Parker, 1990) even though the normative desirability of this has been challenged from many perspectives (e.g. Morris, 1993; Dalley, 1988). I return to a consideration of this in Chapters 5 and 6.

The empirical study of community fell out of favour among sociologists, largely because of the problematic nature of the concept. But during the 1990s a preoccupation with community has re-emerged in different forms. Firstly, notions of 'communities of interest' and 'communities of identity' reflect attempts to recognise empirical differences in the nature of those groupings which provide people with opportunites for social interaction within late twentieth-century western society. But they go beyond simply describing the groups within which people interact. Firstly, they suggest ways in which identity may be formed through association between those who share significant characteristics or experiences (Friedman, 1989). Such identities may be formed in opposition to others and seek to emphasise the difference of one community from another. Secondly, these more recent analyses of communities locate new forms of political action within collective organisation grounded in interest or identity.

These analyses reflect the plurality of contemporary society as well as the reduced significance of location of residence as the sole determinant of communal life. In this formulation, the factor providing the shared experience which is the source of communality may be identity, as in sexual or racial identity; it may be occupational: as in professional communities; or it may be a commitment to a cause, as in social movements such as environmental or peace movements. Once such understandings of community are added to that based on locality, the problem for 'community care', as implicit within policy definitions, starts to become evident. There are three aspects to this. Firstly, those in need of 'community care' may be just those people who are excluded from participating in communities of interest because of factors such as the ageism which excludes older people from work; the stigma attached to mental illness; the debilitating personal impact of mental distress; or the physical organisation of social life which makes access impossible for disabled people. Secondly, since physical proximity cannot be assumed in relation to members of such communities, their availability as resources for the daily provision of care also cannot be assumed. And thirdly, the nature of the relationships between members of such communities may not be such that 'providing care' would be considered an acceptable part of that relationship. However, communities of *identity* may offer alternative forms of support among those excluded from other forms of community. One example of this is the development of both formal and informal supportive networks for people with HIV/AIDS within the gay community. During the course of this book I will consider the significance of such ways of thinking about community for the dual identity of users of community care services as 'consumers' of those services, and as citizens who are members of different communities.

The other way in which community has re-emerged as an organising concept is in the communitarian philosophy developed by Etzioni and others in the United States (Etzioni, 1995). Communitarianism recognises the existence of multiple communities – indeed society is described as a 'community of communities' – but calls for all communities to speak with one 'moral voice' (p. 32) on questions of basic values: 'The moral voice is the main way communities keep moral order . . .' (p. 52). However, in most of the detailed discussion of ways in which the moral voice of community might be expressed, communitarianism harks back to an understanding of community based on families, neighbourhoods and larger socio-geographical entities. Communities of identity are not recognised. The frequency with which the term 'moral' appears in Etzioni's manifesto for communitarianism makes explicit the normative nature of the concept. He refers to 'moral confusion', 'moral traditions', the need for 'moral reconstruction' and 'moral commitments'. The emphasis is on the responsibilities of individuals to each other as members of communities of people living in proximity, rather than the aggressive individualism evident in an exclusively rights-based approach which is much more a feature of American society than it is in the UK (Glendon, 1991).

In seeking to re-emphasise the connectedness of individuals living together, communitarianism can be considered a potentially important corrective to the abstract individualism underpinning certain liberal philosophies. Some of the specific recommendations arising from the communitarian analysis can be welcomed, for example, designing housing developments in a way which enables a mix in the population, specifically including accommodation designed to meet the needs of older people. However, the normative assumptions on which communitarianism is based have been critiqued because of the acceptance of traditional gender subordination and similar critiques could be offered from the perspective of other groups who face structural discrimination. Marilyn Friedman notes:

communitarian theory fails to acknowledge that many communities make *illegitimate* moral claims on their members, linked to hierarchies of domination and subordination.

(Friedman, 1989, p. 279; my emphasis)

By accepting families and geographical communities as its starting point, communitarianism insufficiently acknowledges the way in which such communities exclude 'outsiders' (whether they be people with mental health problems, black people or gay and lesbian people) and can be the source of oppressive practices towards them. If communities are to make moral claims on their members, then these need to be legitimated by communal relationships which do not subordinate particular groups.

Characteristics of community

For the purposes of the discussion in this book certain key characteristics of the concept of community need to be highlighted;

1. Community exists in distinction to the state. It may be considered to be one element of civil society, or in some formulations, to be virtually indistinguishable from it. Community refers to the private lives of people lived through interaction with families, friends and others with whom they engage through voluntary association. Nevertheless, in pursuing the policy of community care, the state has sought to appropriate community and to 'command' it as a resource to be used in fulfilling public policy. Thus the interaction between community and state, and between individual members of those communities and individual workers, serves to construct public policy and to define its meanings in practice.

2. Community implies some unifying characteristic between those people who are members (the term is significant) of the community. The unifying factor may be one of space; of ethnic identity; of professional affiliation; or of sexual identity. The implication is that shared characteristics, interests or circumstances result in shared understandings:

> Community is an understandable dream, expressing a desire for selves that are transparent to one another, relationships of mutual identification, social closeness and comfort.
>
> (Young, 1990, p. 300)

But while alienated strangers in an individualistic culture may yearn for the comfort of shared community, membership also implies exclusion:

> A community is a group that shares a specific heritage, a common culture and set of norms. In the United States today, identification as a member of such a community also occurs as an oppositional differentiation from other groups, who are feared or at best devalued.
>
> (*ibid.*, p. 311)

Those in need of 'community care' are those who have been excluded from communities as traditionally understood both as a result of social policies which have segregated them within institutions, and by discriminatory attitudes and practices within communities. They share experiences and characteristics which can provide a focus for the establishment of new communities of identity. This will be one theme pursued through this text.

3. Community has tended to be used to refer to groups which do not occupy positions of high status within society. This perhaps derives from its early usage when it referred to the 'common people' (Williams, 1976). Sociological studies have identified the way in which disadvantage and oppression can serve as the social glue binding together communities (e.g. Young and Wilmott, 1962). Put crudely, one could say that there has been an assumption that people only need communities when their individual resources are insufficient to meet their needs.

4. Community refers to small scale social organisation, usually assuming relationships sustained by face-to-face interaction. In this context, it has gendered connotations. It is women who are often seen to be the sustainers of communities and who may be both constrained by and the definers of community. It is the space in which the personal and the political interact and in which women may mark out their sphere of influence, or be subject to the expectations of policy makers that they will know their place (Williams, 1993).

5. Community is overwhelmingly, but not exclusively, regarded as a positive concept.

So how is the concept of community employed in *Caring for People*, the White Paper which preceded and largely defined the content of the NHS and Community Care Act? A close study of this document reveals that the term is never defined. The unstated assumption underpinning the approach is that community is, quite simply, 'not hospital'. Community, in the terms of the White Paper, is living at home or 'in homely settings' in regular contact with family, friends and neighbours. It is recognised that ethnic minority communities may have different concepts of 'community care', but these are not defined. Apart from this, community is assumed to apply to locality: community services are 'locally based' in contrast to the 'remote mental hospitals' situated geographically separate from the original homes of most of their inmates. The disputed and shifting nature of the concept is simply ignored.

It is hard to find any explicit statement of what constitutes the community in which or by which care is to be provided. The assumption must be that everyone shares an understanding of this. Implicitly, the source of community care is not the locality but the family. Martin Bulmer's earlier (1987) warnings about the robustness of policies based on unexplored assumptions about the capacity of communities to care, and the ease with which such 'informal' care can be interwoven with care provided by public agencies have apparently gone unheeded.

Care

While *Caring for People* makes no attempt at a definition of community, it does provide some indication of the assumed content of care. Careful analysis reveals the frequency with which the concept of 'care' is qualified. Care may be 'health care'; 'social care'; 'residential, nursing or hospital care'. Does this imply that care is whatever action is carried out, or whatever services are provided by the qualifier? Further analysis would suggest that this is indeed the case. Care may be 'looking after those close to them' in the case of family or friends; or it may be any one or more of a disparate collection of inputs: 'social care and support e.g. for mobility, personal care, domestic tasks, financial affairs, accommodation, leisure and employment.' *Caring for People* also contains an explicit statement of the objective to be achieved through the provision of care – to achieve maximum independence, acquiring/re-acquiring basic living skills and to achieve full potential (para. 1.8).

However, certain elements of the 'care' discussed in *Caring for People* are oddly described in that way. Describing the need for housing, employment and leisure activities as a need for care starts to construct needs which are shared by all citizens as evidence of dependency in the case of selected groups of people. Why have necessities that all of us would take for granted come within the rubric of 'care' in the case of disabled people, older people, people with learning disabilities, and those experiencing mental distress? In part there is a pragmatic answer to this. The closure of institutions which encompassed people's whole lives, providing accommodation, food, employment, leisure activities, and a place in which to worship, meant that all those basic aspects of people's day to day lives have, in the inelegant terms employed by policy makers, to be 're-provided' elsewhere. Hence the provision of such resources has come to be included within the community care policy framework, rather than remaining within the spheres of housing, employment, cultural and leisure policies.

But, underpinning the practical need to ensure that people discharged from long-stay institutions have somewhere to live and activities to occupy their time which can be a source of income, pleasure and the development of skills and identity, there is a way in which defining such needs by reference to care serves to maintain the segregation of people even though they are 'within the community'.

Social services departments are not estate agents nor housing authorities; they are not employment agencies, education or economic development departments. Yet for people with 'special needs' they may serve the functions of all these agencies. What for most people constitute a range of needs relating to different aspects of their personal and social lives which they would expect to be met through accessing a range of public and private agencies, have become incorporated as part of the need for 'care', to be met from – or at least planned by – welfare services.

Leaving aside such unlikely constituents of care as employment and housing, care is no less complex a concept than community. It can be subdivided by reference to the source of care: whether it is provided by paid workers and hence 'formal' care, or whether it derives from pre-existing relationships of kinship or friendship and hence 'informal' care (Thomas, 1993). Within each type of care there are a number of other interpersonal, structural and cultural factors which affect both the way in which care is provided and the way in which it is received, while the interaction between the provision of care in the formal and informal sectors is one of the major issues affecting the successful implementation of community care policy (Bulmer, 1987; Twigg and Atkin, 1994).

It is recognised that there are instances in which distinctions cannot be completely drawn between the motivations of those providing paid care and those of informal carers. Home carers who spend more time than they are paid to do with an elderly person, or a nurse who stays chatting with a patient worried about an operation, are demonstrating a personal concern for that individual which has certain of the characteristics of informal care. In her study of home helps caring for elderly people Warren (1990) demonstrated that women drew on skills, knowledge and experience gained from their positions as housewives and mothers in preparing themselves to take on paid roles as home helps. Once they had taken on this role, some expressed surprise at subsequently finding themselves becoming emotionally involved with the older people and hence drawing on their experiences as caring relatives as well as good housewives. Warren concluded:

Women used a language and ideology to articulate the public domain which was taken directly from the private domain since, in this instance, activities clearly straddled both. They saw themselves as doing work *for* as well as *to* old people, they *cared* as well as *tended*.

(Warren, *ibid.*, p. 85; emphasis in the original)

Waerness (1987) has explained this merging of caring tasks and caring feelings by reference to the concept of the 'sentient actor' – a concept which recognises both the conscious and feeling aspects present within human actors. Care giving, whether paid or unpaid, cannot be undertaken solely on the basis of generalisable scientific knowledge, but has to respond to the individual and particular circumstances of the care receiver. In her research Waerness found that home helps described the most satisfying aspect of the job as being the relationship they established with their clients. Nevertheless, the fact that they were providing care for a particular individual has nothing to do with a pre-existing relationship and the negotiations which led to the carer/cared-for relationship coming into existence were very different from the negotiations which result in a particular family member taking on the care of an elderly relative (Ungerson, 1987).

Within the formal sector, the notion of care has less active connotations than certain other concepts used to describe what professionals do to their clients or patients. Terms such as treatment or therapy suggest an active intervention by a professional who has undergone training and has particular skills which qualify her to use technologies designed to achieve particular outcomes. In contrast to this, care is seen to be something which can be provided without the need for professional training – the job of 'care assistant' which exists in day centres and residential homes is usually an unqualified post. In hospital, the provision solely of nursing 'care' often means that more active forms of clinical intervention are considered unlikely to have any effect and the aim is simply to keep the patient as comfortable as possible without assuming any curative potential. Care tends to be a low status activity, one which is undertaken primarily by women, and one which is subordinate to the work undertaken by the professionals.

In spite of evidence that caring tasks and caring feelings are hard to separate, care has come to be commodified within the formal sector. *Caring for People* talks of the need to make a 'cost effective care choice' when putting together 'packages of care' (para. 3.4.1) for those whose needs are being assessed. The right amount of care needs to be supplied to enable people to achieve their full potential (para. 1.8). Care is something which can be applied for (para. 5.10) by reference to the social services 'gatekeepers' to care (para. 6.9); it can be bought and sold, preferably for the lowest possible price; and it can be incorporated within a 'care programme' (para. 7.7). This 'programme' will define who has responsibilities for supplying the different elements of the care package and who will have responsibility for managing this.

Another way of looking at the commodification of care is to consider the nature of the contracts for social care services developed following the implementation of the 1990 Act. In a study of 60 social care contracts, Smith and Thomas (1993) found that the focus of contracts was primarily on inputs or processes while a significant minority contracted on the basis of outputs or outcomes. The 'inputs' were expressed both in quantifiable form, for example, the ratio of qualified to unqualified staff, and in qualitative terms, setting out the procedures which the care provider should follow in relation to safety and security aspects of care, for example. Those contracts which were expressed in terms of outputs or outcomes were normally expressed in terms of qualitative criteria. They referred to aspects such as privacy, dignity, individuality, consultation and empowerment of residents. Contracts also showed variation in the degree of specifity about the practices which should be adopted in order to deliver such outcomes. For example, a precise approach to defining how privacy is to be achieved was demonstrated in a contract which included the following: 'Staff should adopt a "knock before entering" approach' (Smith and Thomas, *ibid.*, p. 17) The authors of this report observe:

> The nature of social care means that purchasers have legitimate interest in how the care is to be provided. The methods employed to achieve ends are very relevant in social care, particularly where measures of outputs and outcomes are under-developed. However, over specification and a high level of prescription will anger providers, who will view this as inappropriate interference by the social services department in the way they do their job.
>
> (*ibid.*, p. 18)

This expresses the dilemma of defining exactly what 'care' is within the formal sector of social care provision. The notion of care as something which can be defined in a contract, and which can be exchanged and managed is in stark contrast to lay understandings of care as deriving from emotional attachment to another person. But it also jars with the personal experience of many paid workers who find it hard to consider how the care which they show for those who use their services might be specified and quantified to be included within a contract. Caring within the informal sector is usually the consequence of a relationship and cannot be divorced from emotional attachment, whether it contributes to or jeopardises such attachment. The provision of tending care (as opposed to 'caring about' someone, Parker, 1981) may result in the transformation of an existing relationship, literally for better or for worse. It may be that neither the carer nor the person receiving care would choose to link tending with their existing relationship, whether that relationship is one of lovers, spouses, parents or siblings (Morris, 1993). Some may prefer to see tending as something to be bought from paid workers whose time and skill can be bought without the need to enter into a personal relationship (Morris, 1993). An automatic assumption that such care is better if provided by a member of the family rather than by a paid worker is simply not justified. Both the nature of pre-existing relationships and the impact that disablement, dementia or the birth of a child with learning disabilities may have on an existing relationship will affect whether or not tending can become a positive part of that relationship. In many instances, the very fact of an emotional attachment may interfere with the ability of both parties to transform their relationship into something very different.

Nevertheless it is hard to see how 'caring about' can be bought in the same way. The emotional labour of caring is an aspect of caring in its own right as well as underpinning the physical labour of tending. Loving someone when others may find it hard to love them, providing encouragement and reinforcing the self-worth of people whose self-esteem may be battered by mental distress, or refusing to give up on a severely disabled child when others are suggesting that they would be better off in a residential home (Barnes, 1996b) demand particular and unpredictable responses which it is hard to imagine could be bought in advance.

The origin of caring in kinship obligations has been explored by a number of researchers (e.g. Qureshi and Walker, 1989; Finch and Mason, 1993; Ungerson, 1987). While the role of male carers has received some attention from those concerned to counteract assumptions that caring is solely a female task (Arber and Gilbert, 1989; Fisher, 1994), male caring is primarily conducted within spouse relationships. Both emotionally and normatively women carry the major responsibility for providing care to relatives in need of extra support. However stressful taking on caring responsibilities might be, many people simply do not consider they have a choice when a close member of the family starts to need support beyond the usual exchanges which take place within families. It is not only a question of love, obligation or even guilt, in some instances the provision of care is a key part of the identity of the person taking on this role. For women socialised to assume that their role within families is one of servicing and nurturing, caring may be bound up with their identity. For such women 'release' from caring may be experienced as a loss of identity rather than freedom to pursue their own interests (Barnes and Maple, 1992). Analyses of caring which solely consider it as a burden ignore the positive experiences which many carers report (Grant and Nolan, 1993) and Braithwaite (1990) has demonstrated that there are many complex variables which affect the extent to which care may be experienced as a 'burden'.

The reality, in the vast majority of cases, is that community care means care by family members and involves both 'tending' and caring about. Caring relationships are relationships between mothers and daughters, husbands and wives, nieces and aunts. I discuss these aspects of caring in more detail from the perspectives of both care providers and care receivers in Chapter 6.

How, then, have community and care become linked in the development and implementation of community care policy?

The development of a policy

Community care has its origins in a number of different policy and practice developments which gathered strength from the 1960s on.

Community development and community-based social work

The empirical studies of community life undertaken during the 1950s and 60s had their practical application in the policy and practice of community development. Community development was conceived as a process through which community workers would act as facilitators: 'linking up with autonomous groups of people in the locality, or the bringing of them into life where dormant and inarticulate' (Hodge, 1970). Community development was focussed on increasing the resources of communities (as localities) to achieve a range of objectives described by Hodge such as: establishing a good quality of life in new town developments; building relationships between schools and people of all ages in the locality; the mobilisation of voluntary sources of community care; and the development of self-help to augment statutory social services. Hodge distinguished community development from the parallel process of community action, which he conceived as a much more explicitly political process through which the community worker seeks to enable groups to articulate their grievances and struggle to achieve new resources and a redistribution of power.

Cynthia Cockburn questioned whether the linking of action to 'community' was a plausible location for struggle intended to change existing power relationships and achieve a redistribution of resources as a result (Cockburn, 1977). In her analysis of the relationship between corporate management and community development in local government, Cockburn identified three problems with the notion of community action. Firstly, it was the state which had defined the terrain: officials – whether they be local councillors, community policemen or community workers themselves – had been created to respond to whatever groupings emerged as collectivities around which action was being taken; secondly, that community action had, by the late 1960s, become closely related to consumer protection: 'Community action points not to deficiencies in the mode of production but in the products: the goods or services' (Cockburn, *ibid.*, p. 160); and thirdly that community action was defined as classless and viewed as small-scale action on the part of interest groups battling with the Goliath of unresponsive bureaucracy. There are pointers here to what will follow in the analyses of subsequent chapters. My purpose in referring to it here is to suggest why community development and community action failed to become established as mechanisms through which an empowering relationship could be established between citizens and the welfare state at a local level. On the one hand the political element frightened those in power, and on the other community was too nebulous and uncertain a collectivity to support effective political action. However, some aspects of community development were influential for a time within personal social services.

The Seebohm Report (1968) was the origin of local authority social services departments in England and Wales. In this report the community was considered to be both a network of social relationships which provided a source of care, and something which itself needed to be nurtured to ensure its well being. This perspective was influential in determining the services to be provided within the new social services departments, and the way in which those services were organised. Social services departments employed community workers as well as individual case workers, and were structured in a way which was intended to enable them to relate to local communities. Early experience of such organisation suggested the need for review of the effectiveness of such links and the Barclay Report (1982) considered this further. Debates concerning 'patch-based social work' were influential in the late 1970s and early 80s (Hadley and Hatch, 1981) and led to experiments which brought together the range of functions of community-based social services in small-scale, local offices. As a researcher working in a social services department in a large metropolitan authority at the time, I remember poring over maps of the city in order to try to define 'natural communities' around which a reorganisation of the department should take place.

The notion of patch-based social work encompassed both 'getting closer to the community' and a desire to mobilise the collective resources of the community in order to provide care. It sought to engage with existing loci of community activism whether that be found in churches, in working-men's clubs, or in voluntary groups. Exponents of the approach described the philosophy of patch as follows:

The spirit in which these teams approach their work is pragmatic and entrepreneurial rather than professional or bureaucratic. They are simply concerned with using their resources in such a way as to maximise the care provided within the community to those individuals and groups in need. Fully recognizing the existing importance of informally and formally organised voluntary carers in the community, the teams accept that it is an important part of their task to strengthen and develop such voluntary action. To increase the effectiveness of their own direct intervention, in cases where the community cannot cope, the teams endeavour to identify those at risk at an earlier stage and to deploy a larger proportion of their staff in front-line positions where they can provide immediate help.

(Hadley and Hatch, *ibid*, p. 151)

Key organisational requirements were that patch-based teams should relate to small communities of no more than 10,000 people, and that the functional separation of tasks within social services departments – social work, community work, home care, day care and occasionally residential care – should be abandoned in favour of small, integrated teams of workers in which functional divisions would become blurred. The integration of statutory service providers with the local community was encouraged by the appointment of local people to work within patch teams, and, in at least one case known to the author, attempts were made by employers to encourage social workers to live within the area in which they worked. Rather than relying on formal referral systems, workers were expected to pick up 'referrals' in an informal way through day-to-day contacts in shops, pubs and chats on the street.

The short-lived patch experiment provides illustrations of both the positive and negative aspects of 'community' in the context of community care. The preventive philosophy underpinning the significance attached to the easy accessibility of services was considered to lead to a reduction in crisis referrals, as incipient problems could be identified early. The role of statutory services was seen to be supportive of the collective strengths of local community organisations, rather than focusing solely on the privatised version of community care as family care promoted by the Griffiths Report and subsequent policy statements (see below). On the other hand, the very closeness of workers, who had controlling powers as well as supportive functions (in relation both to child care procedures and mental health assessments), had disadvantages for both sides. The idea of having to take a neighbour's child into care was no more popular with social workers than it was likely to be for the family concerned. And, in organisational terms, the identification of 'natural communities' to which social services teams could relate was frustrated by the uncertain and shifting boundaries of those communities. The building of a new housing estate or a change in policy regarding housing allocation could mean that a social services team was left without a community, or found itself relating to a very different type of community from that which it was established to support (Harris, 1988).

De-institutionalisation

While ideas about community-oriented social work were influencing the way in which some local authority social services departments were being organised, central government policies also reflected a commitment to locally based care for people considered to have 'special needs'. The White Papers *Better Services for the Mentally Handicapped* (DHSS, 1971) and *Better Services for the Mentally Ill* (DHSS, 1975) had already called for the abandonment of long-stay institutions and for the development both of local residential facilities and of day services designed to provide occupation for people living at home or in hostels within local communities.

The proposals contained in these White Papers were in part a response to scandals which had been exposed within long-stay institutions. An evocative illustration of conditions within long-stay hospitals for 'mentally handicapped people' was provided by Joanna Ryan and Frank Thomas (1980). The justification for the dehumanising way in which many people were treated within those institutions was based on a belief that mentally handicapped people were not only different, but also lacking in any individuality and rather less than human as a result:

> Being in the institution was bad. I got tied up and locked up. I didn't have any clothes of my own, and no privacy. We got beat at times, but that wasn't the worst. The real pain came from always being a group. I was never a person. I was part of a group to eat, sleep and everything. As a kid I couldn't figure out who I was. I was part of a group. It was sad.
>
> (Ryan and Thomas, *ibid.*, p. 12)

Breaking down institutional practices and the stigmatisation resulting from these was another key strand in the developing thinking about community care. In contrast to the preventive philosophy of community-oriented social work, which emphasised collective community development as well as locally based service structures, de-institutionalisation was overwhelmingly focussed on getting people out of damaging environments rather than on supporting and nurturing the communities into which they were starting to be moved. Rather than seeking to support those already within communities whose resources were insufficient to deal with the impact of poverty, mental distress, age or impairment, the de-institutionalisation programme sought to introduce *into* local communities people who had been separated from them, sometimes from birth, and who were themselves likely to need considerable support in making the transition. The task was a very different one and likely to create strains and conflicts within communities.

The origins of the policy of de-institutionalisation were various. Ramon (1992) has described three factors influencing the policy of long-stay psychiatric hospital closure: (1) evidence of the effectiveness of alternative community-based interventions and medical treatments; (2) political support deriving both from the perceived financial savings to be made by hospital closure, and from the fact that community-based services were considered to provide a more 'respectful' way of treating fellow citizens; and (3) sociological critiques of the segregating and stigmatising effect of total institutions. Ramon's conclusion was that:

> While proposed for a variety of motives, hospital closure nevertheless symbolizes the unifying wish to opt for a less segregated social attitude, of accepting that hospitals were a mistaken form of intervention, and of recognizing that there is a place for people who exhibit madness in our midst.
>
> (*ibid.*, p. xiv)

The professional philosophy expressing the commitment to community-based services for people with learning disabilities and those with mental health problems was that of 'normalization'. This philosophy was initially articulated in Canada by Wolfensberger (1972). It was taken up in this country by people working at the King's Fund who applied the principles to *An Ordinary Life* (King's Fund, 1980). The three key principles elaborated in this programme were:

(i)   Mentally handicapped people have the same human value as anyone else and also the same human rights.
(ii) Living like others within the community is both a right and a need.
(iii) Services must recognise the individuality of mentally handicapped people. (*ibid.*, p. 14)

These principles were also adopted by others working on service developments at a local level (e.g. Welsh Office, 1983, West Midlands Forum, 1987). O'Brien (1986) expounded five 'accomplishments' relating to ordinary life principles which services should achieve on behalf of their users: community presence; valued relationships; choice; competence; and respect. Wolfensberger (1983) later redefined the philosophy as 'social role valorization' and Ramon (1991) applied this concept to a consideration of the related but distinct experiences of people with mental health problems. Social role valorisation emphasises the significance for the self-esteem and social standing of those with stigmatised identities of the extent to which people are valued socially. Thus, it recognises that it is not enough for people to be 'in the community', their role within the community has to be experienced and recognised by others as a valued one.

While attracting some opposition because of the cultural, gendered and class assumptions of what constituted a 'normal life', normalisation and related philosophies nevertheless achieved widespread acceptance during the 1980s as a basis for service developments. However, they have been of most significance with regard to the position of younger adults. They have not addressed the issue of the valued social roles which can be occupied by older people who make up the majority of users of community care services. Perhaps for this reason older people have been excluded from certain community care initiatives which have been based on the normalisation philosophy (Barnes and Wistow, 1991).

The link between de-institutionalisation and community care can be seen as the prioritisation of one notion of community – that of the locality within which ordinary people live – over all others. As Lindsay Prior (1993) has described, the asylums (later renamed hospitals) created in the Victorian era for people with both mental health problems and with learning difficulties had many of the characteristics of communities. A fundamental characteristic of a 'total institution' (Goffman, 1961) is that it contains within it all aspects of people's lives. Prior described the hospital which was the subject of his study as follows:

Originally it contained its own farmland and animals, its own laundry and cookhouses; its own administrative structure, churches, chapels, mortuary and workshops. Later on it incorporated its own surgical facilities, its own school of nursing and many other resources for both staff and patients. The patients, of course, were mainly housed in the villas, and these were designed in terms of an image of suburban domesticity which predominated in both Britain and Ireland at the turn of the century.

(ibid., p. 145)

Other specialist residential accommodation for people with learning difficulties has been explicitly described as comprising 'residential communities' and the living groups within such communities have been designated as families. The following is taken from a funding appeal issued in 1996 by Botton Village in North Yorkshire:

Botton was founded in the 1950s by the pioneering doctor Karl Konig. He believed that people with a mental handicap should have the chance to discover and use their talents and achieve their full potential in a safe and caring community. Since then, the Village has gone from strength to strength. Today it is home to more than 320 people, over half of whom are adults with special needs. Everyone lives in extended families like ours at Rowan. Many houseparents, like us, have their own children which adds to the normal family atmosphere. Families are very important to us at Botton – they are the bedrock of the village and fundamental to our community way of living.

Residential communities share with other geographical communities physical characteristics such as the provision of a range of facilities to meet the leisure, educational, spiritual and other needs of those living in physical proximity to each other. They are also small enough to enable face-to-face interaction of all members. However, they are different in terms of the exclusivity of their membership. Entry to the community is determined by reference to a characteristic such as having a learning difficulty or a sensory disability, which is also the source of exclusion from other communities in which people may wish to choose to live.

The evidence collected by Prior in studying the discharge of people from a large asylum in Ireland, calls into question the equation of 'de-hospitalization' with 'de-institutionalization'. The majority of those discharged were discharged to other forms of institutional care: hostels, group homes or other hospital wards. In the smaller institutions features such as separate areas only accessible to staff, lack of privacy, and the strict timetabling of daily life caused many ex-patients to report that they were still being told what to do and still having their lives run by other people. Another study of the result of psychiatric hospital closure, this time of a county asylum in England (Wistow and Barnes, 1995) also concluded that the nature of the service developed to replace the hospital had effectively meant the replacement of hospital wards by bungalow units in which the same patients lived with the same staff as had been in the hospital. But in addition, Prior found that the nature and size of the social networks of the discharged patients were very similar to their hospital networks. He concluded that discharged patients formed 'a community within a community' and that:

psychiatric patients did not automatically enter into new social worlds because they lived in new or different buildings. Nor were they accepted more openly and readily by the community at large simply because they had a new mailing address.

(ibid., p. 192)

By the time of the Griffiths Report, community care had become much more clearly associated with de-institutionalisation and had become almost entirely separated from notions of community development. Community development, in turn, had become associated primarily with policies such as economic development and housing than with community care (Birchall, 1988; Mayo, 1994). The rejection of institutional care in its existing forms for all but the most needy had led to an emphasis on private care within families. Even though some new forms of collective provision had been developed to provide for some long stay hospital patients, there had not been a re-conceptualisation of what collective provision and collective responsibility might mean within the ordinary environments in which people who had not previously been in-patients were to stay (Dalley, 1988). The Griffiths Report contained the most explicit statement of the privatisation of community care:

Families, friends, neighbours and other local people provide the majority of care in response to needs which they are uniquely well placed to identify and respond to. This will continue to be the primary means by which people are enabled to live normal lives in community settings. The proposals take as their starting point that this is as it should be, and that the first task of publicly provided services is to support and where possible strengthen these networks of carers.

(Griffiths, 1988, para. 3.2)

The 'discovery' of informal care

While the role played by family carers had been recognised by front-line workers and acknowledged in previous policy documents prior to the Griffiths report, the place as lay care as an instrument of public policy was made explicit by the community care reforms of the early 1990s. Roy Griffiths's statement of the centrality of the role of 'informal carers' within the provision of community care was echoed by the White Paper *Caring for People*:

The Government acknowledges that the great bulk of community care is provided by friends, family and neighbours. The decision to take on a caring role is never an easy one. However, many people make that choice and it is right that they should be able to play their part in looking after those close to them.

(Secretaries of State, 1989, para. 1.9)

One of the six key objectives of the White Paper was 'to ensure that service providers make practical support for carers a high priority' (para. 1.11). Carers became a high profile group within national policy guidelines and as a focus for research, campaigns and special projects at both national and local level (see Chapter 5).

This recognition of the role played by families and friends in looking after elderly or disabled relatives has to be understood in a two principal way. Firstly, it is a reflection of the familist ideology dominant within right-wing thinking which asserts that caring is a natural function which should be carried out within domestic groups rather than in any other location (Dalley, 1988). The assumption is that care provided in such contexts is not only best but 'right'. Thus the provision of care within family groups carries moral overtones which can effectively mean that individuals do not feel it is possible to choose *not* to care for a family member. Welfare is seen to be a personal responsibility, with the state having only a residual role in cases where there is a real absence of family to care.

Secondly, there is the economic perspective. It has been calculated that unpaid carers provide a resource worth between £15 billion and £24 billion to the state (Kohner, 1993). Supporting carers to continue to provide care is a cost effective policy. Without the willingness and ability of family and friends to continue to provide care the whole edifice of community care policy would come crumbling down. The widespread support for community care policy was, in part, because it was perceived to be a less expensive option than providing institutional care, but this often depended on the willingness of unpaid or lowly paid carers to take on tasks which elsewhere would have been undertaken by paid staff.

Introducing the market

The 1990 Act was not only concerned with professional philosophies and values relating to the best way in which to provide care to disabled people, older people and those with learning disabilities or experiencing mental distress. It was also concerned with the organisation and financing of services. 1990 no more saw the introduction of 'the mixed economy of welfare' than it saw the introduction of community care. However, the stimulation and development of the mixed economy as a means both of increasing the choice available to consumers, and of reducing the power of welfare bureaucracies, was a central objective of the NHS and Community Care Act. Once again such objectives were anticipated by the Griffiths Report:

There is value in a multiplicity of provision, not least from the consumer's point of view, because of the widening of choice, flexibility, innovation and competition it should stimulate. The proposals are therefore aimed at stimulating the further development of the 'mixed economy' of care. It is vital that social services authorities should see themselves as the arrangers and purchasers of care services – not as monopolistic providers.'

(para. 3.5)

The introduction of market mechanisms was one way in which consumers of community care services were to be 'empowered'. It was seen as a way in which people could exercise choice over the services they received. Empowerment was also an objective of the move towards individualised services: constructing packages of care around individual needs was considered to be more capable of empowering people to live the lives they wanted than providing bulk care within residential settings.

In Chapter 2 I consider the way in which the philosophy of the market started to shape the nature of community care and the relationship between users and services.

Summary

In this first chapter I have discussed the disputed and complex meanings of the core concepts on which community care is based, and I have traced the development of the policy through its origins in a variety of political and professionally driven policy and practice initiatives. In the remainder of this book I consider how community care may, or may not, empower those who make use of community care services. In doing so I consider what 'empowerment' may mean from the perspective of citizens who have been excluded from participation within communities. I also seek to develop an understanding of what both care and community might mean in the context of a community care policy and practice which seeks to empower excluded groups.

CHAPTER 2

Consumerism and citizenship

For those who saw the 1990 Act as the birth of community care, this was inseparable from a re-organisation of the NHS and personal social services intended to subject both services to the presumed disciplines of the market. The Act was as much about making services 'customer-focussed' as it was about securing a shift in services from institutional to community bases. In this chapter I consider the way in which a consumerist philosophy has been applied to health and social care services and how this has been argued to contribute to the empowerment of service users. I then discuss critiques of consumerism which have emphasised the need to recognise the dual role of users not only as consumers, but also citizens, and how this is leading to a development of the concept of citizenship itself.

One feature of community care policy as it emerged towards the end of the 1980s was an emphasis on the private rather than public provision of care. Critiques of the inflexibility and unresponsiveness of collective *forms* of welfare provision had created a situation in which collective *responsibility* for provision was itself called into question. Little consideration was given to the possibility of alternative forms of collective provision which might overcome the acknowledged problems of much institutional care. The assumption was that care provided by family and friends was both the preferred and best option. If it were not possible for that care to be provided directly, then people should be free to choose where to buy care within a welfare market place.

This emphasis on individual responsibilities and privatised consumption of services was not confined to community care policy. A construction of users of public services as individual consumers participating within a market was an all-pervading feature of UK government policy throughout the 1980s and into the 90s. While similar changes have been evident in the welfare systems of other European states and elsewhere, only in New Zealand have they been driven by such an explicit ideological force. Policy in the UK has been informed by a neo-liberal philosophy which, in its most extreme forms, has denied the reality of collectivities. Margaret Thatcher, Prime Minister throughout the 1980s, claimed that there was no such thing as society, while Nozick (1974) argued 'There are only individual people with their own individual lives.'

Neo-liberals or libertarians argue that welfare should be the responsibility of individuals rather than the state. If families cannot directly provide the care needed by older or disabled relatives, then they should purchase the care that is needed in the market place. Taxing citizens to pay for welfare services from which they do not directly benefit is an unacceptable restriction on the freedoms of citizens to spend their money in ways which they determine for themselves. To the extent that the state *does* have a role in relation to welfare, it is to police the market and to provide a safety net in cases of extreme poverty or where the market is unable to provide the necessary services.

Buying welfare services in the market enables individuals to make a rational choice based on individual self-interest. Market exchanges are considered to provide the most efficient means of delivering services and to maximise the freedom of individuals to choose which services they wish to receive. Those services which attract the support of the most consumers will thrive, while those which are unpopular, unresponsive or considered unnecessary by potential consumers will go to the wall.

The manifestation of this philosophy has affected education, housing, economic development and other areas of public policy, as well as health and social care. Proponents have argued that public services can and should be managed in the same way as private enterprises in order to maximise both their efficiency and their attractiveness to their consumers (see Ranson and Stewart, 1994, for a critique of this view). Within public services as a whole, a series of managerial, structural and financial changes have been introduced which are intended to weaken the hold of the public sector over the supply of services and to change the nature of the relationship between providers and consumers of services (Stewart and Stoker, 1994).

These changes have led to fragmentation within local government so that, for example:

- responsibilities for the direct management of schools no longer rests with the local authority but with a Board of Governers;
- competitive tendering has been introduced into a broad range of council services and purchasing or commissioning of services has been separated from their direct provision;
- 'flexible employment practices' have been introduced which mean that the idea of a job for life as a local government officer can no longer be assumed, with a consequent undermining of the power of producer interests; and
- changes in the nature of the relationship between national and local government have taken place, the most visible of these being through the increase in central control of local expenditure by means of capping. This has reduced the scope of accountability between local government and local citizens,

These changes have taken place within the context of a period of financial restraint and the promotion of value for money constructed as achieving more output for less input (Butt and Palmer, 1985). Together they represent a substantial shift in the governance of public services at a local level and they have meant that notions of public service have undergone substantial rethinking. As well as the appeal to increased efficiency and effectiveness, they have been justified by reference to the presumed benefits to service users resulting from limitations being put on the power of producers.

It is not my intention here to consider whether the community care and health service reforms have achieved these intended objectives on behalf of the users of their services. My purpose here is to consider the implications of these changes for the nature of the relationship between those with responsibilities for either purchasing or providing services, and those who find themselves in need of making use of services, or indeed who find themselves being forced into receiving services against their will.

Consumers and social care

While the social care services for which local government has had responsibility have not been subject to the full challenge of market testing, many of the changes in the organisation and funding of community care services introduced by the 1990 Act reflect broader changes taking place within the public sector. The major changes were as follows:

- As the 'lead agency', social services departments were given responsibility for assessing individuals' needs for social care – if necessary in collaboration with medical and paramedical services – and for determining what services should be provided. The post of care manager was created. Care managers design and monitor a 'care package', intended to be tailored to the particular needs of each individual and provided by whatever agency, public or private, has the most appropriate services. At an individual level, this is intended to distinguish between needs assessment and service provision and to ensure that consumer rather than provider interests prevail in determining the appropriate service to be provided.
- In pursuing the 'mixed economy', services are intended to be purchased from the independent sector as well as provided from within social services departments' own resources. This does not imply that such a 'mixed economy' was brought into existence by the 1990 Act. Services had previously been provided by both the for-profit and not-for-profit sector. The difference is in the responsibility of the local authority to stimulate the development of these sectors, encouraged in formal terms by the requirement to

spend 85 per cent of monies transferred from the social security budget within the independent sector.

- At a strategic level, social services authorities became responsible for the production of community care plans, to be drawn up where possible in collaboration with health services and other agencies with relevant responsibilites, for example housing authorities. One particular responsibility in relation to the production of these plans is that authorities are expected to consult with service users and carers during their development. This was another way in which it was intended that the interests of consumers should become increasingly influential.

- Local authorities were given responsibility for the financial support, over and above their entitlement to general social security benefits, of those admitted to residential care within the private and voluntary sector, as well as within the state sector. This has involved a transfer of funding at a national level from the social security budget to the budget of local authorities.

- A new complaints procedure was introduced as were 'arms-length inspection units' with responsibilities for ensuring standards within residential homes. These inspection units are expected to involve lay inspectors, who may include both service users and carers, to provide an independent perspective on quality and standards within residential homes.

Research investigating the initial response of social services authorities to these changes found widespread consensus regarding the central objectives claimed for them (Wistow *et al.*, 1994). However, this consensus was found to conceal three very different models through which authorities were interpreting their responsibilities. Authorities interpreted the role of 'enabler' which they were being encouraged to adopt as: (1) enabling market development; (2) enabling personal development; or (3) enabling community development. While the intention of the government was that social services authorities should become 'enabling authorities' by stimulating the mixed economy, the values underpinning the work undertaken by personal social services departments allowed some authorities to recast their enabling role as one of enabling personal development through achieving improvements in individual welfare; or as enabling community development through:

the mobilization and support of community-based resources, especially those of the informal and local voluntary sectors, in order to foster participation and democratize decision-making.

(Wistow *et al., ibid.*, p. 135)

The latter harks back to notions of community development which had been influential in earlier ideas about community and patch-based social work (see Chapter 1).

Nevertheless, while some authorities were clearly not comfortable with the idea of markets in social care, in their sample of 25 authorities studied in detail, the researchers found only two 'conscientious objectors' who had not taken action to introduce service specifications and contracts between the local authority and independent providers.

The significance of these changes for the individual user of services were considered to be:

* Firstly, that they would enable the provision of a much more individualised service designed to meet the needs of the particular person, rather than requiring the person to fit in with whatever service was available.
* Secondly, that the promotion of the market would create a situation in which increased choice was available to users of services.
* Thirdly, that complaints and inspection procedures would increase the safeguards available to users and ensure increased quality of service provision. These improvements were also seen to flow from the requirement to prepare and publish plans, and for purchasers to enter into contractual relationships with service providers.

Consumers and the NHS

Alongside the changes required within local authority social services departments, radical changes were also being implemented within the NHS. The National Health Service in the UK was the biggest employer in Europe and reflected a major commitment to the principle of publicly provided welfare services. If welfare services were to be transformed through the presumed disciplines of the marketplace, then the NHS had to be a central focus for such changes (Le Grand and Bartlett, 1993). Le Grand and Bartlett describe the contrasting models through which welfare could be produced. In the pre-1990 NHS:

how much was produced and who got the fruits of production were not the unintended consequences of self-interested decisions made by individual producers and consumers operating in a competitive market. Rather they were the outcome of conscious decisions of politicians, bureaucrats and professionals operating in a bureaucratic environment and, ostensibly at least, intending to work in such a way as to further the public interest.

(*ibid.*, p. 1)

Clearly if the Conservative project was to be achieved, such a large-scale challenge to the ideology of the market would need to be overcome. Nevertheless, the National Health Service has always

occupied a special place in the affections of the British people and
even the right-wing Tory governments of Margaret Thatcher and John
Major have stopped short, this far at least, of total transformation into
a privatised health service based on a pure market system.

The changes introduced into the NHS affect the service as a whole,
not just services of direct relevance to the policy of community care.
The major changes comprised:

- A much clearer separation of purchasing and provision than was
  introduced into social services departments. The number of
  provider units directly managed by health authorities has reduced
  steadily since 1990 leaving such authorities almost solely in the
  position of purchasers rather than providers.
- Virtually all hospitals and other secondary health services changed
  from being directly managed by health authorities to become
  self-governing trusts.
- GP fundholders were created as another source of purchasing
  power intended to increase the assumed benefits of competition.
- Doctors were brought further within the control of general
  managers through management of their contracts, reform of the
  merit system, and through resource management initiatives
  intended to subject 'clinical freedom' to budget disciplines.

As in the case of the changes within personal social services, the
NHS reforms were justified not only in terms of increased efficiency and
greater consistency within health services, but also in terms of
increasing consumer choice and delivering a higher quality service to
patients.

Creating consumers

Well before the 1990 Act was being implemented, commentators on
the Left had recognised that a defence of the principle of public
services should not be confused with a defence of the existing form of
those services. In a book published in 1990, Deakin and Wright wrote:

Attention to the needs of producer groups (fortified, in the case of the Labour
Party, by an institutional attachment) has not been matched by an equivalent
concern for the needs of consumers. The belief in collective provision has
tended to become a belief in uniform provision. Defining needs has become
confused with meeting them. Provision has too often become paternalism.
Excessive dependence on using the state, centrally and locally, as the means
for service delivery has fostered an administrative, 'top-down' version of
socialism.

(Deakin and Wright, 1990, p. 2)

Prior to 1990, both analysts and activists on the Left were seeking to develop and to define a new type of relationship between those who produce and those who make use of public services. Part of this involved developing a new language by which to describe that relationship. Contributors to the collection edited by Deakin and Wright sought to understand the different types of relationships which users occupy in relation to very different types of public services, not only social services and health services, but also transport, the police, housing, education and planning. The notion of the 'consumer' of those services was considered problematic by a number of contributors to that collection. Indeed, as Barnes *et al.*, pointed out, certain users of health and social services identified themselves as survivors of oppressive interventions, rather than active users of beneficial services (Barnes, Prior and Thomas, 1990). Nevertheless, the term 'consumer' started to replace 'client' or 'patient' within health and social care services as well as becoming a means of describing users of public services in general. It is important to understand both the ideological and the material implications of the notion of consumers in these contexts.

Le Grand and Bartlett and colleagues (Le Grand and Bartlett, 1993) describe changes in organisation and funding as having created 'quasi-markets' within the health service and community care services, as well as within education and housing. The key differences between quasi-markets and pure markets operate on both the supply and the demand side of the equation. On the supply side there *is* competition between providers, but not all providers are motivated by profit maximisation. Providers compete for customers, although not necessarily for all types of customers, but increasing the number of customers does not necessarily equate with increasing the resource base. On the demand side, money does not directly change hands at the point of service delivery. Purchasers may make either block or spot purchases from providers and such purchases come from a budget allocated from public funds for this purpose. Secondly, the decisions about where such purchases will be made are not up to the direct consumer. They are made on their behalf by purchasing or commissioning agents operating in some cases on the part of individual consumers, but more often on the basis of an overall assessment of the needs of a real or potential group of service users.

Hence, the individual user of services is a quasi-consumer (Barnes and Prior, forthcoming) operating within a quasi-market. To the extent that 'exiting' from services *can* be an effective means of exercising consumer power in relation to health and social care services (see below), the power of exit is more likely to be exercised by agents than by the direct user of services.

The use of contracts as a means of ensuring the availability of services offers a metaphor for the character of the change taking place within public services as a whole (Walsh, 1995). While some public services are amenable to the degree of specification required for contract, this is not the case for social care services. Specifying the outcomes to be achieved through the provision of social care services has always been a problem and one which made the determination of performance measures not only technically difficult, but professionally disputed (Barnes and Miller, 1988; Stewart and Walsh, 1994). Introducing contract mechanisms was not likely to make the task of outcome specification any the easier. One danger in this is that contracts are defined in terms of the input to be provided, with little opportunity to ensure that such inputs would be bound to ensure effective outcomes. In such contexts, the power tends to remain with the providers rather than the purchasers and contract monitoring is difficult to achieve (Walsh, *ibid.*, p. 127). Hence it is hard to see how the use of contracts can empower the end user of services.

Some analysts identify these changes as indicators of a more funda-mental ideological shift towards managerialism in the public sector (Pollitt, 1990; Clarke, Cochrane and McLoughlin, 1994). Managerialist ideology is based on a view of management as the saviour of a public sector hidebound by the unholy trinity of bureaucracy, professionalism and trade unionism. Newman and Clarke (1994) characterise the managerialist credo as one which prioritises management because it is free from the sectional self-interest of the professions and the trade unions, and from the inherent conservatism of administrative bureau-crats. Hence, an emphasis on 'getting closer to the customer' and searching for excellence in service provision places managers on the side of consumers. Flynn (1993) describes the ideal implied by the managerialist ethic as one in which managers are outward-looking, constantly aware of their customers, rather than inward-looking, concerned with internal procedures as administrative bureaucrats tend to be, or directed by the values of peer groups as in the case of professionals claiming professional autonomy in decision making.

This view of management is evident in the exhortation to Health Authorities by the short lived National Health Service Management Executive to become 'Champions of the People' (NHSME, 1992). In their roles as health purchasers, managers within the re-structured health authorites were encouraged to listen to 'Local Voices', that is the voices of their local populations, rather than to be driven solely by professional interests in making choices over which health services to purchase. The intention was to ensure that services were responsive to health needs as expressed by actual and potential users of the service, rather than by the interests of providers. The mechanisms through which such voices were to be heard included market research, focus groups, health forums and public meetings which often involved direct contact between local people and staff involved primarily in managerial and planning posts, rather than professional service providers.

One important feature of the 'Local Voices' initiatives was that they recognised that the population as a whole had a legitimate interest in the nature and quantity of health services to be provided within the area in which they lived. One did not have to be an active consumer of services to have a right to express a view. Most people, at some stage in their lives, will use the National Health Service and thus everyone can be regarded as a potential consumer of health services. This attempt to enable people to have a say in influencing the total supply of services can be regarded as a recognition that choice exercised at the point of use, that is at the point when a person goes to their General Practitioner in order to access secondary health services, can only be exercised within the scope of what is available. Nevertheless, the proposals coming from central government stopped way short of suggesting that local health services should be accountable to local people through either representative or participative democratic mechanisms. Consumer choice remained the pre-eminent mechanism through which individuals could influence the services they receive. However, by the mid-1990s the possibility that public accountability for health services might be enhanced through local authorities taking on the role of health purchaser was being aired in debates involving both policy makers and academics (Cooper *et al.*, 1995).

The celebration of individual choice as a mechanism intended to secure more responsive and accountable services appeared to attract support from a broad spectrum of opinion. Like 'community', 'choice' has been invoked as a mantra repeated largely without questioning whether it was choice that people wanted, rather than confidence that the services available would meet their needs (Barnes and Prior, 1995). Its essential 'rightness' as an objective to be pursued has rarely been questioned even though it may have little meaning in relation to many of the ways in which people come to use services. Barnes and Prior suggest that public service use needs to be considered along five dimensions in order to determine whether 'choice' may play a part in empowering individual service users. These dimensions relate to:

1. The degree of coercion associated with service use.
2. Predictability – can the user determine the likely effects of services in advance of their use?
3. The frequency of service use which will affect the degree of expertise the user develops in determining likely outcomes of service use.
4. The significance of the services in relation to different types of need, and
5. Participation – the extent to which successful outcomes depend on the involvement of the user as co-producer of services.

For example, someone who is forced to enter a psychiatric hospital under a section of the 1983 Mental Health Act cannot be considered to have exercised choice in making use of services, while someone who has been severely injured in a road traffic accident is unlikely to prioritise choice about which hospital to be taken to over the speed of arriving there. In contrast to these situations, if therapy is to be effective it involves the active participation of the person receiving the service in what might be regarded as a co-producer role. The fact that the nature of the relationship between service provider and user is the means through which the service is delivered may mean that an ability to exercise some choice over the therapist *is* an important factor in determining effective outcomes for the recipient of the service.

There is another reason why choice can have only a limited role in ensuring more responsive and accountable public services. In addition to responding to those who make direct use of their services, public services are also intended to reflect the interests of citizens who may never be in the position of using those services on their own behalf. Compulsory detention of people experiencing severe mental disorder is legitimated not only because it is considered to be in the interests of the health of the person so detained, but also because such detention may serve to protect others. More generally, funding services such as health and education through taxation is legitimated because it is in the interests of all citizens that the population as a whole is healthy and well educated. Hence citizens generally have an interest in being able to influence public services whether or not they make direct use of them.

The notion of individual choice is also associated with that of 'exit': if the service user is dissatisified with the service being provided, she may take her custom elsewhere. For this to be a feasible option, a number of circumstances are necessary:

- alternatives need to exist;
- the person concerned needs access to information not only about the existence of alternative options, but also about characteristics of alternatives which might suggest that they would not only overcome dissatisfaction with existing services, but also not substitute new for existing problems;
- moving from one option to another should be practically possible;
- moving from one option to another should not of itself generate damaging disruption.

If one considers the circumstances in which most people use health and social care services, it is clear that all these circumstances will rarely apply. In spite of the market development encouraged by the Conservative government, a major problem for many users of social care services is still finding any available services, rather than making difficult decisions about whether alternative services would meet need more effectively. The significance of interpersonal interaction as a means through which services are delivered means that obtaining information about likely differences between services is highly problematic. And for many people the notion that they will be in a position to shop around for alternatives is simply unrealistic. There are many circumstances in which people make use of services when and because their personal resources are low and a part of the need is for others to take over burdens which are becoming too difficult to carry alone. Perhaps the most clear example of this is the case of an older person suffering from dementia who is admitted to a residential home. There are also many other instances in which describing the way in which people use services as 'consumption' is neither accurate nor helpful and to prioritise consumer choice over all other considerations as a way of strengthening the position of the user *vis-à-vis* the provider cannot be an effective strategy.

Nevertheless, during the 1980s there was increasing evidence that service users were dissatisfied with their lack of influence over the services available to them (e.g. Beresford and Croft, 1986). The prospect that they would be encouraged to express preferences over important aspects of service provision was to be welcomed. In particular, many disabled people saw advantages in the possibility of directly employing their own care assistants as a means of exercising choice over who would provide care, and how it would be provided. At the time of writing, legislation to enable cash payments to be made to disabled people by social services departments for this purpose was about to be introduced (Community Care (Direct Payments) Bill). Yet few users of services have been wholeheartedly advocating the development of choice within the marketplace. Their aims are for the availability of alternatives within statutory services, rather than for competition between the state and the private sector (Barnes *et al.*, 1996a).

The celebration of choice within public policy has a deeper meaning which needs to be understood in considering the significance of the initiatives described in later chapters of this book. Giddens (1991) has suggested that the necessity to exercise choice is one of the conditions of life within the contemporary world; 'we have no choice but to choose' (*ibid.*, p. 81). The exercise of consumer choice is posited as the means through which individuals construct their own identities in a world in which such identities are no longer given through membership of a particular social class, nor are able to be derived from an occupation entered in early adulthood and left on retirement (Bauman, 1991; Beck, 1992). People choose their own lifestyles rather than automatically adopting those of the family and culture into which they are born. Identities can be bought, along with the particular clothes, music, food or intoxicant through which such identities are expressed.

Lindsay Prior (1993) considered the way in which such consumerism may further serve to exclude rather than empower people with mental health problems:

But modern systems of consumption are also aimed at the differentiation and atomization of individuals, and as such result in the endless formation and reformation of social distinctions. And therein lies a problem for people with psychiatric disorders. For, as we have seen, one significant aspect of serious mental illness as it is assessed in the late twentieth century, is the perceived inability of mentally ill persons to manipulate a symbolic order successfully, or at least, with any rational plan. And this observation alone should generate suspicions about the potential of people who are mentally ill to integrate themselves as consumers into mainstream social life. This apart from the fact that the majority of people with serious psychiatric disorders simply do not have material resources sufficient to locate themselves as economic agents in the wider society – the modal disposable income for members of the study group after the deduction of subsistence costs, for example, was just £10 per week. Hence, rather than entering in to the social worlds of the economically active, ex-patients in the community tend to live in a subworld of the disabled and the handicapped and the sick – a subworld in which contacts with mainstream life are, at best, fleeting and superficial.

(Prior, 1993, p. 178)

What Prior is suggesting here is that, not only might people with mental health problems find it difficult to behave as consumers in relation to specific mental health services, but that they are seriously disadvantaged more broadly within a consumerist society. This is relevant in view of the objectives of community care policy and is an issue I will return to later in this book.

Authority and knowledge

One feature of contemporary life which provides a focus for much post-modernist analysis is that of the challenge to traditional authorities. Authority deriving from religion, family, established politics and scientific epistemology is being challenged. Different sources of authority, based on alternative knowledge systems or on experiential knowledge, are being claimed and, in some cases, institutionalised. Such challenges can be experienced as empowering, but they may also be experienced as risky: if no authority is to be trusted, how confident can we be that our decisions are going to be beneficial rather than harmful? And further, if science cannot be trusted to reveal the 'truth'; if there is no basis for shared understandings of how the world works, can there be a basis on which shared life is possible?

Keat *et al.* (1994) have suggested that constructing public service users as 'consumers' is inadequately understood solely in terms of the relationship of exchange within a commodity market. If the objective of consumerism is the production of goods and services which are responsive to demands and satisfy the preferences of consumers, then the concept of 'consumer authority' has to be brought into play. They note:

at first sight there may seem to be something very odd or paradoxical about attributing authority to consumers, for at least two reasons. First, more familiar uses of the concept of authority typically involve its attribution to specific individuals or social groups with a limited and fairly clearly defined membership. Second, and relatedly, its attribution to such individuals or groups is typically based on their claims to have some special abilities, qualifications, expertise, etc., which entitles them to exercise such authority in making – and enforcing – various kinds of judgements and decisions.

(ibid., p. 3)

The implication of prioritising consumer responsiveness over provider judgement is that neither the judgement of professionals nor the rules of bureaucrats should be considered more authoritative than the expressed preferences of the consumer. Extending the notion of customer satisfaction from the supermarket to the school, the hospital or the day centre, brings the authority of the consumer into conflict with the authority of the professional. And professional authority is, *par excellence*, an authority deriving from training, qualifications and membership of associations of peers who legitimate and supervise practice on the basis of internally determined criteria. If such authority is not to be trusted, why then should professionals be in a position to exercise power over consumers, and be paid substantial salaries for doing so?

Within health and social care, the link between professionalism and caring – the 'caring professions' – provides another element to this dynamic. Care and control are dual aspects of the work undertaken by many welfare professionals. The power inherent in controlling functions is explicit and derives from statutory duties such as those contained within child care or mental health legislation. The position of those who find themselves subject to such powers is not that of a consumer able to exit from services if they are experienced as unsatisfactory. The need for protection of people in this type of situation is recognised by the existence of procedures designed to scrutinise the way in which controlling powers are exercised. Mental Health Review Tribunals and the Mental Health Act Commission are examples of this (Barnes, 1996a). However, power exercised through the provision of care may be more difficult to challenge simply because it is less overt. Hugman (1991) suggested that professionals control important aspects of their clients' lives: where they live, with whom they live, what they wear, what they eat, the way they spend their time, through the informal rules existing within residential or day care settings. Marsh and Fisher (1992) described ways in which social workers claimed to be working in partnerships with their clients, but were in fact assuming an authority to determine important aspects of the way in which they lived their daily lives without explicitly negotiating these with their clients. The unequal power relationships inherent in such encounters cannot simply be shifted by recasting clients as consumers.

Re-defining citizens and citizenship

One response to the inadequacy of consumerist philosophy as a means of constructing the relationship between people and services, has been a renewal of interest in notions of citizenship. While couched in the language of citizenship, the Charter movement which formed Prime Minister John Major's big idea and which was intended to put his distinctive stamp on Tory public policy, was designed essentially to promote the individual service user as consumer rather than citizen (Prior, 1995; Prior, Stewart and Walsh, 1993). Indeed, as Pollitt (1994) demonstrated, the ideology underpinning the Citizens Charter was one which was hostile to any idea that citizens should develop a collective voice intended to represent the views of service users:

> The theoretical citizen cherished by the Conservative government is not a member of any pressure group but rather a heroic lone consumer with time, money and information to back up his or her individual choices. This paragon sounds suspiciously middle class – and relatively rare.
>
> *(ibid.,* p. 11)

The Citizen's Charter had the effect of confusing two entirely different concepts: that of a consumer of specific services, and membership of a political community which defines the status of citizen. It identified four mechanisms intended to enable a more informed citizenry able to assert their wishes in opposition to the vested interests of welfare bureaucrats: the privatisation of services; the introduction of contracting with the private sector for services which remained a public sector responsibility; developing choices within public sector services; and consultation with the people who are affected by services (Prime Minister, 1991). These mechanisms derive from rather different views of public service and relationships between those services and 'the public'. The inclusion of consultation and the generation of a broader range of services within the public sector alongside the objective of privatising services is one reason why the Citizens' Charter was not rejected out of hand by many whose political and ideological affiliations were very different from those of John Major.

However, responsiveness to customers cannot be equated with accountability to citizens. It ignores the fact that welfare services are provided out of the public purse in order to benefit all citizens (Ranson and Stewart, 1994). Aggregating the outcomes of the exercise of individual choice at the point of use, cannot be a satisfactory basis on which to determine the pattern of services intended to benefit indirect and potential users and citizens as a whole.

Debates about welfare and citizenship have become increasingly prominent during the 1990s. Like 'community'. the notion of citizenship has been re-discovered and is being re-interpreted as a focus for new thinking about relationships between individuals and the state.

The key strands of the debate which have a particular relevance to a consideration of community care and citizenship are as follows:

1. A development of the notion of social rights.
2. A consideration of the role which procedural rights may play in securing access to welfare and fair treatment by public services.
3. Arguments for an extension of civil rights to groups not already protected by anti-discrimination legislation.
4. The gendered nature of much earlier thinking about 'the citizen' and the development of notions of citizenship which include rather than exclude women.
5. The notion of citizenship not only as a status, but as a practice. This refers to the ability of nominal citizens to participate within civic, social and economic life.

In the following section I will discuss key aspects of each issue in terms of their relevance for developing an understanding of community care in practice. I return to explore the application of these ideas in greater detail in the final chapter of this book.

Social rights

The notion that social rights are as much a right of citizenship as civil and political rights is the foundation on which the welfare state rests. Social rights are concerned with social justice and the obligations which this creates. All citizens should have access to the basic material, cultural and health resources which will enable them to live within society and thus there are positive obligations on citizens to contribute through the tax system so that such resources can be made available (Plant, 1992).

Advocates of the inclusion of social rights alongside civil and political rights as comprising the status of citizenship, assert that social rights should be unconditional:

Civil and political rights are not dependent on living a virtuous life; nor does one have to be a member of the deserving poor to qualify for social rights.

(Plant, *ibid.*, p. 160)

However, such a commitment is disputed by those committed to *laissez faire* capitalism and political liberalism. Right-wing thinkers make a distinction between the negative liberties to freedom from interference enshrined within civil and political rights, and the positive rights to receive resources from the state which are implied by social rights. Not only can there be no absolute right to receive resources which are limited and thus have to be rationed, neo-liberals argue that the obligation on citizens to contribute to the provision of those resources is a restriction on individual rights to dispose of their income in whatever way they choose.

From a very different perspective, the implementation of a commitment to social rights does have problems. While entitlements to specific financial benefits within the social security system can be defined by reference to particular, if disputed, criteria, entitlements to other forms of welfare services are complicated not only by the difficulty in specifying qualifying criteria, but also because prescription of services to be provided conflicts with responsiveness to individual needs. Alcock (1989) argues that the welfare rights model should be extended to other entitlements, but it is hard to see how any statute could be framed in such a way as to define rights to the provision of flexible services. It is, perhaps, for this reason that some sections of the disabilty movement are arguing, in some cases reluctantly, for individuals to receive financial resources to enable them to purchase the support services they determine for themselves to be most appropriate. Such a tactic makes clear the right to receive a service, but leaves the determination of exactly what service is to be purchased up to the individual concerned.

Procedural rights

One strategic response to the resource rationing problem inherent in access to health and social care services as an entitlement shared by all those meeting predefined criteria, is the promotion of procedural rights as a means of ensuring fair treatment. This strategy has been considered in relation to a number of welfare services, including community care (Doyle and Harding, 1992). Doyle and Harding note that governments have been reluctant to implement legislation which provides procedural rights, even though those rights are not accompanied by an absolute right to receive services. The 1986 Disabled Persons Act provided a number of procedural rights, including the right to receive a written statement of the results of an assessment of needs, which have not been implemented. Guidance from the Department of Health following the implementation of the 1990 NHS and Community Care Act revealed a fear that any clear identification of need arising from an assessment would carry with it an obligation on the part of local authorities to provide a service. Local authorities were advised not to make explicit statements of need unless they were confident of being in a position to provide a service in response for fear that they would open themselves up to litigation (SSI, 1992). The result was a series of contortions in the design of assessment procedures and instruments intended to avoid the tricky word 'need'. In such circumstances the achievement of procedural rights in respect of welfare services could be seen to be a step forward.

Proposals relating to procedural rights emphasise the need for:

- information;
- advice, advocacy and representation;
- access;
- promptness;
- handling of individual cases;
- redress through appeals and complaints.

(Doyle and Harding, *ibid.*, p. 74)

While action in these areas would respond to the reported difficulties which many service users have identified (Barnes and Wistow, 1992) and may help, for example, to ensure fair treatment for ethnic minority groups whose access to services is prevented by exclusionary practices, there is a danger that the mechanisms required to protect limited procedural rights divert attention from direct service provision. And ensuring that procedural rights are respected will often not respond to the real concerns of the person on the receiving end of services (Barnes, 1996a). Procedural rights are also clearly service focussed and cannot address the wider experiences of disabled and older citizens seeking to live integrated lives within the community.

Civil rights

The disability rights movement in the UK which grew in the 1980s and had achieved prominence by the mid-1990s seeks to extend the statutory protection offered by anti-discrimination legislation (ADL) from women and ethnic minorities to disabled people. In so doing it has argued that the difficulties faced by disabled people are not the result of their individual functional limitations, but of institutionalised practices which exclude disabled people as a group (Barnes, 1991). The term 'disabled people' is intended to include all those with impairments who experience disability as social restriction. This could include physically, sensorily, intellectually and emotionally disabled people, although not all those with these different types of impairments identify themselves as disabled.

The scope of the legislation which was the focus for ADL campaigns involving the tactics of direct action as well as more traditional political lobbying, was intended to include all spheres of social, economic and civic life. The aims were to make illegal the exclusion of disabled people from mainstream education, from employment, from recreational and cultural venues and pursuits and from political participation. The front cover of *The Politics of Disablement* (Oliver, 1990), written by a disabled activist and academic, has a picture of a man in a wheelchair at the bottom of a flight of steps leading up to a polling station. This provides an unambiguous image allowing campaigners to present a powerful case for action to remove such obvious discrimination. At the start of particular campaigns Vic Finkelstein, another disabled academic and activist, asked 'Where's the steps?' with a view of identifying precisely what were the barriers which each particular campaign sought to overcome and how those barriers might be communicated effectively to those whom activists were seeking to influence.

Arguments for the passage of anti-discrimination legislation have been based on the immorality of not providing the same protection to disabled people as is afforded to other disadvantaged groups. They have also referred to the demographic changes resulting in a population with a much higher percentage of very old people, with a corresponding increase in the incidence of disability, and by reference to both United Nations and European Union strategies aiming at realising the full potential of disabled people (Barnes, 1991). Taken together, the latter two points amounted to an argument that it was neither socially nor economically feasible to exclude a significant proportion of the population from the participation open to non-disabled people.

Mental health user groups have not had a high profile within the civil rights campaigns of the 1990s. This might be considered surprising since, in important respects, the civil rights of those considered to be mentally disordered are more obviously restricted than are those of people with physical impairments. The legal concept of incapacity can mean that people defined as incapable may lose the power to manage their own financial affairs or be unable to enter into a contract. A considerable number of people receiving treatment for mental illness are unable to undertake jury service and, if the presiding officer determines that someone is suffering from mental incapacity, that person will not be allowed to vote in an election. Regardless of the degree of lucidity at the time of an election, patients resident in psychiatric hospitals may be excluded from voting because they fail to meet the residence criteria. Patients detained under the 1983 Mental Health Act can be compelled to receive medical treatment against their will. In other circumstances that could amount to trespass or battery (Law Commission, 1991). However, the focus of the majority of action taken by mental health user groups has been on those services which are intended to meet their health and social care needs, rather than on civil rights campaigns (Barnes and Shardlow, 1996).

Mental health groups have been engaged in campaigns being fought in defence of further restrictions on the civil rights of people with mental health problems. Proposals from the Royal College of Psychiatrists (RCP, 1993) that the ability to treat people compulsorily should be extended to certain people not detained in hospital have been resisted, as has the introduction of the Supervised Discharge Order. One of the arguments against the extension of controlling powers is that such powers are already used disproportionately to detain Afro-Caribbean people (Bowl and Barnes, 1990) and any extension stands in danger of contributing further to discrimination against black people.

The gendered citizen

Feminist discussions of notions of citizenship broaden the debate beyond questions of equal opportunities and equal rights. Winning the vote, and thus the key status of citizenship, has made it possible for the citizen to be considered as a gendered subject for the first time within the last century. However, the implications of that for an understanding of the scope and nature of citizenship are still to be developed. The pursuit of equality should not obscure the importance of recognising the contribution which difference can make to the development of an inclusive citizenship (Bock and James, 1992). This argument can be extended beyond the significance of gender differences to differences based on ethnic, sexual and cultural identities (Phillips, 1993).

Traditional discussions of both the rights and responsibilities of citizens have located these within the public sphere in which the relationship between the individual and the state is most immediately evident. The ultimate duty of the citizen is to be prepared to die in defence of the state; the duty on women to give birth for the state is a more ambiguous citizenship obligation. Indeed, motherhood and citizenship have been seen as mutually exclusive (Pateman, 1992). One effect of including women's lives within a consideration of citizenship is that the separation of public and private lives starts to become less clear-cut and citizenship can no longer be understood as a status which only has meaning beyond the confines of home and family. This is of particular relevance in considering a public policy which depends on the preparedness of women to contribute private, unpaid welfare in their own homes.

One argument is that women should be entitled to benefits in their own right on the basis of this contribution of their unpaid labour. Work undertaken within the private sphere, such as child care and the care of elderly relatives, should receive recognition equal to work undertaken in the public sphere which results in benefit entitlements based on social insurance contributions.

But beyond this, the argument which the women's movement has had some success in promoting, is that the 'personal is the political'. The division of domestic labour within households; the nature of sexual relationships; assumptions about the 'naturalness' of women's nurturing skills and thus about the location of responsibility for providing both emotional and tending care are all political issues which have implications for an understanding of the way in which citizenship is defined and the arenas within which it is practised. It is through their engagement with the 'small democracies' of, for example, schools, child care institutions, or carers' groups, rather than the 'big democracies' of political parties (Siim, 1994) that many women are mobilised for political participation and hence contribute to changes in the practice of politics as well as the issues on the political agenda.

The significance of feminist ideas about citizenship have relevance not only for understanding the position of women on whom community care policies depend to provide unpaid care for family and friends. Firstly, recognising the way in which public policies shape private lives has relevance for all those who have been constructed as care givers or care receivers. Secondly, the participative forms of democracy to which the women's movement has made a substantial contribution provide models which user and carer movements can adopt and adapt to pursue their projects. And thirdly, the challenge to unitary notions of citizenship provided by emphasising the significance of gender difference can contribute to enhancing the citizenship of others whose difference relates to ethnicity, disability or mental distress.

The practice of citizenship

The last aspect of contemporary debates on citizenship which I want to consider for its particular relevance to an understanding of community care as a policy which seeks the inclusion of previously excluded groups is that which concerns the notion of citizenship not only as a status which ascribes rights and imposes obligations, but as a practice which is concerned with the participation of individuals within social and civic life. It is a notion of citizenship which has been discussed as moving from 'being' to 'doing' (Prior, Stewart and Walsh, 1995).

This approach shares some of the insights offered by the feminist analysis of citizenship. In considering those spheres in which the citizen may fulfil the practice of citizenship, a sharp distinction between participation within spheres of activity defined by the state and participation within the much broader institutions of civil society is rejected by Prior and his colleagues. Hence participative citizenship can encompass collective organisation based on shared identities deriving from gender, race or disability, as well as participation within the constitutional processes of the state. Such collectivities may be grounded in concerns which are experienced initially as affecting personal lives, but which are subject to a social analysis which enables common experiences to be understood not simply as private disaffections, but as arising from structural inequalities and from other mechanisms through which particular groups are excluded.

Right-wing responses to the perceived passivity of individuals grown dependent on the safety net provided by the welfare state have included the promotion of the 'active citizen' as a model of civic virtue. The active citizen, according to Douglas Hurd when he was Home Secretary in 1989, is one who brings the enterprise culture into public life. He is someone with time and money to spare who is prepared to make a voluntary contribution to improving the lot of those who do not share in the advantages he experiences. On the Left, a recognition of alienation from political processes has led to rather different solutions being proposed. Some have seen in social movements a new form of political action which can motivate those for whom trade unions and traditional political parties are neither relevant nor meaningful. Others have turned to the more classical tradition of 'civic republicanism' for a model of citizenship practice which recognises collective as well as individual responsibilities and interests.

The challenge is to transform the existing relationship between government and citizens from one in which little exists to give expression to citizens' collective voice beyond the blunt mechanism of the ballot box, to one in which citizens are active contributors to processes of collective decision making.

(Prior *et al., ibid.*, p. 20)

That approach is highly relevant to the pursuit of a community care practice in which those who have been defined as objects of policy making become active subjects involved as co-producers both at the level of policy making, and in the implementation of that policy in day to day practice. It is one which has contributed to the development within public services of counter arguments to the consumerist solutions to inflexible bureaucratic practices offered by the right wing. These have focussed on improving the accountability of services to their publics through revitalising the dialogue which takes place between elected politicians, officers and service users (Stewart, 1996; Stewart *et al.*, 1994), and on a reconsideration of the institutional forms through which welfare is delivered (Jordan and Jones, 1995).

The following two chapters will consider some examples of ways in which that dialogue is being encouraged in practice through the initiatives generated by users of services themselves, and through action being taken within health and social care services. The examples discussed also suggest ways in which the structures and processes of welfare systems are undergoing change intended to shift the balance from producer to consumer interests. Chapter 3 focusses on developments in the self-organisation of groups of people who have been constructed as users of services, while in Chapter 4 I consider initiatives which have come about from within health and social care services in response to a genuine desire to develop more sensitive services, or which have come about as a result of top-down pressures to 'get close to the customer'.

The growth of user movements

Introduction

Throughout the 1980s and 1990s there has been a substantial increase in the self-organisation of people who have previously been constructed as clients of welfare services. While self-help groups and voluntary organisations have a long history within the 'mixed economy of welfare', these new user groups have certain characteristics which to some extent set them apart from previous examples of collective organisations operating within civil society. One such characteristic is that the members of many of these groups are assumed by some to be incapable of self-organisation because of the incapacity thought to be an essential feature of their 'condition'; another is that they identify themselves in opposition to voluntary agencies organised *for* disabled people or other groups, as groups largely composed *of* and certainly controlled *by* such people; while a third is the emphasis they place on collective action both as a means and an end. As such, an underlying purpose is to campaign for the inclusion of people previously excluded from mainstream society, not only socially and economically, but also spatially through containment in long-stay hospitals, specialist residential homes and other accommodation designed for those with 'special needs'.

Many groups operating at a local level are affiliated to national umbrella organisations, such as the British Council of Organisations of Disabled People, People First (people with learning difficulties) and the United Kingdom Advocacy Network (people with mental health problems). Together they constitute a social movement with a significance extending beyond the immediate impact of changes achieved in particular local services. The origins of this movement preceded the embracing of the consumerist ideology within health and social care services and thus cannot be considered to have been caused by a shift of perspective from producer to consumer interests. Nevertheless, some aspects of the critiques of statutory services offered by user groups reflect the analysis that producer interests had become too powerful to enable the provision of services sufficiently sensitive to the needs and circumstances of those for whom they were intended. It has thus been possible for reformers within the statutory services to encourage and support the development of such groups, and for differences in objectives to become obscured or confused.

Analysts (some of whom are also participants) have discussed aspects of disability and mental health movements in the light of theories of 'new social movements' and have drawn different conclusions about the usefulness of such an approach (Oliver, 1990; Rogers and Pilgrim, 1991; Shakespeare, 1993). New social movement theorists (e.g. Melucci, 1985; Touraine, 1985) suggest that it is important to understand movements seeking social change which have emerged in the post-industrial period as different in important respects from those which formed around class interests in an earlier period. Movements discussed in this context are typically environmental and peace movements, and those based on common identities such as women's movements, gay and lesbian movements and black people's movements. New social movements are considered to be different in organisational form, ideology and objectives from class-based movements. For example, their goals are considered to relate to cultural issues which emphasise social relations, rather than goals relating to economic growth and re-distribution. However, Scott (1990) and Kaase (1990) have questioned whether these diverse groups have anything in common other than their position within post-industrial society.

In this chapter I consider the nature of user movements and their wider significance as forces for social change, before turning in Chapter 4 to initiatives taken from within health and social care services designed to involve users in decision making in order to produce more responsive services.

Before continuing this discussion it is important to reflect on the significance of language. I have employed the term 'user' to refer to those who are or could be in receipt of services because of needs associated with physical, sensory or cognitive impairments, mental distress or age. I adopt this term as one which has less ideological content than the term 'consumer' and thus which is intended to offer a neutral description of a relationship between those who provide and those who receive services. Nevertheless the term is not without problems:

- some people reject the term because of its connotations with drug misuse;
- some feel that it implies an active decision to make use of services when their experience is of having been forced into a relationship with services against their will. This is most evident among those who are or have been in receipt of mental health services, some of whom describe themselves as 'survivors' of interventions which they have experienced as oppressive or damaging;
- people may not have an active relationship with services, but nevertheless be active participants in groups established around shared experience of disability or past use of services; and finally

* it is easy to forget that a term which describes a particular relationship cannot describe the whole person. Well before the contemporary preoccupation with 'consumers' Mike Simpkin (1979) warned of the way in which labelling people as 'clients' can serve to homogenise those who receive services and to separate them from providers so that they are assigned to a distinct, and usually deviant, category of persons.

The development of a new language is part of the project of many of those engaged with the movements discussed here. I will continue to address issues related to this throughout the book.

The mental health user movement

In the mid 1980s a book called *The Politics of Mental Health* was published in the series: 'Critical Texts in Social Work and the Welfare State' (Banton *et al.*, 1985). The authors of this text were mental health practitioners and, while they offered an explicitly socialist perspective locating the politics of mental health within an analysis of the social construction of the individual, users of mental health services featured solely as case studies presented as objects of the professional gaze. There was no mention of users as active subjects undertaking their own analysis of the power dynamics within therapeutic relationships, nor organising themselves to support each other to challenge the professional construction of mental health services. Political activity was seen to be of considerable significance, but this was assumed to lie in 'radical struggle within the ordinary practice of mental health work' (*ibid.*, p. 194) rather than among mental health service users.

Rogers and Pilgrim (1991) date the origins of the British mental health users movement at around the same time that this book was published and they note that the British movement lagged behind similar developments both in the US and in Europe. One key event in the mid-1980s was the World Federation for Mental Health/MIND conference held in Brighton which was attended by delegates from the Dutch users' movement. These delegates made a powerful impact on British mental health service users at the conference and subsequently provided help and advice to local groups seeking to organise themselves for the first time. For example, input from the Dutch movement was significant in the establishment of Patients Councils in Nottingham (Gell, 1987), where the mental health user movement now has an influential local group which has also contributed to the development of other local and national groups.

Three years after the WFMH/MIND conference, Brighton was also the venue for another jointly sponsored international conference, this time with the explicit theme of user involvement in mental health services. For this event MIND worked with East Sussex County Council and Brighton Health Authority to co-organise an event called 'Common Concerns'. This brought together users and mental health professionals, and was described by Ros Hepplewhite, then Director of MIND, as 'a turbulent three days, as people's roles and sensitivities and aspirations were to some extent subject to uncomfortable analysis' (Hepplewhite, 1988).

The relationship between user activists and professionals sympathetic to users' concerns has been a continuing theme within the mental health user movement. In a 'Psychiatrists Apologia', Alec Jenner asked users at Common Concerns to recognise what science has to offer those experiencing mental distress, as well as encouraging psychiatrists to take responsibility for supporting the user movement and learn from the insights it can offer (Jenner, 1988). In contrast, the challenge to professional power and credibility which user critiques of psychiatry have constituted have been dismissed by some professionals as 'the ravings of mad men' (Barnes and Wistow, 1994a). Nevertheless, others have recognised the validity of that critique and have become allies, working with users to support the movement and to seek change within mental health services. The term 'ally' has been formally adopted by 'Survivors Speak Out' to describe professionals who have become members of the movement and to distinguish them from full user members. Some groups have refused to enter into dialogue with professionals and actively seek to disempower mental health workers whose interventions have been experienced as oppressive. Others have been prepared to work with sympathetic professionals or, indeed, become involved in decision making structures with professionals and managers who are not regarded as sympathetic, but whom the users are seeking to influence (Barnes *et al.*, 1996a). And there are other groups which largely accept the medical model of mental health and the authority of medical practitioners, while nevertheless asserting that service users should be able to express their views (Rogers and Pilgrim, 1991). These differences indicate the heterogeneity of ideologies evident within the mental health user movement, although a willingness to work with allies within mental health services is evident among most of the groups which have achieved a national profile and influence (see e.g., Read and Wallcraft, 1992; Beeforth *et al.*, 1994; Graley *et al.*, 1994).

The movement does not derive from the professionally led anti-psychiatry movement of the 1960s, nor, with some exceptions (e.g. Davey, 1994) has it given priority to developing an alternative model of mental distress from which to develop models of action. Elements of such a critique are evident within many of the responses of users to existing mental health services, but these are primarily based within the personal experiences of those who have found many services not only detrimental to their mental health, but also profoundly insensitive to their need to be heard and respected. The experience of mental distress itself and of having been a user of services is what brings mental health service users together to validate that experience as a source of expertise which should be respected in determining how services should be provided (Barnes and Shardlow, 1996).

The number and nature of groups which make up the mental health users' movement are constantly changing. At the time of writing, there were four major umbrella groups:

- Survivors Speak Out (SSO) which operates primarily as a network of individuals who identify themselves as survivors of mental health services;
- the UK Advocacy Network (UKAN) which promotes and supports the development of self and citizens advocacy groups across the country, including within the top security 'Special Hospitals';
- MINDLINK, which provides a forum for user members of the national mental health voluntary organisation MIND and which aims primarily at ensuring that there is a user voice influencing the policy and services offered by MIND itself; and
- Voices, which is a user network operating within the National Schizophrenia Fellowship (NSF). NSF has been primarily a support group for relatives of people diagnosed as having schizophrenia. Its policies have often been in conflict with those of MIND because they have sought to put a brake on psychiatric hospital closure, arguing that such closures have put unacceptable demands on the relatives of 'sufferers' who have been discharged. Nevertheless, users who accept the psychiatric diagnosis of schizophrenia have been able to assert their rights to be heard through NSF (Took, n.d.).

Local groups exist throughout the country, not all of which are affiliated to these national organisations. Groups may be linked to particular services: either user councils within hospital wards or day centres, or user forums based on geographical areas and linked to and often supported by community mental health teams. Others exist independently of services with links developed in order to enable influence to be exerted, rather than to receive support. The Nottingham Advocacy Group was one of the earliest groups to establish an independent identity from origins within service specific user councils (Gell, 1987).

Some groups of black mental health service users have been formed, for example, in Leicester and Manchester. The National Black Mental Health Association has sought to enable the voices of black people to be heard on mental health issues (NBMHA, n.d.) But the Association has struggled to secure funding to enable it to provide a co-ordinating role in relation to these groups (personal communication with the Acting Chair of the NBMHA).

Building on the early contact with the Dutch movement, international links have developed and a European user network was formed with prominent involvement from representatives from SSO and UKAN. In January 1995 the first newsletter of 'The European Network of Users and Ex-Users in Mental Health' was published. Articles in this newsletter reflected my earlier discussion of the conflict over language. One of the earliest debates within the fledgling European network was over its name and the newsletter reported an intense debate over whether the term 'survivor' should be included within this. Kersten Kempker argued for the inclusion of the term 'survivor' writing:

We have to accept, that there are people in the network, who try to use the psychiatric system, who call themselves mentally ill. They should accept, that there are also a lot of people, who were brutally abused and battered by psychiatry. We all have to respect the self-definition.

(Kempker, 1995)

The groups themselves are not static in their objectives and activities, but the key objectives relate to: advocacy (both self advocacy and citizen advocacy); influencing the nature and pattern of mental health services; and the provision of support to their members. The particular construction of mental illness as a condition which may result in the sufferer 'losing touch with reality' means that the focus for much advocacy work is on enabling the voices of those experiencing mental distress to be heard and taken seriously. Thus the day to day relationships between service users and those with direct responsibility for their care and treatment is a matter of considerable importance and it is the nature of that relationship which many advocacy groups seek to change. A report produced by a Users Council in Birmingham reported that users experienced medical staff as: 'impolite, arrogant, disrespectful, dismissive of users' wishes' (Barnes and Wistow, 1992a, p. 20). Descriptions of personal experiences of being on the receiving end of psychiatric interventions emphasise the personal disempowerment which advocacy aims to overcome (Chamberlin, 1988; Dyer, 1985; Community Psychiatric Nurses Association, 1987).

The mental health users' movement is grounded in the need to improve the day-to-day experiences of those in contact with the mental health system. It gives priority to ensuring better treatment for people on hospital wards; for those subject to detention under the Mental Health Act; and for those seeking rights to assessment under the NHS and Community Care Act. But those individual experiences have been used to develop a critique of mental health services as a whole and at both local and national level user groups are playing a role in service planning, in contracting, in training mental health workers and in service monitoring and evaluation (see Barnes *et al.*, 1996a and Harrison, 1993, for examples of local groups working to influence services).

Few groups are directly involved in service provision as they are in the United States (Chamberlin, 1988), although some have adopted this approach in preference to seeking to change the nature of services provided by statutory agencies. One example of this is McMurphy's in Sheffield. This took its name from the character in the film *One Flew Over the Cuckoo's Nest* and this was intended to demonstrate a rejection of traditional ways of providing mental health services. McMurphy's operates as a drop-in centre, primarily for younger people with mental health problems, which is run entirely by its members. One part of the centre is for women only. While members provide informal advocacy for each other on occasion, the emphasis is on providing an alternative space where members can spend time and engage in conversations and activities if they wish to, rather than seeking to influence the nature of services provided by statutory agencies. It is described in a review produced in 1995 as being:

based on the principles of self-help and mutual support and is both developed and run by those who use it. It offers opportunities to meet friends, to socialise and to share problems if necessary. We attempt to strengthen individuals' social networks in an attempt to combat the social alienation of the loss of confidence, demoralisation, aimlessness and despair often associated with mental health problems.

(McMurphy's, 1995)

Proposed changes in mental health legislation which would have the effect of extending the compulsory powers contained within the 1983 Mental Health Act provided a focus for campaigning by some groups, although mental health user groups have not had a high profile within campaigns for anti-discrimination legislation led by the disability movement (see below). Some have contributed to campaigns such as the MIND *Stress on Women* campaign (Darton *et al.*, 1994) and other projects which have sought to raise the profile of women's mental health needs and to secure specific changes in services intended to better meet these needs (GPMH/ERC, WFMH, 1994). Some users have worked together to design and conduct research intended not only to explore users' perspectives on services, but also to demonstrate that users are capable of undertaking research and that new ways of undertaking research as well as new ways of providing services are necessary if users are to be empowered (Beeforth, Conlan, and Graley, 1994; Davis, 1992). On a broader front, the movement seeks to raise public awareness about the nature of mental distress to overcome the stigma and fear which surround this, and to enable people who have been users of services to find jobs, get somewhere to live, engage in leisure activities and otherwise participate in the ordinary world.

'People First'

The growth of self-advocacy among people with learning difficulties in the UK has also been influenced by initiatives elsewhere in Europe and in both North America and Australia. While self-advocacy – people with learning difficulties advocating on their own behalf both individually and collectively – is the preferred aim of the movement, the support of professionals and other supporters has been of major importance in enabling the movement to achieve recognition, and it remains important in cases where full self-advocacy has not been possible to achieve. This has been recognised as a danger by professional sympathisers. They are aware of the potential for take-over or transformation of self-advocacy (Flynn and Ward, 1991) as well as more personal dilemmas concerning the way in which they may seek to influence the behaviour of people with learning difficulties experiencing for the first time the freedom to determine how they want to organise their time (Amans and Darbyshire, 1989).

On the other hand, the involvement of non-disabled people has been considered to have a particular significance in the context of movements of people with learning difficulties. This is reflected in the title of a pamphlet written by Paul Williams and published by the Campaign for Mentally Handicapped People. *Our Mutual Handicap* (Williams, 1978) was an early attempt on the part of a non-disabled person to 'put myself in the shoes of a mentally handicapped person'. Not only did it attempt to convey what it felt like to be 'mentally handicapped', it also pointed out the handicaps of others who seek to relate to mentally handicapped people:

Your handicap is great when you come into contact with us, and that fact increases our handicap. When one of us meets one of you, especially if it is for the first time, we are quite likely to lack many of the skills for successful communication. We may not be able to think of anything appropriate to say, or to put it into words, or to control our facial expression. But you also will show a great lack of skill. You will be embarrassed, you won't be able to think of anything appropriate to say, you will tend to talk in an inappropriate tone of voice, you will tend to have a wide grin on your face and ask questions without really being interested in an answer.

(Williams, *ibid.*)

The movement of people with learning difficulties has demonstrated that people who do not have learning difficulties nevertheless lack expertise in important areas and this has challenged professional assumptions about the basis on which it is possible to claim knowledge and understanding. People with learning difficulties may be better at understanding what each other are trying to say than are people who do not have learning difficulties. People whose communication skills are restricted to verbal skills may find it difficult to read behavioural communication or be creative in using pictures and other visual forms in establishing communication. Those who employ abstract concepts may not read in concrete descriptions of life experiences any evidence of an awareness of the meanings of those concepts.

Professional allies have sought to enable people with learning difficulties to tell their own stories in their own way, as well as to learn new ways of understanding the worlds of those who may have difficulty with verbal communication. An important example of the former was an anthology put together by staff at the Open University to provide course material for students (Atkinson and Williams, 1990). This included poetry, photographs, drawings and extracts from self-written or dictated accounts produced by people with learning difficulties with the support of intermediaries in day centres, colleges and in their own homes. Professional allies have also sought to enable the voices of people with learning difficulties to be heard through research. In the final section of the Open University collection the editors considered some of the implications of this approach towards seeking to understand the lives of people with learning difficulties for the conduct of research. They placed their approach (which was not intended to be 'research') within the broad traditions of qualitative and participative research and considered that the experience raises particular questions about:

- the relationship between the researcher, or interviewer, and the story-teller;
- the methods used in the story-telling;
- issues of ownership and control;
- the story of the research itself.

Other examples of researchers seeking alternative ways of understanding the worlds and experiences of people with learning difficulties and communicating these to others were contained in the companion volume to the Open University anthology (Brechin and Walmsley, 1989). One example was of a researcher seeking to enter the world of a deaf and blind young woman by covering his eyes and ears and reproducing her responses to objects which are intended to provide her with stimulation (Goode, 1979).

Elsewhere, Booth and Booth (1994) have used a life story approach to explore the experiences of people with learning difficulties who become parents. Their aim in adopting this approach was to give both credibility and precedence to the accounts of parents with learning difficulties over those of professionals. In a variety of ways, therefore, researchers have sought to ensure that the authentic voices of people with learning difficulties can be heard.

Achieving self-definition and overcoming negative labelling and stereotyping is a key objective of the self-advocacy movement. Other objectives and achievements summarised by Flynn and Ward (1991) are:

- questioning the configuration of power in service settings and the irreproachably well intentioned philosophies of the same;
- exchanging thoughts about their lives, experiences and aspirations through 'participation events';
- initiating self-help groups;
- beginning to contribute to the monitoring and evaluation of services;
- confronting the outlawed topics of preparation for independence, real wages and interesting work, personal freedom and intimate relationships, and the power advantage of parents and staff in service settings;
- and seeking to learn the skills required in order to be heard.

(Flynn and Ward, *ibid.*, p. 130)

This list includes reference to the imbalance in power relationships which exist within the 'primary group' of the family as well as within society more broadly. Self-advocacy is as much about enabling people with learning difficulties to achieve an adult status that is recognised and supported by other members of their families, as it is about increasing their influence over formal services, and in achieving recognition of their status as equal citizens within society more broadly. The potential for conflict which may be enhanced by initiatives which seek to strengthen the voice of people with learning difficulties and those which seek to increase the influence of family carers, is perhaps more evident here than it is in the case of other 'client groups'. I discuss this in more detail in Chapter 6.

The movement also seeks to support people who themselves want to become parents. The sexuality of people with learning difficulties has been the site of one of the most controversial debates around rights to self-determination. There are two broad aspects to this: firstly, concern about vulnerability to sexual abuse and sexual exploitation which may translate into a highly protective response which can result in denying the opportunities for people with learning difficulties to express their sexuality; and secondly, the eugenicist-inspired belief that handicapped people should not be allowed to reproduce because they would produce 'bad stock', or more mundanely, that they would generate the need for a considerable amount of support which would place an unacceptable demand on service providers. The latter argument leads to support for sterilisation as a contraceptive measure.

The issue of sterilisation is dealt with in a recent Law Commission report on mental incapacity (Law Commission, 1995). The report draws a clear distinction between citizen advocacy and substitute decision makers. The authors assert: 'The advocacy movement cannot deal with the legal difficulty which arises when a legally effective decision is needed and the person concerned does not have the capacity to make that decision' (para. 2.44). In this context they recommend that the authorisation of the courts should be required when any treatment is 'intended or reasonably likely' to render the person permanently infertile (para. 6.4).

The legal position with regard to sexuality is important both in terms of the protection from exploitation that it can offer, and in terms of the citizenship rights which can be confirmed or denied. But the issue is much more than a legal one. One of the women whose voice was heard in the Atkinson and Williams (1990) anthology made a poignant observation: 'Staff can have children. People like us need help' (p. 175) Although another saw the ability to have children as confirmation of her adult status: 'I can't remember what it was like to be a child. Everything is the same. But as a grown-up I can have a baby' (p. 31). Becoming parents can be a matter of great struggle for people with learning difficulties, but it can also provide great satisfaction (Booth and Booth, 1994). It is an issue which provides graphic demonstration of the link between the personal and the political in the struggles of people with learning difficulties.

In organisational terms the self-advocacy movement comprises a network of individuals and groups working in different ways to promote the self determination of people with learning difficulties. User groups or councils work within service settings to give a voice to people with learning difficulties in the organisation and management of such services. These are often supported or enabled by professionals and may find it difficult to achieve a high degree of independence from service providers. Nevertheless such groups may provide people with their first opportunity to express their views about the services they receive and they can provide a springboard to wider participation in the movement (Williams and Schoultz, 1984, pp. 198–203).

Many of the early initiatives in the UK which were not based around specific services were supported by the Campaign for the Mentally Handicapped (CMH). CMH organised a number of conferences which were attended by people with learning difficulties and provided opportunities for them to share their own experiences with each other, and to share those experiences with non-disabled people. One way of achieving that was simply through sharing a weekend which involved people living and attending recreational activities together as well as working together. The report of one such conference (Campaign for the Mentally Handicapped, 1973) called for others to take up the idea of such events and to repeat them elsewhere. At this stage CMH saw the major responsibility for ensuring the participation of people with learning difficulties as resting with those who provided services to them. However, by 1986 CMH was publishing material intended to assist those who wanted to develop self-advocacy groups (CMH, 1986).

Citizen Advocacy services bring together unpaid citizens with partners who have learning difficulties with the objective that the advocate will promote and defend the interests of their partner as if they were their own. John O'Brien has described the main characteristics and significance of citizen advocacy in the following way:

a valued citizen who is unpaid and independent of human services creates a relationship with a person who is at risk of social exclusion and chooses one or several of many ways to understand, respond and represent that person's interests as if they were the advocate's own, thus bringing their partner's gifts and concerns into the circles of ordinary community life.

(O'Brien, 1987)

Citizen advocacy is now widely accepted as a means of ensuring that the voices of those who find words difficult are still heard. There are many different schemes in the UK, throughout Europe, Australia and the United States, but in the UK the legislative endorsement of the role of advocates in representing people's interests in relation to services which was promised in the Disabled Persons' (Services, Consultation and Representation) Act of 1986 has not been forthcoming because the relevant sections of the act have not been implemented. In parts of Australia citizen advocacy has followed more of a community development approach than is evident in the UK which has the benefit of enhancing a sense of community ownership of advocacy pro- grammes (Ramcharan and Grant, 1993). The relationship between citizen advocacy, guardianship and more formal legal advocacy is one which was touched on in the Law Commission's (1995) report on mental incapacity, but it is an issue which has yet to be fully resolved in practice.

'People First' started in America and was established in the UK following a visit by a small group of people with learning difficulties to find out about it in 1984. People First in the UK consists both of local groups and a national office which supports the development of self advocacy at all levels.

'People First' is a statement by the members that they are human beings first and that their disabilities are second. People First is a statement that people with disabilities desire to be seen as people who have value and dignity, to be seen as people who can participate and contribute to the community.

(CMH, 1986, p. 4)

People First have been involved in conducting research into users' views of services (Whittaker, Gardner and Kershaw, 1990); they have organised conferences for people with learning difficulties and mixed events involving service providers, policy makers, and researchers as well as people with learning difficulties. They conducted a successful campaign to get rid of 'Little Stephen' – the image used by the charity Mencap to prompt charitable donations from members of the public. They have established groups for black people with learning diffi- culties, for young people, and groups to address the particular experiences of women with learning difficulties. As well as focussing directly on community care policies and services and supporting self advocacy groups, they have addressed issues such as: sexuality and relationships, jobs, the law, and the language used to refer to people with learning difficulties. They also fought a successful campaign with the Charity Commission to achieve recognition as a charity run by and for people with learning difficulties (People First, n.d.).

Another element of the movement to empower people with learning difficulties has been the campaign to introduce service brokerage as a means of challenging professional vested interests (Brandon and Towe, 1989). Brokers act on behalf of people with learning difficulties to negotiate the support and services which they and their parents decide they need. This espouses an explicitly consumerist philosophy and derives from the experiences of Canadian parents of people with learning difficulties in battling with large scale service systems. Not only does it challenge professional vested interest, but also some of the other attempts to enable people to participate within services. Brandon and Towe refer to 'participation' having: 'replaced "community" as the fresh aerosol term to tart up descriptions of jaded services' (*ibid.*, p. 20). However, their response to participation initiatives is somewhat confused. On the one hand they claim that 'Kieran' (the name given to the man whose experiences they discuss) does not want to appoint staff or play a role in managing the ATC which he attends because what he really wants is a job. But on the next page they say he does need to be involved in both the running and management of services and 'through that to their planning and development' (*ibid.*, p. 25). Service brokerage emphasises the rights of individual consumers to determine the services they receive as individuals. Such an objective may be shared by the broader user movement, but the particular model has not been widely taken up.

Disabled people

The disabled peoples' movement has been the subject of a considerable amount of academic analysis and has generated a substantial literature authored by people who are both academic analysts and activists within the movement (see, for example, Barnes and Oliver, 1995; Barton, 1993; Davis, 1993; Hasler, 1993; Shakespeare, 1993). In contrast with *The Politics of Mental Health* (see above, p. 48), *The Politics of Disablement*, published in the same series (Oliver, 1990), was authored by a disabled activist who went on to become the first Professor of Disability Studies in the UK. In this book disabled people are subjects, not objects, and political activity is clearly the province of the disability movement, not located within professional practice. The movement draws its strength from a theoretical analysis of the social construction of disability which locates the 'problem' within society rather than within individual disabled people and thus targets social organisation rather than disabled people as requiring change.

The social model defines both the philosophy and the strategy of the disability movement. It opposes the notion that disability is the result of impairment, with the notion that disability is caused by social organisation which excludes disabled people. It rejects an understanding of disability as a personal tragedy which should prompt compassion, and instead analyses the experience of disabled people as that of oppression and discrimination which should prompt action to achieve social justice. It has been expressed in a number of ways:

The experiences of disabled people are of social restrictions in the world around them, not of being a person with a 'disabling condition'. This is not to deny that individuals experience 'disability'; rather it is to assert that the individual's experience of 'disability' is created in interactions with a physical and social world designed for non-disabled living.

(Swain *et al.*, 1993, p. 2)

The following is taken from the statement of aims and objectives produced by the Derbyshire Coalition of Disabled People, one of the earliest disabled peoples' coalitions to be established in the UK:

We believe the most effective policies are ones which attack the root causes of disability. Our view is that these root causes are to be found in society. For this reason Coalition policy is directed out into society, and aims to promote awareness and take actions which remove social and physical barriers and thus overcome disability.

The contemporary disabled peoples' movement emerged rather earlier than was the case among users of mental health services. The key year which provided the event which triggered the establishment of the British Council of Organisations of Disabled People (BCODP) was 1981 – the International Year of Disabled People (IYDP). The announcement of the IYDP prompted the substantial charitable organisations for disabled people operating in the UK to become involved in organising a series of events and working parties to focus attention on disability, to raise money and to generate new opportunitites for the development of services for disabled people. It provided an opportunity for those prompted by charitable concern to 'do their bit'. One example of an event at a local level serves to illustrate the response of organisations of disabled people such as UPIAS (the Union of the Physically Impaired Against Segregation), to the control of the IYDP by charitable bodies led by able-bodied people. In Derbyshire the Duke of Devonshire threw open his substantial estate to money-raising events involving charitable bodies. Local members of UPIAS sought to be involved in this but their approach was rejected. Out of this experience the Derbyshire Coalition of Disabled People (DCDP) was born. At a national level the challenge to able-bodied control of disability organisations resulted in the establishment of BCODP and the key distinction between organisations *of* and organisations *for* disabled people.

By the early 1990s BCODP comprised over 95 independent organisations controlled by disabled people. The sole criterion for membership of BCODP was that organisations must be controlled by disabled people. It described itself as:

the only national assembly which truly represents the interests of all disabled people including people with physical and sensory impairments as well as people who face multiple dicrimination and oppression such as black and other ethnic disabled people, gay and lesbian disabled people and disabled women. BCODP also supports people with learning difficulties through its close links with People First.

(BCODP, n.d.)

The national organisation publishes books and a quarterly journal *Rights not Charity*, and has established a Disability Research Unit at Leeds University. It also takes the lead on both national and international campaigns and is a member of Disabled People's International.

Under the umbrella of BCODP are groups organised around geographical location: the Derbyshire Coalition and other coalitions such as the Hampshire Coalition and the Manchester Coalition, the Greater London Association of Disabled People (GLAD) and many others; there are groups organised on the basis of other aspects of identity: for example, the Asian Disabled People's Alliance and Gemma, an organisation of disabled lesbians; and groups united by particular campaigning focusses, for example, the Campaign for Accessible Transport (CAT). The unifying characteristic of these very different groups is that the majority control of the organisation rests with disabled people themselves. As is the case with many mental health user groups, non-disabled people can ally themselves and become members of disabled people's groups, but they may not have voting rights nor be able to hold elected office in groups which have constitutional structures.

Since the period of renewed vigour ushered in by the establishment of BCODP in 1981 the disability movement has been involved in campaigning on a wide range of issues which affect all aspects of people's lives (Barnes, 1991). The accessibility of transport services and the built environment has been a continual focus for action, generating some successes in respect of changes in building regulations, although leaving substantial numbers of people effectively excluded from using public transport or being able to become active consumers within the open housing market. Barnes (*ibid.*) has demonstrated that disabled people are disadvantaged both within the public and private housing sectors. A similar disadvantage applies in relation to both public and private transport. Large sections of 'public' transport are in practice out of bounds for many disabled people, while private transport options are also less accessible, not only because mass produced cars are not designed to be used by disabled people, but also because poverty puts car ownership beyond the means of many of those dependent on social security benefits.

Discrimination against disabled people in employment is a significant aspect of the civil rights campaign. Finkelstein (1980) has provided a historical analysis of the changes in disabled people's access to employment related to changes in modes of production. The modernist, teleological assumptions underpinning his analysis of the three phases of production: the feudal, capitalist, and an emerging model which might be based on socialist principles, now has a markedly old-fashioned ring to it. Nevertheless, it does point to the significance of an analysis of the way in which work is organised in order to understand, for example, the failure of legislative require-ments to achieve the 3 per cent quota of disabled people employed within organisations employing 20 or more people. Current campaigns relating to employment being pursued within the disabled people's movement are based on the conclusion that: 'The only policies which might succeed are ones focussing primarily on the demand side of labour, namely on the workplace. These are policies creating a barrier-free work environment and requiring employers to use production processes accessible to the entire workforce' (Barnes, *ibid.*, p. 97).

Disabled people who have experienced segregated education have used those experiences to advocate for an integrated education system capable of educating able-bodied children about disability, as well as providing disabled people with an education which is capable of preparing them to participate as adults in mainstream society. (e.g. Barnes, *ibid.*; Corker, 1993). The media and arts have also been the focus not only for action intended to challenge the negative portrayal of disabled people, but as a source of positive opportunities for disabled people to express their aspirations and develop their own cultural representations (Morrison and Finkelstein, 1993).

While the disabled people's movement has stressed the shared experience of disability as a basis for collective action, Morris (1989 and 1993) has developed an analysis which includes gender as a social construct with significant implications for the experience of disability as of other life experiences. Stuart (1993) has similarly argued for the importance of including race when seeking to understand black people's experience of being disabled.

The social model of disability has provided the basis on which some sections of the disability movement have developed alternative models of services which have, in some cases, been accepted and supported by statutory service providers in partnership with disabled people's groups. Centres for Independent Living, or for Integrated Living (CILs) have been developed as alternatives to the segregation of specialist residential accommodation. Within the UK national meetings took place during the 1980s to bring together disabled people in different parts of the country who were working towards this model and BCODP set up a Standing Committee on CILs. In 1983 international links were established on this topic when UK representatives went to a conference in Stockholm to debate issues with disabled people from the USA and Sweden.

Within the CIL movement in the UK two streams of thought are evident which reflect the distinction between the concepts of 'independent' or 'integrated' living. For example, Hampshire has adopted a Centre for Independent Living with the emphasis on individual choice and personal solutions. One outcome of this is the publication of a source book which gives information and advice to disabled people about employing their own care assistant (Hampshire CIL, 1986). These ideas have become more influential since the passage of the 1990 NHS and Community Care Act provided an opportunity for disabled people to argue that they should effectively become their own care managers and be responsible for determining which support services should be bought from the budget assessed as necessary to meet their needs. The argument is very similar to that being advanced for service brokerage in relation to people with learning difficulties. When work on this book started, direct payments of this type were still not legal in the UK, but the House of Commons Select Committee on Health gave a sympathetic hearing to arguments being advanced by disabled people and a bill to enable such payments to be made by local authority social services departments was going through parliament.

A rather different approach is evident among members of the Derbyshire Coalition who sought to work in a collaborative way with Derbyshire County Council in order to establish what has subsequently been called a Centre for Integrated Living. The collaboration was at times very difficult (Davis and Mullender, 1993), but the centre now operates with a council comprising appointed members from DCDP, the County Council and voluntary organisations. The centre employs both disabled and non-disabled staff and is intended to model the integration which it seeks to enable the disabled people who use its services to achieve:

Whilst the nature of the barriers preventing the full social integration of disabled people in Britain are very complex, in essence it was considered that they stem from the unequal nature of the able/disabled relationship. . . . The concept of 'integrated living' grew out of this analysis. It asserts that the social integration of disabled people will follow when service delivery systems are themselves integrated, i.e., when people who have personal experience of the daily problems of disability are themselves directly involved in service design, delivery and control.

(Quoted in Davis and Mullender, *ibid.*, p. 39)

Campaigning for anti-discrimination legislation brought the disability movement more public attention and support than it had enjoyed before. While at the time of writing, the 1995 Disability Discrimination Act does not have the full force of the proposals introduced as a Private Members Bill by Harry Barnes MP and supported by the disabled people's movement, the government have accepted that discrimination against disabled people has to be dealt with by legislative means (Minister for Disabled People, 1995). However, it was also suggested prior to the Bill being enacted that 'it is possible that when and if the Government proposals do become law that disabled people in Britain will be worse off than they are today' (Barnes and Oliver, 1995, p. 111). This is not only because important limitations are evident in the proposed legislation, including the intention to scrap the quota scheme for the employment of disabled people, but also because of the potential for the consensus among disability groups achieved in the civil rights campaign to be destroyed as some disability organisations are: 'bought with the promise of lucrative jobs on the proposed National Disability Council, extending funding for their organisations, or a place on the honours list' (*ibid.*, p. 113). Less cynically, other disabled people have acknowledged that the experience of women, of gays and of black people shows that getting legislation on the statute book is far from being the end of the matter in the battle to achieve equal rights.

Is there a movement of older people?

When we turn to consider equivalent movements among older people the question of whether we are talking about movements involving people who are in receipt of health and social care services, or whether we are talking about people who share a particular characteristic or identity, takes on an additional significance. Older people comprise the majority of those who use community care services. But the majority of older people do not use services. This group is the only one which is defined by reference to their date of birth and there is a danger that any discussion of the collective interests of older people obscures or ignores the substantial differences associated with class, gender, race and geographical location which apply to people of all age groups.

If our focus is on older people who are users of health and social care services we are talking about people who might ally themselves with disabled people because physical frailty is a major determinant of service use in old age; who might be among the increasing number of older people in receipt of mental health services because they are experiencing depression or because they are suffering from dementia; or who might throughout their lives have been using services designed for people with learning difficulties and who now cause service providers a degree of uncertainty over whether they should be attending older people's day centres or whether they should continue to attend the adult training centre (Walker, Walker and Ryan, 1996). Some older people are active within the movements I have described above, but the administrative separation of services for older people from those provided for 'younger disabled people' and of psycho-geriatric services from general psychiatric services, does not encourage older users of services to meet up with younger people with whom they may share experiences of service use. In this section I will consider examples of initiatives which are concerned with older people *per se,* both as users of services and as older citizens who are seeking to ensure their broader interests are respected.

Thornton and Tozer (1996) have reviewed initiatives, mainly within the voluntary sector, which have sought to involve older people in planning community care provision and in evaluating services. Their focus on the voluntary sector derives from what they describe as the central role of the voluntary sector in representing the interests of users. They note that this is a growth area in the work of voluntary organisations and suggest that, in the case of older people, no distinction between groups *for* and groups *of* older users has emerged.

Some voluntary organisations have addressed this issue directly. Age Concern – which includes service provision, information and advice, training, development and policy work alongside a campaigning role – undertook a process of self-examination in which they addressed the following questions:

But for whom do we really speak? When are we speaking *for* older people and when are we speaking *about* them, but not being their voice? Is there more we could do to ensure that we fully understand the views of older people and present these effectively to the outside world? What other voices do we have?
(Age Concern, 1993; emphasis in the original)

Age Concern Scotland followed this up with a project designed to enable the voices of frail older people to be heard directly. In Fife, panels of frail older people, average age 82 and all substantial users of community care services, have been supported by project workers with the aim of enabling them to speak about their experiences of growing older and of using services and to seek responses from service providers both at the level of specific services and in service planning (Age Concern Scotland, 1994). The particular significance of this project is that it seeks to support collective organisation among people often assumed to be too old, frail or tired to meet together with the objective of seeking change. While evidence suggests that panel members are happy to make a continuing commitment to the project, the practi-calities of making that possible are substantial (Barnes and Bennett-Emslie, 1996). Deaths and hospital admissions also demonstrated the particular vulnerability of such groupings and it is unclear that they could be sustained without substantial input from younger or fitter supporters.

A different model which is intended to enable the representation of older people whose circumstances make it difficult for them to speak on their own behalf is that of citizen advocacy. Ivers (1994) described one such initiative developed by the Beth Johnson Foundation. This involved 'younger older people' as well as people in middle age who volunteered to undergo training and to act as advocates for partners who were in local authority residential homes or who were receiving services in their own homes. While this and other examples of advocacy for older people have produced some important benefits for the older people involved in terms of securing more sensitive treatment and access to alternative service options, it cannot be considered as an example of self-organisation on the part of older people.

The Fife project demonstrated that frail older people can make a collective contribution to service development, but it also indicated the potential vulnerability of collective action involving only those older people who are users of health and social care services. Are older people who are not substantial users of services engaged in collective activity intended to pursue the interests of older people in general, and those in need to services in particular?

Abrams and O'Brien reported on a survey of older people's political preferences and political activity carried out by National Opinion Polls in 1977 (Abrams and O'Brien, 1981). This found that older people were just as likely to vote in elections as younger people, and, bearing in mind the low membership of organisations among the population generally, no less likely to be members of organisations such as political parties, community or neighbourhood organisations, residents' or tenants' associations. There were differences in the level of participation in other types of civic/political activities:

Participation rates roughly equal
Voted in last council elections
Stood for public office
Voted in last general election
Paid an individual subscription to a political party
Taken active part in a political campaign

Elderly participation rates roughly half
Been to a meeting of a local political party
Written a letter to an editor
Urged someone outside the family to vote
Presented own views to a local councillor or MP
Been to a meeting of an interest group or organisation

Elderly participation rates roughly one third or less
Helped in fund-raising drive
Urged someone to get in touch with local councillor or MP
Been elected as an officer of an organisation or club
Made a speech before an organisation or group
Been to a trade union meeting
Taken part in a demonstration, picket, sit-in

(Abrams and O'Brien, *ibid.*, p. 12)

The authors also reported another survey which indicated that older people were considerably less likely than young people to support unorthodox forms of political activity: occupying buildings, taking part in demonstrations, spraying slogans, for example. Current research into older people's participation in different types of political and social action in different European countries may indicate whether the situation described by Abrams and O'Brien is changing as older people's numerical power increases, and the nature of political activity more generally undergoes change. This project has a developmental purpose and has led to the production of a handbook designed to support older people in achieving influence within their communities (Kurt Lewin Institut, n.d.)

Where there has been age-specific political activity among older people this has primarily focussed on pension rights. Elman (1995) described the Townsend movement in the USA in the 1930s which campaigned for pensions for older people as an age-based social movement revolving around 'issues, identities and experiences based in a particular stage of life' (p. 300). Elman also suggested that incentives for involvement derived not only from the practical benefits which the Townsend movement sought for older people, but also from the intrinsic value of participation which compensated for other roles which were no longer available to older people. This conclusion is supported by the evaluation of the very different Fife User Panels Project (Barnes and Bennett-Emslie, 1996) and suggests that, as in the case of the other groups I have been considering in this chapter, exclusion from economic, social and political roles not only provides a focus around which to campaign, but a reason why collective organisation is valuable in its own right.

In the UK pensions also provided an early focus for action on the part of older people. In 1939 the National Federation of Old Age Pensions Associations was formed, followed in the early 1970s by the British Pensions and Trade Union Action Group. However, neither of these organisations was considered to have wielded much influence, in spite of the potential for self-interest to encourage support from younger workers. Their apolitical approach, designed to appeal to cross-party consensus, was considered to reinforce conservatism rather to provide a strong force for change (Walker, 1996). However, by the early 1990s local pensioners' action groups were becoming increasingly active and some affiliated to the National Pensioners' Convention thought to have some 1.5 million members. Changes of policy provided new issues for such groups to campaign around. Action by older people's organisations had an impact on plans to introduce Value Added Tax (VAT) on fuel. The government was forced to back down on the second stage of this plan, leaving VAT at 8 per cent, half of what was proposed originally.

Changes in the health service and in community care services have also provided a focus for action. The greater visibility of rationing decisions within the NHS has exposed ageist policies regarding the low priority given to access to certain forms of treatment for older people. Of particular relevance to the argument being pursued in this book, there has been a growing concern that an emphasis on community-based rather than hospital-based care and treatment is enabling the NHS to divest itself of responsibility for long-term care of older people. The particular significance of that is that services which were previously available at no direct cost to the user because they were provided by an NHS committed to the principle of services free at the point of use, started to become redefined as social rather than health care and thus as the responsibility of local authorities forced to means test and charge for services. Walker (1996) has claimed: 'There is no doubt that many of the more active pensioners are affronted by the undermining of collective provision that was a product of both the inequities of the pre-welfare state period and the national consensus forged during the Second World War.' While the Prime Minister John Major might ask rhetorically of the Conservative Party Conference in 1994 'Is it likely I would take away the security of mind that was of such value to my parents? I can tell you, not while I live and breathe will I take it away' (quoted in Courtney and Walker, 1996), by 1995 the issue of payments for long-term care was being given public airing in news stories about pensioners and their children having to sell their homes in order to pay for care. Jack Jones, President of the National Pensioners' Convention Council, asserted: 'The treatment of frail elderly people in Britain today is a scandal crying to high heaven. . . . As a community, we should care for them as passionately as a good family cherishes its own parents. It should be a major objective of society to secure the relief of poverty, to provide the dignity of security, and to enhance the quality of life of all our elderly fellow citizens' (Courtney and Walker, *ibid.*).

The new era of political action among older people which Walker suggests is marked by 'open dissent' rather than acquiescence is reflected among the range of initiatives listed in the directory produced by the Social Policy Research Unit at York (Thornton and Tozer, 1995). These include projects such as:

- Action Age in Northern Ireland which aims to get issues of concern to older people onto the political agenda and is described as 'Primarily an exercise in collective public advocacy' (p. 73);
- elderly forums within London boroughs which are affiliated to the Greater London Forum for the Elderly and which are designed to ensure older people's views and interests are represented within local government decision making;
- the Strathclyde Elderly Forum which brings together 68 local forums to campaign on issues such as health and community care, concessionary travel and fuel costs at both a regional and national level. It had direct access to the Regional Council (before this was

abolished in 1995) as well as maintaining regular contact with local forums through training days and bi-monthly meetings;
*   the Wolverhampton Pensioners' Convention, which again campaigns on local issues such as library services and abuse of disabled parking spaces, as well as national issues such as coalmine closure, the privatisation of British Rail, and VAT on fuel bills.

Numerically, older people form an increasingly powerful lobby. While there has been only limited evidence to date that this lobby is achieving political influence, within the commercial world there are signs that the commercial benefits to be gained from responding to the needs of older people has been recognised. Saga Holidays has become well established as a travel agency providing holidays exclusively for older people, while a variety of practical aids designed to make personal and household tasks easier for older people are now available in general retail outlets rather than requiring referral to specialist aids stores. A deliberate attempt to influence the market in this respect is a project called 'The Thousand Elders' initiated by Bernard Isaacs at Birmingham University. This involves a panel of one thousand older people who market test products to determine their user friendliness.

Action aimed at creating the social and economic circumstances in which people can lead a good old age is likely to attract more widespread public support than action to improve the circumstances in which people with mental health problems, disabled people and those with learning difficulties can lead a good life. Most of us hope to reach old age – we do not seek to experience mental distress or disablement. The category 'older people' includes people whose life circumstances and interests are more heterogeneous than those of people with learning difficulties, for example, and thus action in a common cause may be more difficult to achieve. Nevertheless, older people may be capable of exercising substantial moral and political leverage in their campaigns.

Pluralism, difference and identity

The descriptions of developments in the self-organisation of users of welfare services illustrate considerable diversity within and between the user movements. To what extent then can they be understood as demonstrating any common features, or any common relevance for an understanding of community care which goes beyond an enumeration of services to be provided and the organisational and financial systems required to support them, and sees it as a means through which disabled or older people can participate as citizens within society? In very general terms the similarities lie in the fact that groups of people who have occupied subordinate and powerless positions are seeking to have their voices heard in decision making forums. People excluded from social, economic and political life are seeking to participate in those spheres as well as to participate in decision making about those services of which they stand in need. They are asserting that people constructed as passive recipients of care can be actors playing a part not only in the production of welfare, but also on the wider social stage. That represents both an ideological and a material challenge to the *status quo*. Having looked in more detail at the nature of the various user movements it is now possible to extend the anlaysis of notions of consumerism and citizenship as they apply to recipients of community care services which was introduced in Chapter 2.

Late twentieth-century society is characterised by a conspicuous pluralism. Difference is celebrated, whether associated with gender, sexual orientation, language or culture. Personal identity has become linked to political action in diverse forms which include the actions of groups such as Outrage in 'outing' public figures thought to be hiding their homosexuality, as well as that of disabled people blocking Oxford Street to protest at inaccessible public transport. But identity has also been seen as the ultimate statement of consumerism: the explosion of choice within the consumer market means that lifestyles can be bought off the shelf and swapped when the fashion changes. In Chapter 2 I quoted Lindsay Prior to suggest that the option of identity formation based on consumerism was not open to many of those for whom community care services are designed. Indeed, a consumerist society may contribute to the exclusion of such groups. While all the groups considered here seek in different ways to have their difference acknowledged within cultural production, and while older people and physically disabled people in particular have used commercial arguments to push for access to shops and for a wide range of products to be designed to be usable by those with physical impairments, the objectives of such groups cannot be understood as lifestyle politics.

Giddens (1991) has distinguished 'emancipatory' and 'life politics':

I define emancipatory politics as a generic outlook concerned above all with liberating individuals and groups from constraints which adversely affect their life chances. Emancipatory politics involves two main elements: the effort to shed shackles of the past, thereby permitting a transformative attitude towards the future; and the aim of overcoming the illegitimate domination of some individuals or some groups by others. (pp. 210–11)

Life politics presumes (a certain level of) emancipation, in both the main senses noted above: emancipation from the fixities of tradition and from conditions of hierarchical domination. It would be too crude to say simply that life politics focuses on what happens once individuals have achieved a certain level of autonomy of action, because other factors are involved; but this provides at least an initial orientation. Life politics does not primarily concern the conditions which liberate us in order to make choices: it is a politics *of* choice. While emancipatory politics is a politics of life chances, life politics is a politics of lifestyle.   (p. 214)

In this formulation, the political activity with which user groups are engaged is clearly emancipatory – they are seeking autonomy of action and the ability to make choices. Achieving the power to define their own identities rather than having those identities defined for them is a fundamental aspect of the emancipatory project with which they are engaged.

While all the groups share the experience of having devalued identities and of having their identities and needs constructed by professional groups, there are also different connotations for each. People with mental health problems are often considered to 'lack insight' and therefore be incapable of defining either themselves or external reality. People with learning disabilities are often infantilised and may be thought insufficiently sophisticated to have a sense of self. Disabled people may reject the identity of tragic hero and understand their experience as having been constructed by a disabling social environment. Older people may share some of the experiences of people with learning difficulties in being treated as children; they may have internalised the cultural devaluing of old age; or they may struggle with the difference between their internal sense of self as remaining the same as when they were younger, and the change in the way in which they are regarded by others.

Together such groups are also asserting that a puralist society must include those whose difference relates to emotional, physical or cognitive aspects of being human. An awareness of injustice is a powerful motivating factor for those who become involved in user movements (Barnes, 1996c) and overcoming material disadvantage is clearly an objective. Nevertheless, such movements offer a more fundamentally ideological challenge. They are not solely concerned with the redistribution of material goods or with changing the balance of power within existing structures, they are also seeking to change the nature of the discourse within which notions of age, disability and mental disorder are constructed.

This is of importance for a number of reasons, not least because it holds the potential for solidarity between excluded groups who could be in competition for attention and for a bigger share of resources. Pluralism as a political philosophy and practice has been criticised because of the danger that it could degenerate into competition between different groups, each trying to prove they are more disadvantaged than the other (Phillips, 1993). Any sense of the 'common good' or of concerns which could provide a unifying theme would be lost as specific and sometimes temporary issues fragmented participants. Phillips has suggested that the tendency to fragmentation has been reinforced by the increasing significance of identity as an organising factor. For example, once ethnic identity rather than commitment to civil rights and racial equality became the focus for the anti-racist movement in the USA:

it began to matter immensely whether you organized autonomously as members of the same ethnic group, what kind of alliances you struck with people from other ethnic groups, and which groups dominated the leadership roles within your organization. (p. 147)

However, she also sees possibilities for solidarity arising from the communicative theory of democracy with its emphasis on public interaction between different groups in a way which can encourage reflection and change. The significance of user movements thus goes beyond what they are able to achieve to benefit those whose identities and interests are represented directly by such groups, to their potential to act as transformative agents altering the perspectives of dominant groups. Thus, the social model of disability can result not only in material benefits such as increasing the accessibility of buildings to people in wheelchairs, but can also transform the way in which disability is constructed by elite groups (welfare professionals) and by dominant lay discourse. Disabled people and others engaged within user movements contribute to change not only by analysis but also by their presence within deliberative structures:

By giving voice to formerly silenced or devalued needs and experiences, groups representation forces participants in discussion to take a reflective distance on their assumptions and think beyond their own interests. When confronted with interests, needs and opinions that derived from very different social positions and experience, persons sometimes come to understand the limitations of their own experience and perspective for coming to a conclusion about the best policy for everyone.

(Iris Marion Young, quoted in Phillips, *ibid.*, p. 158)

Thus while self-organisation among users of services may have been motivated by personal experiences of insensitive treatment by service providers, or by a sense of personal injustice in relation to wider experiences, the significance of such developments extends beyond achieving specific change in the nature of services or, indeed, of achieving protection for civil rights through anti-discrimination legislation. It is important to have this deeper significance in mind as we turn to a consideration of initiatives from within statutory systems which have sought to give a voice to service users.

CHAPTER 4

Changing relationships: hearing the voices of service users

Community care was not introduced by the 1990 Act and, as the previous chapter has made clear, neither was the idea that users of community services should have their voices heard. Nevertheless, not only did the 1990 Act provide a major impetus for organisational and service developments intended to ensure that both social and health services gave priority to 'making a reality of community care', the Act also made consultation with users and carers regarding community care plans a legislative duty. Thus it provided user groups with a means of legitimising their demands to be heard and forced social services departments to consider how they could demonstrate to the Social Services Inspectorate of the Department of Health that they had indeed consulted with users in drawing up their plans. This was easier for some authorities than it was for others. Some had already started to develop mechanisms for consulting with users and with carers; some had been seeking ways of involving users in running services; and some had made an active response to the only partially implemented Disabled Persons (Services, Consultation and Representation) Act of 1986 by co-opting disabled people onto council committees and by supporting the development of individual advocacy.

In this chapter I consider some of the pre-1990 initiatives from within statutory authorities to listen to what users had to say about services, and then what effect the act and related guidance had in increasing the profile, extent and nature of such initiatives. My discussion will be focussed around key texts and major examples of initiatives which have sought to enable users to have their say about services. From an analysis of these examples I identify the major dimensions of change involved, both within and between service organisations, and within relationships between users and services. I develop these points further in Chapter 7.

The Client Speaks

In 1970 a text was published which became something of a social work classic. Mayer and Timms reported a study of clients' perceptions of social work and in so doing demonstrated the different and sometimes conflicting assumptions held by social workers and their clients about the problems to be addressed and hence some of the reasons why social work was not always successful. Their justification for undertaking this research has a considerable resonance in the 1990s when attention to the significance of outcomes of health and social care interventions has become much more commonplace than it was in 1970:

Clearly, until we have investigated consumer opinion we cannot begin to be sure that social work resources, likely to remain in short supply for the foreseeable future, are deployed in the most effective way possible, to say nothing of whether they are achieving the goals for which they were designed.

(Mayer and Timms, 1970, p. 2)

Over ten years later Eric Sainsbury (1983) discussed the ambiguous nature of social work and hence the complexity inherent in studies which sought to measure its success. Sainsbury also noted that the opinion of clients is only one element to be considered within social work evaluations. This discussion was contained in the introduction to a volume which sought to reflect the fact that: 'Nowadays it is difficult to conduct respectable research without incorporating the clients' views' (Fisher, 1983). Four years later an editorial in the journal *Social Services Research* commented on the increase in the frequency with which research exploring users' views of services was being reported to the journal's Annual Register of Current Research:

Such projects are a part of a growing recognition that paternalistic welfare services determined entirely by professional and bureaucratic definitions of what should be provided, are increasingly indefensible. Research alone cannot ensure that the voice of service users is adequately heard in planning and developing services. But it does have an important part to play:

* in demonstrating the gap between what people feel they need and the services they actually receive;
* in identifying the source and nature of dissatisfaction with existing services;
* and in extending expertise and experience of consultation with users rather than other professionals.

(Barnes, 1987)

Throughout the 1970s and 80s researchers working within social services departments in the UK and in universities and independent research agencies had been undertaking research which sought to explore how users experienced those services and how effective users thought they were. Some of that research utilised methods drawn from consumer research conducted within the commercial sector, but other methods, including participant and non-participant observation, were employed to investigate the experiences of users in circumstances where it could prove difficult to ask them what they thought of services. For example, Annette Warner spent a week living in old people's homes in Birmingham in order to understand what it felt like to be a resident and to assess the quality of care provided to residents

(Warner, 1987). She adopted this approach because many of the residents were mentally frail and would have been likely to find a formal research interview a difficult means of communication, and also because she considered residents might find it difficult to be open about their experiences when they were going to continue to be dependent on staff for their care. For rather different reasons, I had used both non-participant and participant observation in evaluations of two family centres for children under five (Barnes, 1981, 1982).

Much of the research of this type was conducted with the intention that the results would directly influence the practice of service provision. Indeed, during this period a considerable amount of such research was carried out by researchers employed within social services departments in order to provide such organisations with an intelligence function intended to contribute to organisational and service development. However, the rationalist assumption that research findings would lead to action has been questioned both in general and in particular. Booth (1988) has challenged the notion that there is a linear relationship between research and decision making; Barnes and Wilson (1986) considered the limitations of dissemination and implementation strategies following the reporting of research conducted within social services departments; while both researchers (e.g., Lewando-Hundt and Grant, 1987) and users themselves (Beresford, 1992; Davis, 1992) have not only challenged the effectiveness of 'consumer research', but have suggested that such research can itself contribute to the disempowerment of users because it treats them as objects of study, rather than active participants determining what should be studied and how. While research had a role to play, clearly other action was required if users' views were not only to be investigated, but also to become influential and to enable users to feel empowered as a result.

Raising Voices

During the second half of the 1980s there was evidence that the idea that users should have their voices heard was starting to take root within mainstream service providing agencies as well as being evident in campaigning organisations and in the work of researchers. Three publications which appeared in 1990 analysed initiatives being taken from within statutory organisations which suggested that the nature of the relationship between service providers and recipients was starting to undergo some kind of change. *Consuming Public Services* edited by Nicholas Deakin and Anthony Wright (1990) considered changes taking place in a range of public services, including social services and health, while *Raising Voices* (Connelly, 1990) and *From Paternalism to Participation* (Croft and Beresford, 1990) were specifically concerned with social services departments. All three publications point to the different origins of the renewed interest in the experience of receiving rather than providing public services which were considered in Chapter 2. For example, Naomi Connelly referred to the considerable scope for confusion and disagreement created by similar messages about user involvement coming from different sources and for different reasons. She also considered that the impending changes envisaged by the *Caring for People* White Paper meant that this was a critical time in which user views would be competing with other factors for influence. If the changes heralded by the White Paper were indeed to be in the interests of disabled people, then the involvement and participation of disabled people had to be an explicit part of the discussion which was taking place.

Croft and Beresford (1990) drew similar conclusions about the potential danger of confusing very different purposes for user involvement:

We have identified two different, sometimes conflicting philosophies at the heart of user involvement; one service provider, the other service user led. If the primary aim of user-involvement is to meet agency needs, people's response to it may be cautious. If it is part of a well worked out process to increase people's say and control over their lives and services, then its prospects are likely to be much more promising. All the evidence suggests that people's attitudes to involvement depend significantly on its nature and effectiveness.

(p. 42)

Croft and Beresford found that just under one third of statutory departments that they surveyed had written policies to involve service users and over 40 per cent had plans to review the situation. They found a large variety of different practical applications of a commitment to user involvement, operating in different contexts and at different levels. They identified user involvement in:

- service planning and policy development
- inspection
- quality assurance
- evaluation and research
- developing and providing their own services
- assessment
- as case managers, designing their own support packages.

(Croft and Beresford, *ibid.*, p. 10)

Connelly (1990) distinguished three levels at which the involvement of disabled people was taking place: (1) having a voice in her/his own circumstances; (2) having a voice in reacting to services currently being used or contributing to their design and management; and (3) making an input through participation in training, planning or advisory groups. She noted that while involvement in decision making about their own circumstances was basic to any sense of personal empowerment, involvement at the third level might be considered more significant because it implies involvement in roles other than as users of services and holds the potential for the development of entirely new types of service.

Barnes, Prior and Thomas (1990) in the Deakin and Wright collection also distinguished different levels at which user involvement in social services might be pursued:

* in contacts between individual workers and users
* in contacts between discrete groups of workers and users (e.g. in a children's home)
* at the level of the management and planning of a particular service (e.g. children's residential care)
* departmental service/resource management and planning
* committee management and policy development
* local authority-wide and inter-agency management and policy development
* national policy development (e.g. legislation, resource allocation).

(Barnes *et al., ibid.*, p. 108)

As well as looking at initiatives which had the specific aim of increasing the control or influence users have over services, Barnes *et al.*, also considered organisational and other factors likely to affect the extent to which users could influence services, and they also considered the legal framework which provides some, if limited, rights to users of services. Thus it was suggested that factors such as clear rights to services and locally organised, flexible services, as well as both individual and collective mechanisms for the expression of voice, would be important in increasing user control. While the authors suggested it was possible to point to important initiatives being taken in individual authorities, the overall environment was considered to remain substantially unfriendly for a shift from producer to user control.

During the 1980s at least two initiatives which sought to involve service users aimed to go beyond the somewhat *ad hoc* developments taking place in many areas. In 1983 in Wales, the All Wales Strategy for Mentally Handicapped People (AWS) was launched with the aim of encouraging and supporting the move from institutional to community-based care for people with learning difficulties. This strategy included a commitment to consult with and otherwise involve people with learning difficulties and their carers and was studied by researchers working at the Centre for Social Policy Research and Development in the University of Wales, Bangor, and by the Mental Handicap in Wales Applied Research Unit in Cardiff. The second initiative was the Birmingham Community Care Special Action Project

(CCSAP). This was a three-year project running from 1987 to 1990 involving the whole local authority and the five health authorities then responsible for health services in Birmingham. The project aimed to develop an inter-agency approach to community care which was also based on the needs and wishes of users and carers. An evaluation of CCSAP was funded by the Department of Health and carried out by myself and Gerald Wistow at the Nuffield Institute for Health at Leeds University. In the remainder of this section I will consider these two large-scale initiatives in order to draw some conclusions about the nature of user involvement prior to the implementation of the 1990 NHS and Community Care Act.

The All Wales Strategy

The All Wales Strategy was an exercise in large-scale planning. It was a top-down initiative emanating from the Welsh Office which sought to ensure that services for people with learning difficulties (mental handicap as this was referred to when the strategy was launched) throughout Wales were based on the same principles of de-institutionalisation and normalisation. Its objective was a change in the nature and pattern of services throughout the country and thus it required local planning and service development which was consistent with the overall strategy.

Well before the 1990 Act required user and carer involvement in community care planning the All Wales Strategy placed considerable emphasis on 'consumer participation at all levels in the planning and management of services' (McGrath, 1989). Although as McGrath pointed out, in common with other protestations of a commitment to participation, it did not define what this meant, nor did it address the question of the extent to which this represented a shift in the balance of power from professionals to users. What it did do was to specify the different levels at which 'consumer' involvement could take place: individual planning; county and local planning; and service monitoring.

Somewhat belatedly, in 1989, a consumer involvement sub-group was also set up to advise the panel overseeing the implementation of the strategy. This was in part a consequence of the uneven progress being made in putting the commitment to consumer involvement into practice. This group produced a report which started to define key issues such as 'who are the consumers?' It distinguished people with mental handicaps and their informal carers as two different stakeholder groups and highlighted the fact that parents had been able to achieve much higher levels of participation in the strategy than had people with learning difficulties themselves. However, the sub-group included within their definition of consumer stakeholder groups providers of statutory and non-statutory services, thus somewhat confusing the issue.

The report also addressed the question 'Why is consumer involvement important?' In so doing it raised the issue of power:

By involving consumers in the planning and management of services, we can begin to ascertain how far they are meeting the needs of those who use them. Consumer involvement can also act as a lever to start changing the traditional balance of power between providers and users which has usually operated in favour of the former.

(Consumer Involvement Sub-Group, 1991)

But the group did not include this as an issue to be explored directly within the framework proposed for reviewing consumer involvement initiatives. Nor did it return to the need to define explicit purposes for involvement in addressing the key issues to be considered in the further development of user involvement strategies.

At a local level throughout much of the strategy 'consumers' in practice usually meant carers of people with learning difficulties. McGrath (1989) reported that one county within Wales brought people with learning difficulties into planning groups, but, on the basis of her analysis of the problems of carer participation, she questioned whether this would be the best way of obtaining the views of people with learning difficulties about the future directions services should take. The consumer involvement sub-group's report provided brief details of projects seeking direct involvement of people with learning difficulties themselves. Most of these operated either at an individual level, concerned with user involvement in individual programme planning or with the establishment of individual advocacy shemes, or at the level of user input to specific services: for example, user councils in day centres or a quality action group set up to assess how effectively a family aide service was meeting its stated aims. There was only one reported initiative which aimed to develop user involvement at a county-wide planning level by establishing a People First network.

The discussion of the development of People First in Chapter 3 suggests that the Welsh experience is typical. Building from involvement at an individual and service level to more strategic involvement is important as a means of enabling people to develop skills and confidence in arenas with which they are familiar, before asking them to engage in larger and more distant planning arenas. However, when the consumer involvement sub-group published their report in 1991, they were still posing the question of whether the AWS should make a clearer distinction between the interests of people with learning disabilities and their families, and whether such interests should be represented separately, rather than making a clear statement that such interests should be distinguished.

Grant (1992) concluded that the achievements for users and carers within the AWS were dissimilar and used the experience of evaluating user and carer participation in the AWS as a basis for proposing a framework within which user and carer involvement can be separately analysed and evaluated. The confusion about who were the 'consumers' to be involved in planning and management was in part a result of the lack of definition of participation or the objectives to be achieved through this. As Grant (*ibid.*, p. 65) noted: 'Involving users or consumers in community care services, for example, can and is used to overcome the organisational excesses of bureaucracy, but need not necessarily be directed towards the empowerment of individual consumers.' His analysis of the accomplishments and challenges for users (rather than carers) which came from the AWS identifies accomplishments primarily in the areas of service changes which have the potential for supporting personal development, rather than in attaining a presence within decision making forums which shaped the overall development of services:

Accomplishments for users
- Development of opportunities for personal growth and development
- Improved access to services for individuals
- Better targeting of resources to needs and aspirations of individuals
- Enhancement of self-esteem through participation in socially valued activities
- Increased influence for individuals in decision making about service packaging and life choices
- Cultural shifts in service settings from paternalistic models to systems that promote both participation and calculated risk taking for individuals
- Opportunities to provide valued services to the community, in partnership with the community

Challenges for users
- Uneven territorial development of opportunities for personal development
- Minority of users with individual plans
- Surface or tokenistic involvement which is devaluing
- Involvement restricted to forums which do not hold service providers to account
- Marginal involvement in forums dominated by parents or other informal carers
- Exposure to unrealistic expectations about capacities for involvement
- Ensuring that representatives' views are transmitted in the planning and development of services

(Grant, 1992, p. 69)

While the AWS was recognised to have been more successful in developing models of carer than user involvement, the experiences of parents and other carers nevertheless demonstrated that there was much to be learnt about how best to enable widespread involvement which satisfies the very different motivations of those who wish to take part. Stuart Humphreys (1987) reported that in one county parental involvement peaked at 30–40 per cent of those entitled to take part in planning processes and then steadily declined. He identified factors which prevented people from becoming involved in the first place:

1. The rural nature of the county which made travelling to meetings difficult;
2. The pressures of caring making it difficult to get away;
3. Some older carers were seen to have well established routines of care and they had little desire for changes which might upset a hard fought for equilibrium;
4. Others were described as 'retired lobbyists', people who had played an active role earlier in their lives but now felt it was time for younger carers to take over;
5. Others had distanced themselves from service providers because they felt them to have an uncaring attitude;
6. Others had only a vague idea of what the strategy was about and had insufficient information or understanding to enable them to participate.

In addition to these factors, which meant that the majority of carers did not become involved in the first place, others withdrew at different stages and those who did remain sought very different models of involvement. In some cases an initial optimism that change was on the way was frustrated. Since the motivation to participate was to secure tangible benefits, when this did not happen quickly carers withdrew. Others whose motivations to participate were more complex stayed even though they could see no immediate direct benefit:

there are a smaller number of participants who are sustained in their efforts by an element of political idealism: a desire to make hitherto apparently autono-mous officers within the service providing agencies more accountable to the mandators – this is the wishes of parents and the mentally handicapped. The AWS which stresses the need for parents and other interested parties to be consulted and listened to, provided them with a legitimate platform and thereby energized a latent political force which may be termed democratic radicalism.

(Humphreys, 1987, p. 31)

Humphreys described the democratic radicals as a group who would not compromise the nature of their relationship with service providers. They demanded an equal partnership and on occasions when they were frustrated in this aim adopted political tactics, including the use of the media, to seek support for their position.

Yet another group, described as the 'patient participators', were not considered to bring a political perspective to their involvement in the strategy, but were people who brought their particularistic knowledge of the experiences and wishes of their sons and daughters to bear on the initially confusing subject of multi-agency service planning and development. As their knowledge of bureaucratic processes and structures grew, they were able to make an increasing contribution to the debate, but, unlike the radicals, they were more content to remain as junior partners and thus were considered less challenging to the status quo.

McGrath (1989) also reported reasons for non-participation and the reactions to involvement on the part of carers in AWS workgroups. She suggested a number of practical changes likely to increase levels of participation including: smaller, informal, local meetings; grounding participation in carers' direct experiences; establishing accountability structures; providing training opportunities for those for whom participation was a new experience; ensuring an effective internal communication system was in place; and ensuring that professionals who meet with carers adopted an openness and preparedness to admit mistakes which can generate trust between different stakeholder groups.

Many of these detailed experiences in Wales were reflected in the Birmingham project to which I now turn.

The Birmingham Community Care Special Action Project (CCSAP)

While the remit of the AWS was restricted to people with learning difficulties and their carers, the Birmingham CCSAP sought to develop community care policies and services for all groups of users and carers. At the time the project was launched Birmingham City Council served a population of approximately one million and employed approximately 53,000 people. Five health authorities employed another 25,000 people. The project was thus a wide-ranging one designed to promote user involvement and cultural change in the development and delivery of mainstream services within the large and multi-cultural metropolitan area.

The first task of the project was to produce a set of principles which would both govern its activities and serve as a statement of intent. These are set out in Box 1.

These principles were strongly influenced by the principles of normalisation which had previously been adopted as the philosophy underpinning the development of services for people with learning

---

Box 1   CCSAP project principles

- People who have special needs because they are elderly, have a mental handicap, mental illness or a physical disability, should be valued as full citizens with both rights and responsibilities. They are entitled to be consulted and to have opportunities to influence the pattern of services on which they depend, to meet their individual and changing needs;
- People with special needs should have access to services which promote the greatest degree of self-determination on the basis of informed and realistic choice;
- People with special needs have a right to support and participation in the community which does not exploit or disadvantage others; and
- People with special needs have a right of access to services which support this participation as valued members of the community. The services should be free of stigma associated with their use.

(Quoted in Barnes and Wistow, 1991)

---

disabilities within the city and the surrounding region. CCSAP sought to apply those principles through a range of activities which were designed to secure user-led change in community care for all user groups. In practice, however, while sub-projects explored user involvement and user-influenced service development in relation to services for people with mental health problems, for disabled people, and for carers, it did not directly develop initiatives involving older people. The main initiatives undertaken during the three-year life of the project included:

- consumer research seeking the views of people with mental health problems;
- a pilot citizen advocacy project for people in a psychiatric hospital which was due for closure;
- the development of users councils for people with mental health problems both in hospital and in community-based services;
- a series of public consultations with carers and a programme of developmental work arising from this;
- a review of day services for disabled people, undertaken through consumer research and consultations with physically disabled people and, separately, with people with sensory disabilities;
- a service development initiative within day services for people with learning difficulties and a strategy designed to enhance employment opportunities for disabled people;
- a variety of activities designed to help people find out more about services, and about their rights to them.

As well as providing opportunities for users' voices to be heard in relation to particular services, CCSAP adopted a way of working which aimed to build commitment at senior and Chief Officer level to the implementation of project principles. Those principles also required a commitment across the whole local authority and from the health authorities. It sought to involve local authority officers from Education, Social Services, Libraries, Recreation and Community Services, Economic Development, Planning, Architects and Housing departments, working together in task groups as well as in groups established to co-ordinate project activities. While most of those involved with CCSAP considered the user involvement dimension of the project central, its inter-agency approach was also considered significant at the time in demonstrating that community care should not solely be the responsibility of social services and the health authorities. By demonstrating the role that, for example, the Economic Development Department could play in improving employment opportunities for disabled people (Barnes and Wistow, 1995a), and in involving the city's engineers and architects in addressing issues of mobility and access, Birmingham recognised that the experiences of disabled and older citizens are affected by the actions or omissions of a wide range of public servants, and was modelling an approach to community care which acknowledged people as citizens within a wider community as well as users of specific care services.

In approaching the evaluation of CCSAP it was necessary to deconstruct a number of the assumptions on which the user involvement initiatives of the project were based. Firstly, why involve users? I have referred above to Connelly's and Croft and Beresford's discussion of the different origins and ideological positions underpinning the apparent consensus in favour of user involvement. This analysis has subsequently been further developed by Beresford and Croft and by others (see also North, 1993; Wistow and Barnes, 1993; Barnes and Walker, 1996) in the light of the actual changes resulting from the NHS and Community Care Act:

the consumerist approach is essentially service-led, beginning with the service providers' needs, not the consumers', the democratic one is *citizen*-led. It is concerned with people having the chance to speak directly for themselves. These two approaches to involvement have different origins and objectives. The politics of liberation don't necessarily sit comfortably with those of the market-place.

(Beresford and Croft, 1993)

However, CCSAP, in common with the All Wales Strategy and other initiatives at the time, did not embark on a detailed analysis of purposes to be achieved through involvement before seeking models through which involvement could be implemented. The project was a time-limited one and its director clearly saw the task as one of action not analysis. However, this meant that participants seeking to develop user involvement initiatives under the CCSAP banner were sometimes seeking rather different ends which could, and did, come into conflict. Early in the evaluation we identified two broad categories of purpose for user involvement initiatives: (i) those which seek to improve the quality of services by making them more sensitive or responsive to the needs and preferences of individuals who use them; and (ii) those which seek to extend the capacity of users to participate in decisions about the design, management and review of services.

But in addition to these two rather different purposes which service users and providers were seeking, additional objectives were suggested by different stakeholders during the course of the evaluation: (i) to help solve individual problems relating to the receipt of services; (ii) to enable people to 'get things off their chests' and hence to feel better. This can have both positive or negative connotations.

For example, we found evidence of different expectations and priorities regarding the purpose of consultation held by carers and service providers involved in the series of carer consultations (Barnes and Wistow, 1992b). Perhaps because this was the first time that many of them had been consulted, many carers saw it as an opportunity to resolve particular problems relating to their own use of services, or to find out about services and improve access to them, rather than as an opportunity to start to shape wider service development. Those organising the consultations described their purpose in terms of finding out from carers about their experiences as carers and as users of services, in order to start to identify ways in which services needed to be improved generally. Both parties sought to become better informed by the other, but the consultations were not initially set up as information sharing events. Carers' thirst for information was later recognised in a series of events focussing on information exchange, rather than consultation.

The experience of the mental health user councils also demonstrated different perceptions of purpose held by professionals and users. One view expressed by a service provider was that the opportunity to have their say within the user councils offered a therapeutic, 'ventilating' experience for users. This was not accompanied by any commitment to take action in response to the views expressed (Barnes and Wistow, 1994a). Clearly, service users' expectations were that their views would be taken seriously and that a key objective for enabling those views to be expressed was the generation of user-inspired change in services.

The second question we had to address in conducting the evaluation of CCSAP was: 'Who are the "users"?' (also raised by the AWS). As I discussed in Chapter 3, the term 'user' is a controversial one and one which is not readily accepted by all those who receive services. Different ways of thinking about who constitutes a 'user' have been discussed by Jenny Morris and Vivien Lindow (1993). CCSAP made a clear distinction between initiatives designed to give a voice to direct service users and those designed to give a voice to carers. The project also sought different and separate ways of securing the involvement of different groups of service users. There was a recognition that different methods were needed to engage with people with differing circumstances and characteristics. Nevertheless, both in Birmingham and nationally, the programme of consultations with carers achieved the highest profile of all CCSAP's activities and for some defined what constituted 'user involvement'. This experience may be compared with that of the 'All Wales Strategy'.

However, we considered that further sophistication was required in understanding the notion of 'the user' and the implications of this for user involvement. The concept of service use is a relational one and it is also useful to conceptualise 'users' in ways which indicate some of the differences in the way people 'use' services. During the course of the CCSAP evaluation we developed the following classification:

• Voluntary and Involuntary Users
• Short-term and Long-term Users
• Individuals as Allies or Competitors
• Individuals and Group Interests
• Actual and Potential Users
• Users and Carers
• Users and Citizens

CCSAP made a deliberate decision not to focus on potential as opposed to actual users, nor on citizens who were not also users of services (Barnes and Wistow, 1991). This decision was in part a pragmatic one, based on an awareness of the resources available in comparison with the size of the task. Nevertheless, this decision put two constraints on the success of CCSAP as an overall strategy for user involvement. Firstly, it caused some difficulty in relation to disabled people who were not 'users of services', but who were invited to participate in consultations about those services. Secondly, it meant that the project could neither address the actual and potential problems caused by opposition to the integration of disabled people within the community (the 'Not In My Back Yard' syndrome), nor could it seek to build a constituency of support for the development of high quality community care services among voters and local community charge payers.

The methods CCSAP developed to secure involvement primarily emphasised group rather than individual interests and, at the individual level, user involvement initiatives remained somewhat under-developed (Barnes and Wistow, 1992a, b and e; Barnes and Wistow, 1994b). This resulted in a degree of dissonance in the experience of carers who were being consulted collectively about how services might be improved, but still experienced difficulty in influencing the services they received on a day-to-day basis (Barnes and Wistow, 1992c).

The significance of the involuntary nature of contact between users and services emerged in the initiatives designed to enable people with mental health problems to have their voices heard (Barnes and Wistow, 1994a). However, the position of other 'involuntary users', for example, those reluctantly using respite care services in order to give their carers a break, was not really explored. Elsewhere, Marsh and Fisher (1992) have sought to develop an approach to practice which acknowledges the involuntary nature of many encounters between users and providers of social services, while still enabling users to negotiate interventions and participate in decision making.

Whatever the purpose of involvement, and in whatever context their views were sought, it became clear that users and carers would be dissatisfied unless action followed. To that extent, there was a broad consensus that a major purpose of involvement was achieving service improvements. Many of the service improvements identified by users and carers in Birmingham were quite specific improvements in service quality, for example, ensuring that any changes to service provision, such as a change in the time home helps were to call, would be notified and agreed in advance. Others represented a more fundamental change in service design and philosophy and thus presented more of a challenge. For example, mental health service users were seeking both more understanding and more say in the nature of the treatment they received from psychiatrists. They were seeking more information about the range of treatments available, and the ability to exercise choice in an area traditionally reserved for clinical judgement. The more conservative psychiatrists who came into contact with this attempt to assert autonomy responded with a defensive stance which sought to deny the validity of users' views. It became evident from certain elements of CCSAP's work that, even where there was a commitment to listen and to learn from people who use services, it remained possible for service providers to select from the views of users and carers, those messages which (a) they felt capable of responding to, and (b) which 'fit' with professional thinking. There was a concomitant danger that the more difficult messages, or those which are viewed less favourably would get lost.

As well as ensuring that messages were heard, it also became clear how important it was to establish effective mechanisms for translating those messages into action. Carers in Birmingham clearly judged the consultations in terms of their effectiveness in securing change (Barnes and Wistow, 1995), as did carers involved in working groups established as part of the All Wales Strategy (McGrath, 1989). While there was considerable frustration on the part of some carers about the slow pace of change in Birmingham, others recognised that the actions which *had* been taken in response to certain of the issues raised by carers, the need for better information, for example, plus the mechanisms which had been established for continuing involvement, constituted a real departure from the situation which existed prior to

CCSAP (Barnes and Wistow, 1993). They acknowledged that service development is a slow process, but saw new opportunities to influence this which needed to be grasped. These opportunities can perhaps be seen as the development of procedural rights reflecting their right to have some say in decision making.

While the carers' programme included the development of mechanisms intended to implement change, the initiatives to hear from users of mental health services suffered from a failure to develop effective mechanisms for ensuring that user views would have an influence on services (Barnes and Wistow, 1994a). A particular factor in this context was the professional defensiveness which greeted what were perceived to be the 'angry and unreasonable' voices of users of mental health services. But those who took the lead in establishing the user councils also acknowledged that they had not given real thought to the question of what to do with the issues raised by users. Immediate issues, for example, about activities available to users of a day centre, could be dealt with locally. Broader issues concerning the nature of services and treatment available within them, which presented a more fundamental challenge to both professionals and managers, failed to be resolved in part because there was no agreed process or forum in which they could be considered.

Lessons from the pre-1990 user involvement initiatives

What then were the key issues emerging about the changes in relationships between health and social care agencies and their users which were starting to take place before the 1990 NHS and Community Care Act? The main issues can be summarised briefly:

1. The Birmingham project identified the need to adopt a broad perspective including a wide range of institutional players if community care was to become the responsibility of the community as a whole. At some points the project also drew in private sector employers. This has important implications for an approach which seeks to enhance the ability of users of community care services to participate as citizens within their communities.

2. Developments both in services and in models of and opportunities for user involvement are necessary if people's expectations for change are to be met. Participation can be empowering in itself and it can represent an opportunity both to hold providers to account and to enable a presence for those often excluded from decision making processes. It is necessary to develop different ways of involving different groups of users if such opportunities are not to be limited to a small 'elite' group and as experience

of involvement develops (on both sides) the nature and scope of involvement will also need to develop. Some participants value involvement in its own right because of the personal and political recognition this affords, but many will need evidence of direct and immediate benefit in terms of improvements in the services available to them if they are to remain involved and if they are not to become cynical about the possibility of change.

3. In initiatives which seek to hear a number of different voices it is always likely that some voices will be heard more loudly than others. Both the AWS and CCSAP were able to involve greater numbers of carers than other service users. This affected both the change agenda identified, and what might be considered effective models of involvement. Involving users will not result in a unified 'user view' being expressed and there is the danger to which Anne Phillips (1993) has referred that disadvantaged groups will compete with each other by claiming that they are worse off than others. If such differences are not to lead to fragmentation it is important that such 'low level' opportunities for participation are supported by democratic renewal at higher levels.

4. As well as the development of collective models of involvement designed to influence service managers, policy makers and planners, there is also a need to change relationships between service users and front line providers: doctors, community nurses, social workers, day centre workers. Developing new types of professional practice requires changes in pre- and post-qualifying training as well as changes within operational agencies.

5. As users start to play a part in decision-making it becomes more important that their input draws strength from groups controlled and led by users themselves. CCSAP was a provider-led initiative, but sowed the seeds of user-controlled groups among carers and people with mental health problems. The AWS started to encourage People First networks in order to support the involvement of people with learning difficulties in county-wide planning. Support for such groups must be part of a longer-term strategy for involvement.

6. The various purposes of involvement held by users, professionals and managers start to emerge as the experience of involvement develops. While some of these different purposes may be capable of being met in a complementary manner, others are likely to be in conflict. A strategy for involvement needs to make explicit the various purposes to be served and to enable negotiation to take place around these.

7. Community care is a policy which has implications for communities and citizens in general as well as for people identified as having 'special needs'. The involvement of citizens who are not users of services is necessary if negative attitudes which can get in the way of integration are to be addressed. Further emphasis on

working with local communities is called for as user involvement strategies develop.

After the 1990 NHS and Community Care Act

By the mid-1990s user involvement had moved from being the 'new idea' which progressive authorities were adopting in order to renew and revitalise their relationships with those using their services, to a legislative requirement; a prerequisite for obtaining research funding; and a job description for officials within both health and social care agencies. If the claims of statutory agencies were to be believed, virtually everyone was doing it, although on closer inspection just what people were doing and the degree of change it represented showed considerable variation.

The descriptive and evaluative literature on user involvement increased dramatically in this period. In order to consider what was happening after the passage of the 1990 Act I will review five examples of projects, initiatives and research which demonstrate some of the different contexts in which user involvement was developing post-1990:

1. A series of projects undertaken as part of the National Health Service Management Executive Programme 'Developing Managers for Community Care' and brought together under the heading: 'Involving Users and Carers in Inter-Agency Management Development' (NHSTD, 1993).
2. The 'Local Voices' initiative, also taken by the NHSME which resulted in a series of local initiatives to involve people in defining health needs and priorities undertaken by health authorities (NHSME, 1992).
3. A project published as *Taking Part in Community Care Planning* (Osborn, 1992) which was concerned with the way in which voluntary organisations and user groups might be assisted to engage in planning within the new system.
4. A research report entitled *Squaring the Circle* (Ellis, 1993) which considered what impact the requirement to involve users and carers in individual assessments was having.
5. *From Margin to Mainstream* (Goss and Miller, 1995), a project funded by the Joseph Rowntree Foundation which aimed, as its title suggested, to assist the move from user involvement as a 'special project' to an integral part of community care manage-ment and development.

Involving users and carers in inter-agency management development

Following the passage of the Community Care Act the Department of Health developed a number of initiatives designed to assist local agencies in its implementation. As its name implies the 'Developing Managers for Community Care Programme' was concerned with management development and training. Although it was centrally co-ordinated by what was then the NHS Management Executive, the programme was undertaken through a series of local initiatives intended to produce demonstration programmes which could then be disseminated in the form of training materials to be used more widely. Local operational, academic and training agencies were invited to submit proposals for projects addressing a series of management development needs raised by the new community care arrangements. One such area of management development needs was considered to be in the area of user and carer participation:

User and carer participation is at the heart of the 'Caring for people' reforms. This cannot simply be added on to other community care agendas. In order that services are planned on the basis of what people want and need, participation must be developed throughout community care agencies as an essential part of their work. This applies equally to training and development as it does to service delivery.

(NHSTD, 1993, p. 1)

This element of the programme thus had two dimensions: firstly, involving users and carers in management training and development; and secondly, training managers to work with users and carers in order to enable them to develop services which would meet needs effectively. While in practice the two may not always be entirely separate, it was important to distinguish both purposes and to consider the practical and methodological implications of both. User involvement in training represents more of a challenge to traditional notions of the relationship between professional and client, than does training managers in methods of user participation. As trainer the user is the expert and the manager the student in a more explicit role reversal than might be the case in, for example, joint planning forums in which managers and users might be considered partners.

At the same time, the pay-off for users who become involved in management training may be even less immediate and certain than for those who participate in service development initiatives. Why should users devote their time to management development? The managers concerned may not be responsible for the services received by user trainers and any effect of their training on services will be mediated by a whole host of factors which make outcomes very uncertain. This dilemma was addressed in one project undertaken as part of this programme (Barnes, 1993). One result of this developing commitment to involve users in management training is that some user groups have taken this on board and a number have set up independent training and consultancy organisations to provide this service. Users provide training on the basis of fee payment as would any other trainer.

Common to all the projects undertaken within this part of the programme was the provision of opportunities for managers to experience working directly with users and carers. During the workshop and other sessions in which this happened managers and users addressed together the questions of what user-led or user-sensitive services would look like, as well as what were the current experiences of those who used services and what impact such new ways of working had on both managers and users. Examples of the type of issues addressed in different contexts were:

- Does user-led mean that control moves away from the provider to the user?
- Do negative attitudes towards disabled people result in low self-esteem and status as second-class citizens, is this at the heart of poor service provision to users?
- It is often easier to stay with what you know – many managers feel threatened by change. How can this be overcome?
- What qualities and skills do carers require of service managers?
- What can help partnerships between managers and carers work?

A theme running throughout the work undertaken was the need to acknowledge the significance of the personal dimension within the provider user relationship. Carers identified the importance to effective working relationships of personal qualities such as: empathy; commitment; sensitivity and openness, as well as management skills. Acknowledging and addressing managers' fears about change, and the need for a shared value base were identified in another project. This suggests that the establishment of trusting relationships is a prerequisite for change. Trust is a reciprocal relationship which requires the valuing of the knowledge and understanding which each brings to the encounter (Barnes and Prior, 1996).

Local Voices

Local Voices was one of the first initiatives which linked citizen involvement to the 'purchaser–provider split' in health services. It was addressed to District Health Authorities and Family Health Services Authorities newly designated as health purchasers and at this stage with a limited and decreasing role in the direct provision of health services. The notion of health purchasing was that this should be based on an assessment of health care needs. Such needs could be determined through the application of epidemiological methods and through analysis of referrals to health services, but Local Voices was intended to ensure that local people's views were also part of the assessment. The initiative related to all types of health services, including those at the interface between health and social care.

The NHSME document outlining the initiative was specific about the reasons for involving local people in purchasing decisions and suggested both public relations and political reasons as well as an information gathering function intended to improve service relevance:

There are a number of reasons for involving local people in the purchasing process. If health authorities are to establish a *champion of the people role,* their decisions should reflect, so far as practical, what people want, their preferences, concerns and values. Being responsive to local views will enhance the credibility of health authorities but, more importantly, is likely to result in services which are better suited to local needs and therefore more appropriate. There may of course be occasions when local views have to be over-ridden (e.g. on the weight of epidemiological, resource or other considerations) and in such circumstances, it is important that health authorities explain the reasons for their decisions.

   Moreover, as health authorities seek to bring about changes in services and make explicit decisions about priorities they are likely to be more persuasive and successful in their negotiations with providers if they secure public support.

(NHSME, 1992, p. 3; emphasis in the original)

This statement could be read as a recognition within the NHS that the lack of locally elected democratic structures such as those which exist within local authorities is a deficit which needs to be compensated by the development of other mechanisms through which local people could express their views. However, the document makes no reference to such mechanisms as means through which health authorities might be accountable to local people, but the penultimate sentence of the above quotation does suggest an awareness of the need to give account, if not to accept the full consequences of accountability through the ballot box. Subsequently there has been some debate about whether the logical conclusion of this position is that local authorities should take over the role of health purchaser (Cooper *et al.,* 1995). However, at the time of writing there seemed no immediate prospect that either of the two main political parties would adopt this as a policy position (The Labour Party, 1995).

   Local Voices resulted in a number of initiatives which sought to consult with local people generally, as well as users of specific services. It may be that, because health services are more widely used and attract a greater degree of public interest and concern than do social care services, it will always be easier to generate participation among local citizens who do not have an immediate selfish interest resulting from their current use of services than it is in relation to community care services. The principle that health services are of interest and concern to all and thus all should be able to have their say in them is an important one and one which still has to be fully accepted in relation to community care. Thus, for example, the Local Voices document reported local initiatives which sought input from local community groups; from employers and employees; from panels made up of people identified through questionnaires circulated to all households; from people in local black and ethnic minority communities; and from focus groups selected using market research techniques, in addition to initiatives targeted on users of particular services and people with specific health care needs throughout the area.

Methods adopted to involve people in Local Voices initiatives were drawn primarily from different research methodologies including survey methods; qualitative methods such as focus groups and in-depth interviewing; action research; and from public relations and market research (NHSME, 1992, Sykes *et al.*, 1992). The report contained few examples of initiatives based on community development methods.

Taking part in community care planning

One effect of the increased emphasis on hearing the voices of service users was to call into question the ability of voluntary organisations, organisations *for* rather than *of* disabled people and other users of community care services, to speak on behalf of users. In Chapter 3 I referred to Age Concern's attempt to consider with whose voice the organisation was speaking when seeking to influence policies and services for older people. Other 'traditional' voluntary organisations also found themselves challenged by user-led groups to recognise that disabled people and others were speaking on their own behalf and that consulting with voluntary organisations over community care plans could not be assumed to mean that social services departments had carried out their statutory duty to consult with users and carers. As service providers voluntary organisations could also find themselves on the receiving end of critical feedback from their own users.

At the same time the mixed economy of welfare assumed a significant role for voluntary organisations within the new community care arrangements and the NHS and Community Care Act specified that voluntary groups both representing the interests of users and providing services to them should be consulted. The Act stated that in developing and reviewing community care plans the local authority shall consult:

such voluntary organisations as appear to the authority to represent the interests of persons who use or are likely to use any community care services within the area of the authority or the interests of private carers who, within that area, provide care to persons for whom, in the exercise of their social services functions, the local authority have a power or a duty to provide a service;

such voluntary housing agencies and other bodies as appear to the local authority to provide housing or community care services in their area;

and such other persons as the Secretary of State may direct.

(section 46(2))

What then was the role for voluntary organisations in community care planning? Averil Osborn, then Senior Assistant Director of Age Concern Scotland, sought to address this issue and produced guidance for voluntary and user groups about what community care planning meant for them and some of the practical implications of becoming involved within it.

While the statutory requirement is to consult with different groups, Osborn advised voluntary groups to seek *involvement* in the planning process, rather than simply respond to invitations to be consulted about it. She considered involvement to be a more active description of the relationship to be achieved than consultation and, since neither the act nor subsequent guidance specified how the planning process should operate, nor how consultation should be conducted, Osborn suggested there was scope for voluntary organisations as well as local authorities to propose methods which would allow early participation in the development of plans, rather than reactive feedback to proposals from statutory authorities. She noted that many other bodies were likely to have interests and involvement in the process including health authorities; other local authority departments and private provider agences. The aim for voluntary groups, she suggested, 'is to achieve a partnership not only among these interests but also with recipients of services' (Osborn, 1992, 'Why consult?', p. 4).

The guidance noted that, while definitions of users and carers contained within the act appeared to be very specific, in practice they were based on a series of judgements at local level which determine whether any particular individual is assessed as needing a service and hence can become a 'user'. Similar opportunities for differences of interpretation exist in relation to the definition of who is a carer. Osborn suggested that one responsibility of voluntary groups was to use a variety of methods to make contact with the wider range of potential users and carers who had not yet become users of services. As well as research, community work and community development approaches were likely to be important ways of achieving this.

Osborn suggested:

Given the need to be clearer about who the users and the carers are, and the question as to when a service is a community care service, voluntary groups need to address whether they are involved with such users and carers and whether they believe they are operating a community care service. If involved with carers or users, there are questions to ask as to whether they represent these people in any way.

Users groups may well have a mix of members, not all of whom would be regarded by the social services or social work department as 'users'. It may be important to decide whether or not this matters in relation to what the group is able to contribute to the planning debate and the development of better services.

(Osborn, *ibid.*, p. 70)

Through confronting both the assumption that voluntary groups represent the interests of users and/or carers, and the spurious specificity of the definition of users and carers contained in the act, Osborn highlighted some of the important ambiguities of the legislative requirement to include users' views within community care planning. Nevertheless she saw this as an opportunity to which voluntary groups should prepare themselves to respond. She also suggested that, as well as contributing to the formal planning process led by the statutory agencies, voluntary groups could extend con-sultation and involvement through using a variety of different approaches with which they are familiar. These could include: open meetings through which views could be canvassed; special consultative events bringing together all those concerned about particular problems or groups; using the media to interest and inform people; and community development work 'to find out what people want by "involving and doing" '.

Squaring the circle

Involvement in needs assessment was the other main area through which users and carers were to be enabled to influence community care services. Kathryn Ellis undertook a detailed study (Ellis, 1993) of assessment practice in two local authorities following the publication of the White Paper *Caring for People* in order to explore both the attitudes and behaviour of providers alongside the views and experiences of users and carers. She noted in her introduction to the report of the project that assessment is not only about competing perceptions of need, but also about differential power. Her study thus contributes to an understanding of the micro level political as well as professional implications of opening up provider judgements to lay challenge.

The person making a community care assessment finds herself looking at least two ways. On the one hand she has heard the exhortation that service provision should be needs led and that services should fit the person, rather than the person be fit to the services; but she also knows that she is in the front line in the apparently permanent campaign of resource rationing. She is to contribute to user empowerment by enabling users to participate in the assessment process, but she is also to be aware of her responsibilities as a gatekeeper to public resources.

This is not the only dilemma she faces. She is also to take note of the different and possibly conflicting need of those providing unpaid care to the person who is being assessed. If she has had contact with the disability movement she is also likely to be aware of a fundamental critique of assessment which defines this in terms of needs for care, rather than focussing on an individual's needs in relation to her ability to participate within the broader social, economic and civic life of the community in which she lives.

Ellis's work demonstrated that an important factor inhibiting any sense of partnership in the assessment process was a lack of openness on the part of practitioners making assessments. This could take a number of forms: some appeared to use instinct or moral judgement as a basis on which to make decisions about who was most deserving of help; others would on occasion withhold information in order to 'protect' people or fail to make allocation criteria explicit and thus leave users puzzled at the line of questioning that had been pursued with them; others clung to professional language and concepts as a way of maintaining a professional identity and distance from the user; while in other cases assumptions about the role played by an informal carer might not be checked out and negotiated and thus the practitioner might make a wrong judgement about the level of support required in particular circumstances.

The effects of this lack of openness and exchange on users included: difficulty in making demands because they did not have a sense of what type of help they might expect; frustration at the impossibility of exploring problems without a meaningful context in which to do this; an experience of having to fight for what they felt they needed; and an enduring cynicism about the social services department.

Ellis concluded by discussing five strategies for change which would be necessary in order to effect 'the radical shift from provider-led to user-led assessments which are necessary if user and carer participation is to become reality' (Ellis, *ibid.*, p. 39). The five strategies involved: changing the language of assessment; training; making rationing explicit; broadening definitions of need; and empowering users and carers. These strategies recognised the challenge to professional values and attitudes which need to be achieved and the acceptance that a shift to user-led assessments would involve not only changes in the way in which professionals are trained, but also a recognition of the essentially political nature of assessment in the context of resource constraint. Explicitness over rationing was seen to provide opportunities for the development of alliances to fight for more resources, as well as to provide a context in which rationing decisions could be challenged through the official complaints procedure. People need to understand their entitlements and receive the assistance of an advocate if this appeared necessary. Ellis also considered the importance of enabling community care assessments to take on board much broader definitions of need which consider people's whole lives rather than simply consider service and care deficits. This would match much more closely the priorities of disabled people and would contribute to the broader understanding of community care which is the theme of this book.

From Margin to Mainstream

From Margin to Mainstream was an action research initiative which sought to support the development of user and carer involvement in four local authority sites and to learn the lessons of this experience. It was funded by the Joseph Rowntree Foundation which had become a champion of user involvement and used its considerable research funding capability to promote good practice in this area. Case study sites were chosen because there had already been some pilot work and the authority wished to move from the 'special project' status to making involvement 'an everyday part of the way all services are planned and delivered' (Goss and Miller, 1995, p. 4).

The four sites demonstrated different models through which user involvement was being developed at this stage:

- In Dyfed (Wales) a co-operative of disabled people extended a user-run information service and took an active part in community care planning; in re-thinking assessment processes; developing a complaints procedure; and in delivering training.
- The Hereford project focussed on older people with mental health problems, or with dementia, and their carers. It concentrated on how the older people could be involved in the assessment process and on establishing an effective dialogue between carers, workers and the older people themselves.
- A Charter for People with Disabilities provided the focus of work in Sheffield. This resulted in a process reversal in which disabled people set out their own business plan and invited local authority representatives to discuss it with them.
- Consultations with users about a new day centre in Sutton (London) developed into a user managed learning centre for disabled people. The board provided the service under contract to the local authority. Another initiative which arose from this was the recruitment of people with mild learning difficulties to act as buddies and advocates for people with severe learning difficulties.

The emphasis in this work was on achieving change and the most important change to be achieved was considered to be in the nature of the relationship between users, carers and staff. Many of the messages coming out of these projects are those with which we are now familiar:

- the significance of partnership based on equal, but different expertise and perspectives;

- the importance of values and personal qualities such as trust, mutual respect, commitment and honesty;
- a recognition of the different service agencies which have a role to play in meeting community care needs;
- the need for change throughout organisations if partnerships between users and providers are to be developed and supported.

From Margin to Mainstream placed a strong emphasis on the need for training: not only seeing users as trainers, but also enabling users, carers and staff to train together. It acknowledged that changing relationships is likely to mean changes among all those involved:

The case study sites stressed the need to listen to and understand the point of view of staff and to treat them as 'whole people'. They talked about helping staff to feel empowered, to work with users and carers to increase their own influence and sense of being listened to. One user stressed the need to 'recognise that working together is a two-way learning experience, we have to show interest in where they are coming from and remember that they may have little experience of working with disabled people.'

(Goss and Miller, *ibid.*, pp. 48–9)

The report also included practical exercises to assist people in developing the partnership relationships being advocated.

Conclusion/summary

This chapter has considered examples of moves to enable users and carers to have a greater say in services which developed prior to the 1990 Act and those which followed on from this. By the mid 1990s there was considerable experience of consulting with users, although rather less evidence that user involvement had become integral to decision making processes. Experience had demonstrated that change was necessary in different spheres:

- User-led services implied structural changes within and between organisations. Users' needs do not fit comfortably into administrative categories through which services have traditionally been organised. Nor could change in one part of the organisation be sustained without cultural and practical changes within the system as a whole
- Changes in professional skills and behaviour needed to be brought about through training which emphasised partnership rather than the separation of professional and user.
- Changes in inter-personal relationships between service providers and recipients would also be necessary. The empowerment of users constitutes a personal as well as a professional challenge for

people who have regarded themselves as experts. User empowerment requires relationships based on trust and reciprocity.

- In order to enable those who had been excluded from decision making processes to make an effective contribution to them, capacity building among individual users and user groups would be necessary. Hence the self-organisation of user groups needed to be supported alongside the developments of mechanisms through which users could participate in organisational processes.

While user involvement was considerably more developed by the mid-1990s than it had been in the mid-80s, power was still effectively located within large-scale welfare bureaucracies. The size of the task implied by developing community care as an empowering service option was perhaps more evident than it had been when the architects of the 1990 Act were doing their work.

CHAPTER 5

Private lives and public policy: the self-organisation of carers

In Chapter 3 I looked at examples of the way in which people defined as users of health and social care services have organised themselves both to achieve influence within those services and to achieve wider objectives relating to civil rights and citizenship. Here I turn to look at developments in the self-organisation of those who have come to be defined as 'carers' of those service users; to consider whether the nature and objectives of carers' organisations are consistent with those of users; and to consider how such developments point to the need for an enhanced conception of citizenship which includes private as well as public lives. I also consider what carers are saying about community care and how this has affected public policy in this area. In Chapter 6 I look more closely at the way in which service purchasers and providers view carers, and how this affects decision making at a local level about whose voices will be heard in consultations about community care.

A growing recognition of the significance of 'informal care' has been a major factor in the development of community care policy at both national and local level. During the last ten years carers have been 'discovered' by policy makers and have been urged to 'come out' by organisations such as the Carers' National Association which has developed both as a pressure group and as a support group. But once again we have to delve rather further back than the events immediately leading up to the passage of the NHS and Community Care Act in order to find the origins of the self-awareness of carers that they had common interests and common experiences which needed to be represented in policy and service development.

It is also important to consider the growth of such an awareness in a sociological as well as a policy context. Why should the position of 'family carer' have come to be regarded as something around which a pressure group organisation should develop? Why should the position of a wife looking after her elderly husband who had had a stroke, or parents providing the additional support needed by a child with learning difficulties, have come to be seen as anything other than something to be taken for granted as part of what is expected within family relationships? In order to answer these types of questions it is necessary to explore broader sociological critiques of 'the family' as well as to consider both demographic and policy shifts which were affecting the particular experiences of families in which there was a disabled or frail elderly person.

The National Council for the Single Woman and her Dependants

In 1963 the first organisation which sought to represent the interests of those subsequently to be known as carers was established as a result of an initiative taken by the Reverend Mary Webster, an unmarried woman who had given up her work in the early 1950s to care for her elderly parents (McKenzie, 1995). At this time a high proportion of women were unmarried because the Second World War had wiped out a large number of young men, leaving a generation of women with a shortage of marriage partners. Hence, there was a plentiful supply of women who had never been married and thus were 'available' to provide care to older people whose numbers were increasing because of improved social conditions and improved and more accessible health care. Mary Webster recognised that her experience was unlikely to be an unusual one and when her parents died she started to explore the experiences of other single women who were in similar circumstances. She wrote a letter to *The Times* and sought to engage the interest of the Churches:

I am anxious to mobilise the redoubtable energies of the Federation in what I consider to be a very neglected social matter. More than ten per cent of the women in this country who are over 40 are unmarried. Because of changing economic circumstances, most of them follow a salaried occupation. Many of them also have responsibilities for dependants. Because they have to earn their living, as well as undertaking the tasks of caring for others, life for them is often difficult.

(Mary Webster, *Federation News*, May 1963, vol. 10, no. 2)

Once she had started to make visible the experiences of single women like herself she received an enormous response from others who were in a similar situation or who recognised that they were likely to be so in the future. It was suggested that the scale of the response was not only evidence of the extent of single women's involvement in informal care, but also of the opportunity it provided for a group who felt ignored, unvalued and powerless to organise on a collective basis. Baroness Seear, who later became President of the Carers' National Association, observed that 'many women saw the organisation as a kind of single women's trade union' (quoted in Kohner, 1993).

Elizabeth Wilson (1977) has described the post-war period as a time during which the task of rebuilding the family in the context of a protective welfare state meant that the roles of women as wives and mothers was being given a particular prominence. Those who had been neither wives nor mothers were excluded from the ambiguous benefits of a return to traditional roles for women after they had been forced into the factories and into the land armies during the war. Women were seen to be liberated from much of the drudgery of housework by the availability of new household appliances, and relieved of the anxieties caused by poverty and ill health by the post-war settlement which resulted in the establishment of the National Health Service and Beveridge's welfare state. Prime Minister Harold Macmillan's assertion that 'You've never had it so good!' represented the dominant perception of the 1950s and early 1960s as a period of increasing prosperity and ease. In this context the dominant image of women was that of wives and mothers happy to return to their domestic roles. However much such an image might have been at odds with the reality of women's experiences, single women who were combining paid work with responsibilities for looking after elderly relatives did not share in it. An organisation which represented their experiences and interests was seen not only as welcome for the specific improvements it sought in their practical and financial circumstances, but also as the start of a more fundamental critique of assumptions about the nature of the family which underpinned the Beveridgean welfare state and which were picked up in later feminist critiques of community care (e.g. Finch and Groves, 1985).

The National Council for the Single Woman and her Dependants (NCSWD) sought to achieve legislative and policy changes which would benefit single women carers, and to provide support and advice to such women. Methods adopted included: commissioning research into the experience and circumstances of single women carers and hosting conferences to publicise results, as well as campaigning and lobbying at national and local level. From an early stage the organisation was successful in gaining the support of some powerful public figures which was considered to have been important in its successes in achieving financial improvements in the lives of many carers. At a local level: 'Branches served as the eyes and ears of the organisation at the grass roots' (McKenzie, 1995, p. 86). While the national organisation primarily focussed on the need for legislative changes in relation to the financial circumstances of carers, local branches were more directly concerned with the availability of health and social care services.

The major achievements of NCSWD are regarded as being the introduction in 1971 of the Attendance Allowance, payable to those needing constant care at home, and, in 1976, the Invalid Care Allowance, paid directly to carers. The origins of these benefits in campaigns led by an organisation representing single women is evidenced by the fact that the Invalid Care Allowance was payable only to single women. This was based on the assumption that the allowance was remuneration for lost earnings as a result of the woman having had to give up work in order to care. Married women were assumed not to work but to be dependent on their husbands' earnings. In this, as in other parts of the benefits sytem, the welfare state was based on profoundly sexist assumptions about women's roles and positions within the family (Land, 1985). It was only in 1986 as a result of an appeal to the European Court of Justice that entitlement to the Invalid Care Allowance was extended to married women (see below).

The successes of the NCSWD started to prompt contact from married, widowed and divorced women who identified themselves as being in similar positions to that of single women carers. Eventually it became impossible to sustain such an exclusive membership and the title of the organisation was changed to 'The National Council for Carers and their Elderly Dependants'. This still separated the experience of those who cared for older relatives from those who cared for younger ones. While the experience of adults in mid-life taking on the care of an elderly parent for many years could be constructed as a more than usual family responsibility, looking after a disabled child or providing a quasi-nursing service to a partner impaired as a result of accident or chronic ill health were simply part of what being a parent or spouse meant. In the case of older parents who needed additional support because of advancing frailty there is some implicit if not explicit negotiation over where this responsibility should lie (Finch and Mason, 1993). When it is a child or partner it is almost entirely taken for granted where responsibility lies (Barnes, 1996b; Parker, 1990; Ungerson, 1987).

When the Association of Carers was founded in 1981 on the principle that it should represent all carers, regardless of sex, age, marital status or relationship to the person they cared for, there was some opposition not only from professionals who wanted things organised around the 'condition' of the person receiving care, but also from some members of the National Council who were unhappy about a shift of focus away from carers of older people. The NCCED in fact remained in existence until 1988 when it merged with the Association of Carers to form the Carers' National Association.

'A stronger voice'

During the 1980s the carers' lobby became increasingly influential at a national level as well as continuing to provide a focus for self help in the expanding network of local groups. The Association of Carers was founded both on personal experience (its founder was Judith Oliver whose husband was disabled) and on the analysis of research into the experiences of carers which demonstrated that:

if you broke the experience of caring down into the emotional issues, the physical issues, the environmental issues, the financial issues, then all carers were really experiencing the same kind of stresses and suffering the same kind of problems.

(Oliver, quoted in Kohner, 1993, p. 8)

Subsequent research would suggest that such a claim ignores

important differences in the experiences of women and men carers (Ungerson, 1987), of black carers (Atkin, 1991), of those caring for partners rather than for parents or children (Parker, 1993), as well as differences in the extent to which caring is experienced as 'burden' (Braithwaite, 1990). But shared experiences and shared identities, rather than internal differences are important in establishing a constituency which can form the basis of a powerful pressure group and the subsequent successes of the carers' lobby would have been less likely had there not been a single organisation representing the interests of all carers.

As I discussed in Chapter 1, by the mid 1980s the policy of community care was beginning to receive an increasing amount of attention not only from policy makers but also from researchers. Academic interest in 'the family' was starting to extend to include consideration of the way in which families were assumed to be the natural source of care for elderly and disabled members, as well as of the socialisation of children. Informal care offered a substantial new area for research and the number of research projects exploring the experiences of informal carers and their relationships with formal services burgeoned (see e.g. Parker, 1990, Twigg, Atkin and Perring, 1990). Policy assumptions about the potential for interlinking formal and informal care started to be questioned by academic analysts (Bulmer, 1987; Waerness, 1987), while others looked more closely at the notion of 'caring networks' and the resources available within communities to provide care (Walker, 1987, Wenger, 1991).

Research and pressure group activity were being developed hand in hand in some instances. In 1985, following an initiative launched by the Department of Health under the heading 'Helping the Community to Care', the King's Fund Informal Caring Unit was established in London. This unit combined information giving and gathering, research and service development. Ten years later Carers' Impact, the successor to the Caring Unit and an alliance of local authority, health authority, and voluntary sector organisations, held its first national conference entitled 'Carers in the Mainstream?'. The Director of the Carers' National Association at the time of writing, Jill Pitkeathley, was a founder member of the Carers' Impact Steering Group.

The focus on the financial circumstances of carers which had been a primary concern of the NCSWD continued to be pursued by the Association of Carers (AoC) in the campaign for the extension of the Invalid Care Allowance to married and cohabiting women. In 1982 a steering group was established to pursue this campaign which stood to benefit 96,000 women if it were successful (Kohner, 1993). The campaign was based on a test case brought by a married woman caring for her mother who had senile dementia. This woman was selected by the AoC and invited to pursue her case with the support of the Association. The case was based on a directive issued by the EEC requiring equal treatment in social security systems. As in other cases, the UK government was reluctant to accept European rulings on social policy and it took an application to the European Court of Justice to force a change of policy. The government backed down the day before the European court ruling in 1986.

While the 'Caring Costs' campaign continued to emphasise the personal financial implications of caring and the amount which informal carers save the state by providing unpaid care, during the latter part of the 1980s attention shifted to the policy review process which culminated in the passage of the 1990 NHS and Community Care Act. The 1986 Disabled Persons Act provided the first legislative recognition of the role of carers when it required local authorities to take account of carers' abilities to care when assessing the needs of people seeking community care services from social services departments. Much of the work of the AoC and subsequently of the Carers' National Association can be seen as making authorities aware that it is not only the direct service user who has needs which should be met, but that carers also have needs which should be both taken into account and responded to.

Informal care and the state

Much of the success of the carers' lobby hinges around the fact that it was clearly in the government's interest to acknowledge the role played by informal or family carers. The success of community care policy depended on informal carers being prepared to continue to undertake the primary caring responsibility for their relatives and friends. It was no accident that Jill Pitkeathley was invited to become a member of the group advising Roy Griffiths as he worked on the Department of Health commissioned report *Community Care: Agenda for Action*, nor that, during the deliberations which led to the publication of the Community Care White Paper, Ministers from the Department of Health made their way to Birmingham to hear from the Community Care Special Action Project what carers were saying about their needs and their views of community care in practice (Barnes and Wistow, 1991). The apparent convergence of interests is clear in the following statements from the Griffiths Report (1988) and *Caring for People* (1989):

Publicly provided services constitute only a small part of the total care provided to people in need. Families, friends, neighbours and other local people provide the majority of care in response to needs which they are uniquely well placed to identify and respond to. This will continue to be the primary means by which people are enabled to live normal lives in community settings. The proposals take as their starting point that this is as it should be, and that the first task of publicly provided services is to support and where possible strengthen these networks of carers.

(Griffiths, 1988, para. 3.2)

While this White Paper focuses largely on the role of statutory and independent bodies in the provision of community care services, the reality is that most care is provided by family, friends and neighbours. . . . Helping carers to maintain their valuable contribution to the spectrum of care is both right and a sound investment.

(Secretaries of State, 1989, p. 9)

From the perspective of the state informal care is to be preferred both because it is a more cost effective option and because it is the natural and hence the best option. Underpinning an unwillingness on the part of the state to accept the full resource responsibility implied by meeting the needs of disabled and elderly people, is an ideological position on the respective roles of the state and the family (Dalley, 1988). This position can be sustained because there is little evidence of a powerful lobby arguing that collective forms of provision should be preferred over individualised services. Jill Pitkeathley is quoted as saying:

I've never known such consensus around a set of proposals as there was around Griffiths'. Everyone, on the whole, agreed with the proposals.

(in Kohner, 1993, p. 20)

Carers' organisations were campaigning for increased recognition of the role played by carers and increased support for this role. They were not, with one important exception, campaigning for the extension of residential rather than community services, nor for a reassessment of the possibilities of alternative forms of collective provision such as that suggested by Dalley (1988). The one exception was the National Schizophrenia Fellowship, an organisation primarily involving parents of people with a diagnosis of schizophrenia, which argued for the retention of psychiatric hospitals rather than the development of community-based mental health services.

Certain feminist critiques of community care policy reflected not only the way in which community care contributed to the oppression of women by reinforcing gendered assumptions about caring roles, and by adding to the emotional and material burdens of many women who had to combine both paid work and unpaid caring work, but also a socialist belief in state welfare systems which were starting to unravel as a result of pressures coming from the left as well as the right of the political spectrum (Deakin, 1987). Such critiques were influential in arguing for policies which recognised and supported women's roles as carers and, in some circumstances, which could support the expansion of male responsibilities for caring. However, they were themselves subject to critique from feminists within the disability movement for the way in which disabled and older people were constructed as dependants and burdens on their carers (Morris, 1989). Arguing for the retention of institutions which were experienced as oppressive by those admitted to them could not be the response to an analysis of the oppression experienced by informal carers. Nor could the experience of all carers be defined as oppressive. While caring is a 'labour' it is also very often a 'labour of love' and the carers' lobby sought primarily to find an accommodation with the state which would enable genuine caring relationships to be maintained without the burden of care becoming overwhelming.

What do carers want from community care?

There is little evidence from research into carers' needs and experiences, or from the campaigns of carers' organisations, that families are seeking to give up their overall responsibilities for providing care and support to older or disabled relatives. In some instances both those providing and those receiving 'care' are asking for specific tasks to be undertaken by paid service providers, although *which* tasks vary according to personal circumstances and preferences. Some would not want personal tending to be provided by a stranger, but do want help with practical domestic work so that they can have the time to undertake more intimate tasks involved in personal care. Others, often spouses, find that having to deal with incontinence and other highly intimate physical needs can interfere with their relationships as lovers and partners (Morris, 1993). They would prefer such tasks to be undertaken by a professional in a way that separates physical tending from sexual relationships. The general point emerging from this is that carers want to negotiate with services in order to reach an accommodation about who does what. They are not happy with a system that demands allocation to dependency categories which carry with them specified amounts and types of help which may bear little resemblance to their perceptions of their needs (see Chapter 6).

One part of the carers' lobby has adopted a somewhat different position. The National Schizophrenia Fellowship (NSF) is made up primarily of the family members of people diagnosed with schizo-phrenia (although it does also have groups involving people with schizophrenia themselves). NSF has opposed the speed with which psychiatric hospitals have been closed in the UK, in the absence of a well developed community mental health service as an alternative. Some of the public statements from the NSF have demonstrated a firm opposition to the policy of community care and have led to a polarisation between themselves and some mental health user groups.

Those who provide intensive care over long periods of time to older people, disabled people, people with mental health problems and to those with chronic illnesses are asking for opportunities to have breaks from this which can benefit themselves and those they are caring for. Examples could be quoted from many studies of carers' experiences of the importance of 'respite' which can provide each with a break from the other. The following comes from work in Birmingham undertaken as part of an evaluation of the Birmingham Community Care Special Action Project:

Carers described caring as a 'demanding job' and as being hard work, in some cases growing harder as the carer herself was growing older and her strength was being drained away by constant demands. They talked of getting fed-up with it and being 'touchy and edgy' because of the pressures. In some cases this becomes frustration and resentfulness 'Why him/me/us?' . . .

Caring has an impact on the relationship between the care giver and the care receiver, as well as on the way the carer feels about her/himself:

I love my husband very dearly, but there were times when we could scream at each other. Because we were fed up with each other and yet we knew we needed each other and we didn't mean it.

I knew myself, I just felt I couldn't cope any more; I couldn't go on. But I kept putting it off because I was disgusted with myself to think that I couldn't manage.

(Barnes and Wistow, 1992b)

Carers are asking for their close and intimate knowledge not only of the person they are caring for, but also of ways in which they are able jointly to solve problems and find solutions, to be recognised and respected. For example, parents with daughters or sons with learning difficulties emphasise the importance of the understanding which comes from familiarity with their children's behaviour. The ability to recognise and interpret feelings which cannot easily be expressed in spoken language, and the development of different forms of communication with those for whom words do not come easily may be a particular advantage gained from living in close proximity for many years with family members. A frequent complaint is that such knowledge and the experience and skills which derive from this are ignored or dismissed by the paid workers with whom carers come into contact (Barnes, 1996b).

Yet many carers have not actively chosen to take on this role and, while some describe considerable satisfactions to be gained from caring (Grant and Nolan, 1993), many also feel that they are expected to do too much and that there is insufficient recognition for what they do (Barnes and Wistow, 1992b). They are asking that their input be recognised and, if they have to give up jobs or the prospect of promotion in order to take on a role which saves the state a considerable amount of money, they should not be further penalised by the additional costs of caring. The Caring Costs Campaign which was launched in 1992 by the CNA aims to secure an independent income for carers. From her study of the costs of informal care, Caroline Glendinning found:

The analysis of household budgeting and expenditure patterns which was carried out in this study took full account of the resources contributed by the disabled person. Nevertheless, in many instances at least some of these extra disability costs still fell on carers to meet out of their own financial resources. In addition, some carers incurred extra expenditure because they provided their elderly or disabled relatives with a higher standard of living than s/he would have been able to afford from her/his income alone. In the poorer households, hidden 'costs' were experienced by carers, including foregoing of items of consumption in order to meet the disability costs of the disabled person, and the psychological 'costs' of their own financial dependency.

(Glendinning, 1992, pp. 110–11)

The latter point reflects the fact that adult children had become financially dependent on the welfare benefits of their elderly or disabled parents because they had had to give up jobs in order to provide care. They would experience considerable difficulty in finding work following the death or admission to residential care of the person they cared for, and would also in these circumstances lose the marginal advantage of the benefit income.

Caring is experienced as physically and emotionally demanding work. Those who care for people with mental health problems in particular can also experience the effect of the stigma attached to mental illness and the impact of mental distress on family relationships can be devastating (Smith and West, 1985). On top of the emotional and physical demands, getting access to benefits and services is experienced as a battle or an uphill struggle which may sometimes be too exhausting to attempt. Information about services and entitlements has to be sought out rather than being offered and, as carers have said in many studies of their experiences of services, you have to know what question to ask before you stand any chance of finding out a useful answer (e.g. Twigg *et al.*, 1990). Often those service providers to whom carers turn in the first instance, in particular general practitioners, are themselves unaware of other services which might be available and unwilling to share their professional knowledge in a way which would allow carers to develop their own problem solving strategies. Some carers have suggested that lack of information is a deliberate strategy for rationing services (Twigg and Atkin, 1994), while others have expressed considerable distress at having to make complaints or threats in order to get access to services when they know they are entitled to them (Ellis, 1993). The benefits system is complex and confusing, and appealing against apparently arbitrary decisions can be a humiliating experience (Twigg and Atkin, 1994).

I worked with two groups of carers for a year to involve them in the evaluation of the Birmingham Community Care Special Action Project. Analysing the content of the discussions that took place enabled us to come up with criteria which defined what carers considered to be a high quality community care service. The general criteria shown in Box 2 were identified as expressing carers' views of the characteristics of a sensitive community care service.

Box 2

1. Carers should be able to define their own needs.
2. All services should be accessible from one point within the system: carers should not have to repeat their stories to different people as they get referred from one to another.
3. Assessment of needs would lead to relevant services being provided.
4. Services would be provided immediately after the need has been identified and agreed.
5. Choice of services, particularly respite care services, should be available in order to meet the different preferences and requirements of those admitted to care.
6. Adaptations to homes should be carried out quickly, and there should be a follow up service in case things go wrong.
7. Benefits should not be structured so that carers are penalised for encouraging independence.
8. Benefits and other financial assistance should not assume that other family members will provide care (e.g. sitting time) free.
9. Carers should be able to spend time talking about the effect on themselves of caring for a disabled relative or friend.
10. Services should not be interrupted when people go on leave or change jobs.
11. Home care services should recognise the importance to the self-esteem of elderly or disabled people of having a clean house, and should provide a service which includes house cleaning.
12. Service providers should negotiate with carers when home visits should take place.
13. Carers should be confident that care provided outside the home is consistent with the quality of care which they provide.
14. Carers need to be confident that service providers are planning future services to meet future needs.

(From Barnes and Wistow, 1993)

In these panel discussions, as in interviews conducted with carers for research purposes, carers were reflecting on their own needs as people with major responsibilities for meeting the needs of others, as well as on the direct needs of those they care for. Carers are often aware of the potential for conflict between their own needs and those of the people they support. Respite care is a good example of this. Carers need a break from caring but they know that often the person they care for does not want to be 'pushed out' into a respite care home to enable this to happen. They face the dilemma of forcing their relative to do something which will make them distressed or unhappy, or risking their own health by not taking a break. But to what extent is this conflict inherent within care giving and care receiving relationships rather than being a result of inadequate or insensitive services? If respite care provided positive experiences for those being cared for, would there be a problem? Item 7 in Box 2 makes a similar point. Parents of disabled adult children are sometimes criticised by service providers for being unwilling to encourage them to get jobs. But if family incomes are dependent on benefits which will be cut if the disabled person obtains a low-paid job at less than the level of benefit income, then such a response can be considered a rational response to the needs of the family as a whole.

There are other examples of the way in which services are organised, or the way in which people are treated by service providers, acting to exacerbate rather than resolve the potential for conflict between the needs of carers and those who receive care from them. The earliest experiences of parents of disabled children can lead to a lack of confidence. One mother of a daughter with learning difficulties with whom I worked spoke of following nursing staff round to ensure that her baby was given sufficient food after the hospital matron had said soon after her daughter's birth, 'Forget about her' and a nursing sister had said, 'Children love you and leave you. Buy yourself a dog, a dog will be your best friend.' This had left her with a feeling of working in opposition to paid carers, rather than experiencing professional help as supportive of a joint project concerned with maximising her child's capacities.

The stereotype of parents of children with learning difficulties is of over-protective parents who do too much for their children and who are unwilling to let them take risks. However, a father in a group I worked with recounted how care staff in a respite care home would use hoists to lift his son into bed because health and safety regulations meant they were not allowed to lift him, while at home his parents encouraged him to move as much as he was capable of in order to get what physical exercise he could. Hence they encouraged their son to do what he could to get into bed with their support, rather than using mechanical aids which required little effort on his part.

Such examples suggest it is important to consider why differences between the needs of those who provide and those who receive care may be experienced or constructed as conflicts. As we saw in Chapter 3, the empowerment sought by people with learning disabilities includes empowerment within the family as well as in relation to services, but, as I argue in the following chapter, interdependency is an essential feature of being human and it is probably not helpful to equate empowerment solely with independence. The language of community care is itself a source of difficulty. The concept of 'carer' is one which has been considered to construct the care receiver as dependent and as a burden to the one providing care. It does not sufficiently acknowledge the reciprocity that may exist within caring relationships, nor the nature of the relationships which existed prior to the start of 'care'. I develop this point in Chapter 6.

A self-conscious awareness of the need to reconstruct the relationship between 'carers' and those they 'care for' is evident in an advertisement placed by the charity 'Scope'. Formerly 'The Spastics Society', its change of name evidenced the unacceptability of demeaning language to disabled people. Alongside a photograph of a young man holding a baby the text reads:

Susan has cerebral palsy. I don't want to be a handicap to her.

I used to mollycoddle Susan. Not for her benefit, but for mine. Scope's School for Parents made me realise I had something to learn. Namely that cerebral palsy affects the ability to control movement. Not to grow up. Find out what Scope does for parents in your area. . . .

Encouraging wives, daughters, lovers, husbands or friends to identify themselves as carers has been an important objective of the carers' movement. It has been seen to be a vital means of raising awareness among those who provide care that they are entitled to services and financial support, and it has also been necessary as a means of achieving legislative recognition for the work that carers do. By naming carers as an identifiable sub-group within the population it has become possible to include reference to their needs and circumstances in community care legislation. But such naming can serve to disguise the other, very different relationships that carers may have with care receivers. It may also separate them from each other in ways which may result in competition between interest groups, rather than alliances between all who have a shared interest in ensuring effective 'community care'. Judith Oliver has argued that the carers' lobby has had common cause with the disability movement:

We were on the side of disabled people and acting in their interests too. Because from the start, we argued that disabled people deserved better than to be looked after by one (usually), exhausted (usually), possibly resentful person who was being used as a doormat by statutory authorities. We were saying that the system did neither side any good. It tied disabled people to one person who might not even be the person they would choose to have care for them.

(Oliver, quoted in Kohner, 1993)

However, not all would agree that action taken on behalf of carers has benefited disabled people. There has been opposition from within the disability movement to the introduction of legislation aimed at carers because the demands of disabled people are based on notions of 'rights' rather than 'care'.

The objectives of the carers' movement have not been restricted to service improvement and ensuring that the needs of carers themselves are acknowledged and responded to. In seeking recognition as experts in caring they are challenging the right of professionals to define the nature of their 'problems' and to determine the appropriate response to them. In this respect their project shares with user movements the aim of asserting the authority of experiential knowledge alongside and, if necessary, in preference to that of professional knowledge. As I outlined in Chapter 1, the concept of 'care' contained within policy pronouncements is beset by as many confusions as that of community. While in practice individual paid care providers often learn that the separation of physical labour from the emotional content of caring is not possible, the commodification of care in 'care packages' seeks to define the provision of care on the basis of contract rather than trust (Barnes and Prior, 1996). The conflicts revealed between the interests of carers and those they care for derive from the problems of subordinate relationships (Waerness, 1987). As long as care-giving is conceived as a one-way relationship it will always risk the construction of one party as dependent on the other. But there is considerable evidence of reciprocity in care-giving and care-receiving relationships. Waerness (*ibid.*) also argues that both rationality and emotionality, normally regarded as dichotomous and exclusive, need to be brought together in 'the rationality of caring' in order to understand what 'good caring' consists of. Thus:

Expertise in childrearing, according to the rationality of caring, is dependent both on practical experience in caregiving work and on personal knowledge of the individual child in question. When mothers exchange advice and support concerning problems of childcare, they can therefore at the same time insist that it is easier to bring up the second child than the first, and still say that each child has to be treated quite differently.

(Waerness, *ibid.*, p. 220)

This understanding is something which front-line paid care providers may learn, but which is likely to be frustrated by the rules and procedures within which 'caregiving' bureaucracies require them to work. Home carers forbidden by their employers to undertake any task which involves dealing with electrical equipment, for example, changing light bulbs, or which involves climbing on steps, such as cleaning the top of cupboards, find themselves in a position of either having to refuse to do exactly the tasks which their elderly clients find most difficult to do for themselves, or disobeying rules and risking censure. Treating each 'client' differently is incompatible with rules which define the type and amount of support which can be provided by reference to allocation to particular dependency categories. I have heard many examples of carers saying that the help they have been offered seeks to replace that which they feel capable of providing, whereas they are refused help with those tasks which they find particularly difficult or from which they are seeking to be freed in order to concentrate on the care which reinforces their relationship with the person they are providing care for. The maintenance of reciprocity in caring relationships is threatened when public care-giving services are experienced as inflexible, stigmatising and of poor quality. Waerness concludes:

Strengthening the values inherent in the rationality of caring is, therefore, in today's welfare state, not a question of replacing public *paid* care with informal *unpaid* family care or voluntary work. Rather, it seems to be a question of what possibilities there are to reorganise the public care system in such a way that practical experience in caregiving work and personal experience of the individual client can be an independent basis for greater influence, at the expense of professional and bureaucratic control and authority.

(Waerness, ibid., 2. 227; emphasis in the original)

Underpinning all that carers' groups are seeking to achieve in terms of practical improvements in community care services of benefit to themselves and those they care for, is a recognition of both the quantity and quality of work they undertake. They are claiming recognition as 'co-producers' of care (see Chapter 6), and they are claiming recognition of the experiential knowledge which they bring to caring and from which they want 'professional' carers to learn. Both factors provide legitimation for claims to be involved in the planning of community care services. A ten-point plan reflecting carers' needs has been set out by CNA:

- An income that covers the cost of caring
- Recognition of need and their contribution
- Services tailored to individual circumstances
- Reflecting racial, cultural and religious backgrounds
- Opportunities for a break
- Practical help: home help, adaptations, etc.
- Someone to talk to
- Information on benefits and services
- Opportunities to explore alternatives to family care
- Services designed through consultation.

Changes in demography and policy mean that more people will experience being in the role of 'carer' at some point in their lives. The 1990 General Household Survey found that 6 per cent of all adults in the UK were looking after a sick or elderly relative – 24 per cent of those in the 45 to 64 age group had caring responsibilities. The Carers' National Association has estimated that there are nearly seven million carers in Britain. Increasingly caring for sick or disabled parents is something which young children experience. Local studies of child carers in Tameside and Sandwell have led to estimates that more than 100,000 children are caring for their parents. Not only does this have an impact on the lives of individuals, it has a wider impact on the social and economic structure of society. Interruptions to careers or an early end to working life reduce earning power and hence the spending power of those taking on unpaid caring roles. Caring which is unrecognised and unsupported can lead to physical illness and emotional distress which leads to carers themselves becoming 'clients'.

The demands of caring can severely curtail opportunities to engage in other activities and to take on other roles.

Carers and citizens

What does this mean for the citizenship of carers? It has been suggested that the 'citizen' has historically implied a male individual with rights and responsibilities relating to civic duty existing in the public sphere. The ultimate responsibility of the citizen is to lay down his life in the defence of the state, a responsibility which women have been excused by most western states. Less dramatically, but of considerable relevance to a much larger number of people, is the exclusion of women until well into the twentieth century from the right to vote. Women's capacity to bear children marks their difference from men not only in biological terms but also in terms of their relationship with the state. While their prime responsibility is to produce new citizens, women have been excluded from citizenship by the view that their roles lie within the private sphere of families rather than the public world of both the state and civil society. Hence action is required to enable women to enter the public sphere on equal terms with men. Another view is that since the political duty of women is to bear and raise children, motherhood is itself a civic duty and the objective should be an extension of the sphere of citizenship, rather than an extension of women's sphere of action (see Pateman, 1992, for a discussion of these different positions).

Discussions of the position of women as mothers have a broader relevance for a consideration of women and men as carers. Insurance-based social security systems which provide for the social rights of citizenship are based on the notion of 'contribution'. Paid employment provides the means through which contributions are made since financial contributions are deducted from the wage packet. Within the Beveridgean welfare system women were not seen as capable of making contributions in this way and thus were not entitled to the same rights to receive benefits as their husbands. But this did not mean that women did not have a contribution to make to 'social citizenship':

The paradoxical contribution demanded from women was – welfare. This was not the public welfare of the 'welfare state', but the contribution of private, unpaid welfare in their homes. Women, as mothers, nurture the next generation of citizens, and, as wives and daughters, tend to the sick, the infirm and the aged. The welfare state has always depended upon women's contribution, but it remains unacknowledged and set apart from (political) citizenship. In the present period of 'privatization', women's private tasks assume an even greater importance.

(Pateman, 1992, p. 23)

The contributions which carers make to the welfare state are contributions in kind. They provide more than an alternative to state provided welfare. In many instances state welfare provides relief and technical assistance, through respite care, day care and the provision of equipment, for example, rather than being the primary source from which many of the needs of older people, disabled people and those experiencing mental health problems are met. The 1990 General Household Survey revealed that 55 per cent of those in receipt of informal care did not receive regular visits from health or social care professionals. In 1995 the CNA quantified the contribution made by carers to the welfare state: the total value of the in-kind contribution of informal care was estimated at £30 billion. They calculated that if 10 per cent of carers were to discontinue the care they currently provided, an additional £2 billion would immediately need to be added to the social security budget to pay for the replacement care.

But the contribution of carers is not only in the provision of welfare to family and friends and the consequent financial saving to the state. As carers have developed a collective identity and have gained confidence in that identity, they have started to make a contribution not only through the individual care they provide to particular individuals, but through participation in decision making about the nature and design of services. Both the All Wales Strategy and the Birmingham Community Care Special Action Project provide examples of this at a local level, while the influence of the Carers' National Association on the *Caring for People* White Paper is evidence of the national impact of carers' organisations. At this point their contribution as citizens moves from the private to the public sphere. Siim (1994) discusses the different ways in which women may be mobilised as citizens in comparison to men. She refers to 'citizenship from below' and the forums in which 'citizen–parents' are motivated to mobilise to influence schools and child care institutions. Similarly, carers are motivated to mobilise to influence state institutions which have immediate relevance for the quality of their lives and the lives of those they care for. They start to play a part within a changing local governance which seeks renewed legitimacy for state services through more direct accountability to users of state services, and through incorporating knowledge gained in the private sphere to enhance the quality of services provided in the public sphere. In the final chapter I consider the implications of such action for a renewed concept of citizenship.

Conclusion

By the mid-1990s carers collectively had been recognised as a significant force within the production of community care. At an individual level, at the time of writing, their rights and needs had just received legislative recognition through the implementation of the 1996 Carers Recognition and Services Act, and throughout the country carers' groups at a local level were playing a part in influencing the nature of services provided by health and social services. The Carers' National Association was well established at a national level, not only to provide support to local groups and to individual carers, but also as a powerful lobby within policy making arenas. Nevertheless, the growing strength of the carers' lobby was not welcomed by some of those who were active within user movements. Recognition of the separate and sometimes conflicting interests of users and their carers had been growing and some saw the increasing influence of carers as detrimental to the interest of users. In the next chapter I consider the way in which those new relationships between formal and informal care providers, and direct service users, are being played out within health and social care agencies.

CHAPTER 6

Users, carers and community care

In previous chapters I have discussed separately the growth of influence of those who use community care services, and of those who provide much of the 'informal care' without which the policy could not be sustained. Here I consider the three-way relationship between family carers, those to whom they provide care, and the statutory services responsible for delivering community care. I address the potential for alliances to be more readily struck by formal care providers with family carers than with service users. I conclude by arguing for a better recognition of the complexity and reciprocity of caring relationships as a basis for a practice of community care which can empower both those who receive services and those who provide unpaid care.

Formal care providers and family carers

The first task of the Birmingham Community Care Special Action Project (CCSAP) (which was discussed in some detail in Chapter 4), was to produce a set of principles which would both govern its activities and serve as a statement of intent. Those principles made no direct reference to carers but included the following:

People with special needs have a right to support and participation in the community which does not exploit and disadvantage others.
(quoted in Barnes and Wistow, 1991)

In spite of the lack of any direct reference to the needs and experiences of carers themselves, the most high-profile of the initiatives which CCSAP undertook during its three-year lifetime was a series of public consultations with carers and a programme of developmental work arising out of that. The carers' consultations formed the subject of a number of articles in the professional press (Jowell, 1989; Jowell and Wistow, 1989; Prior, Jowell and Lawrence, 1989), of presentations at conferences, and of representations to government ministers during the preparation of the White Paper *Caring for People*. Both David Mellor and Virginia Bottomley visited Birmingham in their role as Health Ministers and met with carers and project staff. Within Birmingham, the carers' consultation programme was influential in determining people's view of CCSAP as a whole. A lasting outcome was the establishment of a Carers Unit, at first within the Central Executive Department within the city council, and later transferred into the Social Services Department. Two panels of carers established during the evaluation of CCSAP continued to meet as a forum through which carers' views could regularly be fed into both health and local authorities, and these panels produced a Carers' Charter which was adopted by statutory authorities within the city. Carers' Weeks continued to be an annual event within the city and became the focus not only for information sharing and support for carers, but also the opportunity for social events to give carers a break from providing care.

The Birmingham Carers' Charter asserted ten rights of carers; as listed in Box 3.

Box 3   The Birmingham Carers' Charter

1. Carers have the right to recognition of their contribution, their own needs and that they are individuals in their own right.
2. Carers have the right to be consulted and to be involved at every stage of service delivery in order that services are provided which reflect their own and the users' individual circumstances.
3. Carers have a right to a service which reflects their racial, cultural and religious backgrounds, is anti-discriminatory and ensures that carers are not disadvantaged.
4. Carers have the right to accessible information on services, welfare benefits, financial assistance, policies and procedures.
5. Carers have the right to have time to themselves and their own needs addressed. They should have opportunities for a break both short term and long term.
6. Carers have the right to practical help to ease the task of caring. This help could include such things as domestic help, nursing care, equipment and adaptations, continence services, respite and day care and help with transport. *Help can be required 24 hours a day.*
7. Carers have the right to guidance and in some instances training in how to cope with the particular condition of the person they are looking after.
8. Carers have the right to receive support for what is most often a stressful and isolating experience. The support networks should be identified at the onset and should continue during and after the caring task is over.
9. Carers have the right to explore alternatives to family care based on informed choice both for the immediate and long-term future.
10. Carers have the right to make comments, suggestions and complaints in relation to any service received.

Why was it that a project which sought to develop *user* involvement put so much of its resources into initiatives involving carers rather than direct service users? Experience elsewhere suggests that Birmingham was not unusual in this. As we saw in Chapter 3, the All Wales Strategy (for the development of services for people with learning difficulties) was more successful in involving parents of people with learning difficulties in its various planning initiatives than it was in involving people with learning difficulties themselves. Other evidence from studies of user involvement following the implementation of the NHS and Community Care Act also identified a tendency on the part of assessors and care managers to give priority to the views of carers over the people they care for (Hoyes *et al.*, 1994).

Throughout the 1990s there has been a proliferation of initiatives at national and local level which have sought to give support to carers and to enable them to become more influential within community care. In the previous chapter I referred to 'Carers' Impact', developed with the support of the King's Fund Centre in London. This involved a series of locally based projects, supported by consultants, some of whom were carers themselves, and others who had direct experience of working with carers. Local projects included: service development initiatives; initiatives to involve carers in planning and training; the development of Carers' Forums; support for carers at particular times or in particular circumstances, for example, around hospital admission and discharge; and projects seeking to develop support for particular groups of carers, for example, black carers. In November 1994 Carers' Impact held its first national conference entitled 'Carers in the Mainstream' which was reported as having consisted of 'a lively day's debate about how to place support for carers at the heart of community care. . . . From the statutory providers of services there was a real desire to work in closer partnership with carers in order to tackle the inevitable challenges that lie ahead if we are really going to make community care work for carers and the people they care for' (*Carers' Impact Bulletin*, Winter 1995).

In addition to Carers' Impact, the Princess Royal Trust for Carers was launched in 1993 and this too provided funds for locally based projects intended to develop support to carers. One example of this was the Carers' Centre established in Sheffield which was influenced by the Birmingham Carers' Unit. The Sheffield Centre provides information and advice services to carers, a telephone support service and a drop-in facility.

The King's Fund Centre also worked with statutory authorities who wished to develop work with carers. One example was the Yorkshire Carers Project, established in 1991 with the Yorkshire Regional Health Authority. This project had the following aims:

- To assist Health Authorities to develop and implement policies which improve services to carers through the services they provide or purchase.

- To assist Yorkshire RHA through its Priority Services Group (PSG), to identify and implement at local and regional level good practice in services relating to carers and further develop its policy guidance.

(Duff, 1994)

There has been widespread evidence of considerable goodwill on the part of policy makers and service providers who have sought either to improve the support they offer to carers, or to involve them in policy making. There are a number of reasons why service providers may find it easier to develop new ways of working with carers than with service users. One major reason is that those who wish to consult with or involve service users may not have the skills to communicate effectively with people who can be hard to contact and/or unused to talking about their needs in a way which fits with the needs of service planners. In McGrath's (1989) analysis of user involvement in planning in the All Wales Strategy she questioned whether it was realistic to expect people with learning difficulties to become members of planning groups based on professional and bureaucratic methods of working. For those who find talk difficult, who are unused to formal meeting procedures, and who are unable to read lengthy and complex documents, participation in the usual planning forums operating within health authorities and local government is likely to be an unrewarding experience. On the other hand, those used to operating in this way can find it difficult to devise more accessible mechanisms which involve new methods and skills in communication, and which expose them to unusual voices, not usually heard in such contexts.

In an initiative from within the voluntary sector in Scotland, the failure of statutory agencies to engage for the purpose of community care planning with frail older people who are unable to leave their homes without help was recognised. This led to the development of a method of groupwork designed to explore older people's views and experiences in order to contribute to service planning and evaluation (Age Concern Scotland, 1994). This 'User Panel' project involved frail older people with an average age of 82 who were regular and substantial users of community-based health and social care services. They met on a monthly basis, facilitated by workers from a voluntary agency which campaigns on behalf of older people. The project generated very rich data concerning older people's views of services and suggestions for ways in which they might be improved. But it involved very intensive methods of working, pursuing issues identified by the older people themselves during the course of conversations about their lives, and proceeding at a pace with which they felt comfortable. Some local service providers expressed frustration that they were unable to 'use' the Panels to respond to issues on *their* agendas and within a time scale which they could determine; they also questioned whether the panel members could be 'representative' of users of their services because they were articulate and assertive in expressing their views of services (Barnes and Bennett-Emslie, 1996).

It is certainly the case that skills which may not normally be expected of service planners and managers are demanded if such officials are to engage with people who have often been excluded from decision making, not only about service planning but also about services designed to meet their individual needs. The methods required to involve excluded groups and groups for whom talk is not an available method of communication can be very intensive and time-consuming. From a practical perspective it may be much easier to involve carers who, despite severe constraints on the time that they can be available and the need for arrangements to 'cover' them while they are not available to provide care, can nevertheless get to meetings under their own steam. Moreover, once at the meeting, carers are often very articulate in expressing their views based on considerable experience of care providing and, in many instances, campaigning.

But there may be other reasons why professional service providers are more comfortable working with carers than they are with disabled people, with older people, those with mental health problems or with learning difficulties. Carers do not threaten their professional authority and knowledge in the same way that disabled people or people with mental health problems can. In a study of mental health user councils which were developed under the remit of the Birmingham CCSAP, it became clear that the angry voices of users who were highly dissatisfied with the way they were being treated in a psychiatric hospital in the city generated dismissive or defensive responses on the part of some providers. The views expressed by service users went beyond specific dissatisfactions with particular aspects of their treatment and called into question the practice of psychiatry itself:

Two fundamental challenges were being offered by much of what the users involved in these councils had to say: firstly to the effectiveness of the medical interventions which were being offered, and secondly to the accountability of the doctors involved.

(Barnes and Wistow, 1994a)

That such challenges were being offered by people who could be deemed 'incompetent' by virtue of their mental disorder to make basic decisions about whether or not to receive treatment, contributed to the blocking response of some professionals. Elsewhere mental health service users and disabled people have also suggested that providers are fearful of what users are saying and feel threatened by this (Barnes *et al.*, 1996). The threat may be both to professional competence and authority, and, in some instances, to continued employment. While there is some evidence that more trusting relationships are developing between well established user groups and service purchasers and providers who have grown used to working with them, there is an impression that such acceptance is contingent upon the groups not taking what is perceived to be a too radical stance (Barnes *et al.*, 1996).

Similarly, disabled people have experienced the effects of professional defensiveness in response to their arguments for alternative service models. At the macro level one effect of an acceptance of the social model of disability is to reconstruct clinicians as technicians rather than healers. The skills of engineers, architects, and designers in creating an accessible built environment and domestic tools and equipment which can be used by those whose manual skills and mobility are impaired, may be prized above those of the surgeon seeking techniques to repair a damaged spinal column. If care management is a role which can be filled by an 'untrained' disabled client, what does this imply about the value of the professional training which a social worker may have received prior to appointment to such a role? If disabled people are to employ their own care assistants to undertake those tasks which they have decided they require in order to maintain their independent lives, then the whole structure of professional assessment leading to the determination of what service is to be provided, as well as the role of social services departments as large-scale employers and managers of care assistants, is undermined (Oliver, 1996).

In contrast, there is much less evidence that the expression of carers' views leads to defensive responses to an implied or explicit challenge to professional knowledge. Indeed, there was a degree of surprise in Birmingham that carers were not being more challenging nor asking for considerably more than they were in the consultation meetings undertaken by CCSAP. There was a sense that what they were saying was entirely reasonable and that the inadequacies they were pointing out were system failures to which providers were grateful to be alerted. Much of what carers were saying indicated a wish to benefit from professional knowledge, rather than a questioning of it. It was only when there was a suggestion that some of what carers were saying implied that they be recognised as 'clients' in their own right, with needs of their own which public authorities had a responsibility to meet, that there was a degree of alarm. And that alarm was prompted by the resource implications of such a position, rather than by a perceived threat to the authority of the welfare bureaucracies, or of professional groups within them.

Not only is there a higher likelihood of 'professional' identification between paid and unpaid carers, there is also a potential for personal identification. Many paid care workers can anticipate that they too will experience being 'informal carers'. It is easy to think that as a daughter or son you are likely to be in the position of having to take on the care of an elderly relative. Many are already in that position. The *Carers in Employment* report published by the Princess Royal Trust for Carers in May 1995 reported that 15 per cent of all people at work also care for someone at home. There is no reason to assume that at least 15 per cent of those employed within the caring professions do not also have personal care-giving responsibilities. Self-interest prompts action to ensure that services are sensitive to carers' needs.

It is also much less threatening to personal identity to recognise that you may find yourself taking on the role of a carer, than to think that accident or chronic illness may lead to disability; to acknowledge that the fact that 25 per cent of the population is likely to experience mental illness at some stage in their lives means that professional care providers may find themselves on the receiving end of psychiatric services; or to think ahead to a time when increasing age and frailty may leave you without a valued role and dependent on others for personal care needs. Identification of oneself as a potential recipient of the services you and fellow professionals provide opens up dangerous territory. The language of welfare separates those who provide and those who receive services (Simpkin, 1979). Service recipients are 'other', they are 'not us' and to think that the boundary may be permeable threatens not only the professional distance which workers are taught to maintain, but the very fact that such a division exists. Bauman (1991) discusses this type of threat in his analysis of the phenomenon of 'strangerhood'.

Relationships between carers and services. Who are services for?

The relationship between formal services, informal carers and disabled or older people is a triangular one:

formal services

informal carers ———— **disabled/older person**

We need to consider further the nature of the relationship between carers and services and how this may impact on the nature of the relationship between the informal carer and the care recipient.

In 1989 an important article was published in the *Journal of Social Policy* entitled 'Models of carers: how do social care agencies conceptualise their relationship with informal carers?' Julia Twigg (1989) described three models which provided different frames of reference for the way in which those working in social care agencies understood their relationship with carers. Workers could view carers as: resources, as co-workers or as co-clients.

As resources, Twigg identified a way in which carers were seen to comprise the 'taken for granted reality against which services are structured' (*ibid.*, p. 56). This model reflects the Griffiths view that informal care is the best means of providing support to enable people to live within 'normal' social settings, and the role of the state is to buttress and where necessary fill in the gaps of family and other informal care. In Twigg's terms, social care agencies fulfil a residual role which is normatively secondary to the role of informal care. A dilemma inherent in this model is that carers are 'an essentially uncommandable resource that cannot be created by policy decision, nor can they be turned on or off by patterns of incentives or disincentives' (*ibid.*, pp. 56–7). However, action on the part of social care agencies intended to make carers feel recognised and valued could help nudge this resource into a position in which it is more amenable to command. Hence, demonstrating goodwill and openness to influence *from* carers could be seen as a strategy for enhancing influence *over* carers.

Such action could comprise material incentives such as services which are intended directly to support carers, such as carers' support groups and information services; and the provision of respite care to provide temporary relief from caring tasks (Twigg, Atkin and Perring, 1990). But it could also comprise action intended to demonstrate to carers that they are influential in determining the way in which services are to be delivered to those who are recipients of care. This involves deliberately acknowledging the interdependence between paid and unpaid carers in the provision of a 'package of care' and developing alliances between them.

In the second model, carers are already seen as quasi- or semi-professionalised. Located within a model which sees the aim as the 'interweaving' (Bayley, 1973) of professional and informal care, 'Carers here become co-workers in the care enterprise' (Twigg, 1989, p. 58). Leaving aside the critiques of the notion of interweaving which cast doubts on the feasibility of knitting together actions derived from very different relationships and motivations (Bulmer, 1987), the co-worker model implies that informal and paid carers are colleagues and the 'client' is left occupying a powerless position in relation to an alliance of carers.

The third model is one in which carers become 'co-clients'. I have already noted a reluctance on the part of social services to accept responsibility for carers as clients because of the resource implications of creating another 'client group' with actual or implied rights to services. Twigg considers another perspective on this:

To regard carers as co-clients, therefore, threatens, on the one side, an imperialist take-over of what are normal processes of life; and on the other, a swamping of the social care system with 'ordinary misery'.

(Twigg, 1989, p. 60)

In order to justify accepting carers as co-clients, carers have to be evidencing levels of physical or emotional stress which would place them at risk of becoming 'real' clients, capable of being categorised as, for example, a 'mental health case', or a 'frail elderly person'. Within this framework, providing recognition and support for carers, listening to their views, and enabling them to exert some influence over the nature of services provided not only has the benefit of sustaining carer input and preventing the person being cared for ending up as a 'burden' on state services, it also prevents another client being created.

Ironically, the likelihood of a carer becoming a client may be greater when they cease being a carer. For some, the role of carer becomes an important aspect of their identity. They may have given up paid employment in order to take on the role of full-time carer and when the person they care for dies, may find themselves without a job, un-needed in their capacity as carer, and at a time in their lives when it is difficult to take on new roles. Carers themselves may be reluctant to assume the role of *client*, although carers in Birmingham clearly articulated their need to be given consideration in their own right. When their role as carer is no longer necessary because of death or admission to long-term care, this is often experienced not as a relief from burden, but as a loss not only of the person, but of the role. The negative impact on self-identity can prove detrimental to ex-carers' mental health (Barnes and Maple, 1992). Thus carers' needs may outlast the needs of those to whom they provide care. One way in which people can find a role for themselves when they are no longer carers themselves is by becoming active in carers' organisations, either to provide support to other carers, or to use their experiences to influence services for the benefit of others.

Whichever of Twigg's three models is dominant within health and social services agencies (and she notes that each is an ideal type, unlikely to be present in 'pure' form in any particular agency), each suggests that there is a strong motivation on the part of service providers to ensure that informal carers are recognised, valued and supported. The concept of partnership between paid and unpaid carers may be easier to achieve in practice than partnership between paid carers and those who are constructed by reference to their dependency on services. Ellis makes the point:

As collective protection against the contingencies of old age, sickness and disability is redefined as fostering an unwelcome dependency, and state responsibility is reconstituted as enabling family, friends and neighbours to take those liabilities on, so a new morality is arguably emerging within community care. Positioned as the 'deserving' (Twigg and Atkin, 1994) is an active citizenry of carers who must be supported in discharging their duties towards a second-class citizenry of older, sick and disabled people.

(Ellis, 1995, p. 2)

In the language of social exclusion rather than of citizenship, carers are to be included while those who are the recipients of their care are excluded.

Relationships between care givers and care receivers: dependence and reciprocity

The separation between care giver and care receiver is a useful administrative device to enable service providers to categorise client and carer and so determine to whom their prime responsibilities lie. Is it a useful or indeed an accurate reflection of the social and inter-personal realities of the lives of those receiving services from health and social care agencies?

In Chapter 5 I discussed the way in which people who thought of themselves as wives, daughters, sons or lovers had been encouraged to identify themselves as carers in order to build a collective awareness of their experiences and to campaign for action to improve their situation. The building of a collective identity as carers had a similar political purpose to the development of collective identities among disabled people and people with mental health problems. It enabled issues to be named as a preliminary to the development of campaigns for action, at both national and local levels, to improve material circumstances, enhance a recognition of the role played by carers and develop influence over policies and services. However, identity formation can be an oppositional act. Identities are often secured in opposition to 'others' (Phillips, 1993, p. 147), creating exclusive groupings which impose a unidimensional analysis on complex and overlapping identities.

Can a disabled person also be a carer? At what point does a mutually supportive relationship between elderly partners or spouses become unbalanced, identifying one as the care giver and the other the care receiver? Is care giving always in one direction? Framing the issue in this way indicates that political objectives may distort the subjective realities of interpersonal relationships. Recognising that individuals within a relationship have distinct and separate needs should not ignore the significance of relational dynamics, nor assume distinct and conflictual interests where these do not exist. It is necessary to look more closely at the relationship between those designated as carers and those designated as care receivers in order to understand the significance of this relationship for a community care policy which is not exploitative, and which enables appropriate influence to be exercised by those most directly involved.

The caring relationship is as varied as any other type of relationship. It may be interdependent; reciprocal; exploitative; based on love, guilt or duty; seen as an extension of an already existing relationship or as a burden taken on unwillingly. There are three aspects of this which I will consider here: reciprocity; dependence or interdependence; and choosing whether to provide or receive 'care'. In each case the nature of the interpersonal relationship can itself be affected by community care policies and the way in which they are implemented.

Reciprocity

Few relationships are sustainable without some degree of reciprocity. Qureshi and Walker's (1989) study of caring relationships among older people and their families explored a number of aspects to this and concluded: 'reciprocity was clearly one of the main foundations of the caring relationship.' (*ibid.*, p. 159). It could consist of:

• a mutual exchange of confidences which evidenced an emotional closeness defining the relationship;
• help given by relatives to the older person which was considered to be an exchange for help received in the past;
• help given by the older person in the present, for example, in looking after children, which demonstrated that the relationship was not one-sided.

While some relationships were described as having always been one-sided, for the majority of those included within the Qureshi and Walker study, the role reversal involved when children started to care for older parents led to caring responsibilities being defined as a debt owed for past assistance. Duty and love mingle in varying amounts to result in a sense of obligation, causing some carers to feel that they should not seek assistance. That sense is reinforced by the expectations of service providers that relatives will be there whenever they are needed, and by actions which force them into this position. For example, older people can be discharged from hospital with little advance notice, on the assumption that adult children will make arrangements to receive them at home (Barnes and Cormie, 1995). As children didn't they expect their mother to be there when they returned from school?

Another way of considering the notion of reciprocity within caring relationships is to look at the satisfactions which carers gain from caring itself. Some may receive no direct help in return, nor feel that the care they are giving is being provided in return for past help in the other direction, yet nevertheless experience some satisfaction from being a carer. Grant and Nolan (1993) studied sources of satisfaction among carers by means of a postal questionnaire to members of the Carers' National Association. They found that satisfaction could co-exist with high levels of stress in a complex interplay of responses, which means that understanding caring solely as an experience of burden or oppression is inadequate.

Grant and Nolan found that satisfaction could derive from a number of different sources, of which repayment for past services was only one. Satisfactions could derive from inter-personal factors, such as: pleasure in the act of giving; maintaining the dignity and self-esteem of the person cared for, characterised as 'altruism as reciprocity'; satisfaction deriving from expressions of appreciation made by the person being cared for; the improved affinity resulting from the closeness involved in caring; the satisfaction of meeting needs for tending and nurturing (a response which was received mainly from women); satisfaction deriving from being able to honour marriage vows (it was mainly men who responded in this way); and satisfaction which derived from feeling that, if the positions were reversed, the care receiver would care for the carer. This could be considered as an example of latent reciprocity.

Grant and Nolan also identified satisfactions which had an intra-personal or intra-psychic source. At the most basic level these were associated with '*psychic needs for protection from negative self-perception* such as guilt or the desire to feel wanted or needed' (p. 153, emphasis in the original), while other statements suggested that caring provided a means through which people could make sense of their lives. I have already discussed the way in which caring can come to comprise a significant element of personal identity.

A third category of sources of satisfaction could be categorised as negative rather than positive. Carers derived satisfaction from feeling that they were able to protect the person they cared for from what they perceived to be negative consequences or outcomes, such as being admitted to a nursing home. More positively, in some circumstances carers were able to derive satisfaction from assisting in the personal, physical and educational development of children, and from seeing improvements in the condition of relatives, friends or lovers who were not expected to show any improvement.

The significance of reciprocity is in danger of being ignored if caring is constructed solely as a burden, and if policies over-emphasise separate and conflicting needs, rather than the need to sustain a relationship in adverse circumstances.

Dependence or interdependence

An awareness of the reciprocities which exist within caring relation-ships indicates the need to reconsider the notion of 'dependence' of one person (the cared for) on another (the carer). There are a number of aspects to this.

Service providers who have learnt to encourage independence among people with learning difficulties sometimes assume that they are working in opposition to parents who wish to maintain their adult children's dependence on them. By concentrating on the individual and prioritising a concept of independence as separation, they fail to recognise the significance of interdependencies in family relationships and the way in which maturity can be defined by the ability to enter into effective interpersonal relationships as well as an ability to make independent judgements (Kaplan and Surrey, 1986).

As the work of Grant and Nolan suggests, descriptions by carers are full of ambiguous feelings about the nature of the relationship. One example is contained in an interview response I have already quoted:

I love my husband very dearly, but there were times when we could scream at each other. Because we were fed up with each other and yet we knew we needed each other and we didn't mean it.

(Barnes and Wistow, 1992b)

While that reflection could describe any number of different marital and other types of relationship, it has a different significance in the context of something that is defined as a 'caring' relationship because of the potential both for the exploitation of the carer and the abuse of the recipient of care.

Service providers have been at pains to recognise the importance of considering the needs of carer and 'cared for' as distinct. However, some carers have objected to the notion of separate assessments as these do not take account of the nature of the relationship as well as the distinct needs of each person within it. This can be particularly true of spouse relationships. Gillian Parker's study of partners who became carers after one partner became disabled after marriage was prompted in part by personal experience of facing the possibility that she would need to become a carer of her husband (Parker, 1993). She reflected on the way in which disability requires a renegotiation not only of a person's sense of self within themselves, but also their sense of self in relation to those closest to them. The emotional and practical renegotiations which need to take place within spouse relationships in which one partner becomes disabled cannot effectively be understood as resulting in a complete separation between the needs of each partner.

In some instances the provision of care is the means through which a loving relationship is expressed and to oppose the needs of the care provider and the care receiver in such situations is to introduce a potentially damaging dichotomy. Morris (1993) quotes one example of this:

When I'm in hospital the nurses do the kind of things that Andrew does for me but it's not the same . . . it just feels different . . . you know they're very good at it and kind and I can chat to them . . . but with Andy it's different. It's very hard to explain but I think it's got a lot to do with knowing that we haven't got long together and that he can make me feel comfortable and feel alright . . . it sounds soppy but really I think it's an expression of our love for each other . . . you know it's the ultimate 'being there for someone'.

(pp. 72–3)

At the same time as independence has been prioritised as a key policy aim of community care, dependency has been constructed as both moral weakness and an indicator of resource burden. Substantial amounts of time and effort have been invested in determining how to fit people into dependency categories which will determine whether they are entitled to receive services and, if so, the level and type of service they can receive. Thompson and Hirst (1994) review the dominant approaches to this. Need is related to levels of ability in undertaking personal care and household tasks – 'Activities of daily living' – leading to an allocation of an individual to a dependency category. Subsequently they can be referred to, as Thompson and Hirst do in their article, as 'an individual in the "toileting" group', or 'moderately to severely dependent people (that is, in the "toileting", "transferring" and "washing/dressing" groups).'

Much of the effort to define dependency is based on a medical model which defines levels of physical and psychological functioning by reference to individual pathology. But it may also be accompanied by moralising judgements which, perversely, can assign services to people precisely because they demonstrate self-reliance and independence (Ellis, 1993). Elsewhere Ellis (1995) also points to the gendered nature of judgements which can arise from this. Women may be more reluctant than men to admit to being in need of help from others because their lives and identities are linked to meeting the physical and emotional needs of others. Underpinning the whole approach is the administrative requirement to justify rationing decisions, rather than a genuine attempt to engage with the ways in which both parties within caring relationships negotiate their roles and develop strategies to deal with their difficulties. Such strategies will not always be successful and may result in the oppression of one partner. People may need help to understand when this is the case. But designating one partner as the dependant and the other as the active citizen discharging her duties in order to prevent another person becoming dependent on the state is unlikely to resolve any conflicts which may develop.

In view of this it is unsurprising that disabled people have objected to being constructed as 'burdens' – both on informal carers and on state services – and have opposed moves to give increased recognition to informal carers which are based on this construction of them as burdened by those they care for. At the same time, receiving intensive and intimate care from family members or from lovers *can* have an adverse effect on such relationships. Disabled people may prefer to receive such care from a paid carer rather than from an 'informal' carer not because the informal carer experiences the role as burden, but because it transforms the relationship and, in the worst cases, leads to a damaging emotional and physical situation (Morris, 1993). The onus on service providers is to be capable of responding supportively to circumstances in which care giving is an expression of love, and those in which care giving can endanger the expression of love. Policies which require care receivers to be assigned to dependency categories, which then determine the level and nature of the service they are entitled to receive, are unlikely to enable that degree of sensitivity.

Can a care recipient also be a care provider? Walmsley (1993) considered the way in which the person 'cared for' may also have caring roles which demonstrate that identifying a person with one or other role can be highly misleading. She described the experiences of seven people with learning difficulties, one example of which is quoted below:

Deirdre recounted to me her role as an unmarried daughter at home in a small village when she was in her thirties. Not only did she describe herself as caring for her elderly mother, she also ran errands for her neighbours, sat with an elderly friend when she was frightened by thunderstorms, and looked after people's pets when they were away on holiday. Now a resident in a staffed Group Home she helps out with the less able residents, sitting with them when staff are busy, accompanying one to voluntary work in a playgroup, and sharing the domestic tasks.

(Walmsley, *ibid.*, pp. 132–3)

In considering the significance of caring roles undertaken by people with learning difficulties Walmsley discussed how such roles can make an important contribution to the development of an adult identity. In particular for women, caring may be experienced as less of an oppression than as the source of acceptance and value. The feminist analysis of caring as oppression and burden has been criticised as deriving from the particular perspective of white, able-bodied, middle-class women. It is a perspective which may not take sufficient note of the experience of black women for whom 'caring for partners, children and older relatives can be experienced as a way of resisting racial and class oppression' (Graham, 1991, p. 69), nor of disabled women who may long for the opportunity to look after lovers, husbands and children, but who are denied such opportunities.

Similar points were raised in work I undertook exploring opportunities for empowerment of people with learning difficulties within family relationships (Barnes, 1996b). Parents of adults with learning difficulties identified a number of valued roles which their sons or daughters undertook and which made a positive contribution to the lives of their family members. They cared for young nieces and nephews; acted as best man or bridesmaid at siblings' weddings; provided company for a grandparent; and provided emotional and moral support during family conflicts. Such roles may be more accessible than the conventional 'public' roles, in particular as paid workers, through which adult status is normally ascribed. A concept of citizenship which relates solely to action within the public sphere ignores the significance of everyday life as a means through which citizenship can be expressed. The argument is similar to that which has been made about the gendered construction of citizenship which I have discussed earlier (Pateman, 1992). This is not to deny the significance of exclusion from more public roles and the necessity of action to overcome such exclusion, but to argue for a concept of citizenship which values a broader range of action through which it can be expressed. (I return to this point in the final chapter.)

Motherhood, in particular, is a role denied to many women with learning difficulties. And when some do become mothers, they very often find themselves constantly under scrutiny and at risk of having their children taken into care if they make what is considered to be a mistake in their mothering (Booth and Booth, 1994). The challenges which people with learning difficulties have to go through in order to become and remain parents should warn us against an easy assumption that the roles of carer and cared for are fixed and discrete identities, and that the role of carer is always unwelcome. The parents with learning difficulties whose stories Booth and Booth tell in *Parenting under Pressure* had to put up with a level of intervention in their lives which would be regarded as entirely unacceptable by most parents:

During the course of a week, five different workers would call at the house to check on the baby. All visits were recorded in a book kept in the living room. The entries were often derogatory in tone and praiseworthy comments were rare ('Julie was in a bad mood today and I had to tell her off for not hoovering the carpet').

(Booth and Booth, *ibid.*, p. 57)

Yet these parents who were considered to be needy and themselves requiring care and supervision wanted very much to be able to provide care to their children and were desperately unhappy when their children were removed from them 'into care'. Morris (1993) looked at the experiences of parents who are physically disabled and the support they require to enable them to look after their children. In these circumstances the support may be practical: physical adaptations to the home to enable a mother to sleep upstairs next to her daughter, or help with transport to take children to school, for example. While such support is less supervisory and less explicitly questioning of disabled people's capacity to parent than is the case in relation to parents with learning difficulties, nevertheless there is still an issue of the extent to which disabled people are in control of the help they receive or are subject to professional decision making about what help is considered to be appropriate. They may also find their parenting abilities being questioned (Morris, *ibid.*, p. 90).

Choosing whether to provide and receive care

Much of the feminist analysis of caring is based on evidence that women often become carers by default. It is not a role that they choose to enter into, but one which it is assumed they will take on because of normative expectations about innate nurturing abilities and appropriate gender roles. Whether or not they gain satisfaction from being a 'carer', the fundamental choice of whether or not to care is not one which they have freedom to exercise. In contrast, emerging evidence of the experience of some disabled people suggests that they may be denied the choice to *become* carers because of their presumed incompetence, and that their children may seek to maintain links with their parents even though those parents have been denied the opportunity to care for them (Booth and Booth, 1994, p. 43).

The 'decision' to become a carer cannot be considered to be the result of a 'rational choice'. Finch and Mason (1993) and Ungerson (1987) have explored the processes by which one family member is negotiated into the position of taking on primary caring responsibilities for relatives. Factors affecting these processes include: the perceived priority of certain kinship relations; gender; the significance of marital status; geographical proximity; other caring responsibilities; and mutual affection. Often the negotiations which take place within families are implicit rather than explicit, while in other cases 'alternatives' are seen to be effectively absent. In such cases the person who ends up in the caring role is unlikely to feel that they have exercised any choice at all. Even in those situations where the decision about who is to be the primary carer is strongly influenced by the strength of a positive pre-existing relationship, the carer may regret or resent the fact that other family members provide little or nothing in the way of support. Parents of children with learning difficulties who may be considered to be the self-evident first choice as carers of their children also talk with sadness of the lack of understanding and support that they receive from other members of the family. Few seek to stop being carers, but many wish for relief and support from elsewhere within their kinship and friendship networks. This is one reason why carers' groups are important to them. Within such groups they receive understanding and both emotional and practical support from others who share similar experiences.

Spouse carers occupy a particular position:

> at an ideological level in our society, marriage is regarded as the supreme caring relationship, rivalled perhaps only by the mother/infant bond. Marriage vows (to which all the caring spouses referred) act to reinforce the idea that one of the fundamental responsibilities is to care 'in sickness and in health'.
>
> (Ungerson, 1987, p. 51)

The taken-for-granted nature of caring within spouse relationships can ignore the fact that spouse carers are among the oldest of all carers and thus may be physically least able to manage the physical labour of tending. And, as I discussed above drawing on the work of Jenny Morris, there are relationships in which the necessity for physical tending can interfere with the sexual intimacy of spouse and other partnership relationships.

Within such implicit negotiations, what space is there for the person in need of care to express their wishes about the source of that care? While giving and receiving care can be an expression of love and intimacy, it can also 'stifle dependency and lead to an emotionally damaging and physically dangerous situation' (Morris, 1993, p. 74). Those who are in need of assistance with very personal aspects of their daily lives are potentially vulnerable to physical and emotional exploitation. The latter may not be intended, but can arise from a situation in which the carer needs to feel the person receiving care is dependent on them in order to meet their *own* needs. A community care policy which prioritises family care as best, and views paid care as a poor substitute, runs the risk of forcing both care providers and care receivers into a situation which one or other, or both, would prefer not to be in, and which, in the worst cases, can result in harm.

For both family carers and those in need of assistance in their daily lives, one outcome of greater involvement in determining public policy regarding community care might be to emphasise the necessity of choice about whether or not to provide or receive 'care' within this relationship. A mass exercising of such a choice would undermine the whole basis of current community care policy, but, while many would welcome having a real choice, there is little evidence that the outcome would be to 'exit' from informal caring relationships. But what both care providers and those in need of assistance are asking for is more sensitivity to the very different relationships within which care is provided and received, and flexibility on the part of statutory services to respond to those very different situations.

Conclusion

Community care implies that an increasing number of people who would previously have been separated from their families within institutions are now living with the families into which they were born. Some are creating their own new families. In such situations the role of carer and cared for will not always be entirely separate. In addition, the frequently agonised over demographic changes, whereby the number of older people has increased in absolute terms and proportionately to the numbers of younger people in the population, mean that the experience of caring for an older relative is an increasingly common one. Families in which caring responsibilities are both more intense and more long lasting than the provision of parental care to children until they reach independence are becoming more 'normal'. 'Ordinary life' often includes living with people with 'special needs'.   ·

A wholesale rejection of the notion of 'care' in favour of an emphasis on rights, which is evident in some of the literature coming from the disabled people's movement (e.g. Wood, 1991), is not an adequate response to this situation. While the achievement of civil rights would make an important contribution to disabled people's inclusion within the communities in which they live, it would not address the personal and interpersonal significance of caring as an aspect of the interdependencies of human relationships. As well as evidence of abuse by carers and of resentment on the part of those made to feel a burden, there is substantial evidence that people want to care and that people benefit from receiving care. The danger with current community care policies and practices is that, rather than giving appropriate support to families with a disabled or elderly member, they are making life more difficult by forcing people into separate and opposed camps.

CHAPTER 7

Building new relationships

Throughout this book I have been discussing the development of a community care policy which includes among its objectives the empowerment of service users. It has also been my objective to consider this policy – one concerned with meeting the needs of people who through age, impairment, mental health problems or learning difficulties have most contact with those parts of the welfare state established to deliver health and social care services – within the context of broader shifts in the relationship between state and citizen which have taken place in the final decades of the twentieth century. I have described initiatives within national and local service and policy structures which have sought to develop more flexible and responsive methods of service delivery and which have provided opportunities for influence by those in receipt of services. These initiatives have been distinguished from action among service users themselves. Users have been motivated in part by a wish to improve their capacity to influence services, but their action also needs to be understood as part of political and cultural changes taking place within a society in which diversity and difference are enabling the creation of new identities and new communities.

In the final two chapters of this book I adopt a more speculative approach to consider the implications of these shifts for the community care of the future. The aim is not one of crystal ball gazing, but an optimistic attempt to consider how concepts of 'care, communities and citizens' might be reconstructed in ways which better reflect the aspirations as well as the needs of older people and those with physical or sensory impairments, learning difficulties or mental health problems. In this chapter I focus on characteristics of the new types of relationship which are being forged between users, family carers and services and service systems, and in the final chapter I broaden the focus to consider implications for communities and for citizenship within those communities.

Community care: empowering users as effective consumers or active citizens?

Consuming mental health or social services, however adeptly, communicates an entirely different outcome than engagement in a process of participation as a producer. There is a striking parallel between consumers of services and consumers of commodities: both are out of control of what they consume; both stand outside the determinants of the process of production; both act in response to a definition of their needs outside their conscious control; and both are passive recipients of the interaction which reproduces exisiting power relations.

(Rose and Black, 1985, p. 37)

In Chapter 2 I explored the way in which notions of consumerism and citizenship had been conflated (perhaps deliberately) in central government policies aiming to transform the relationship between state and citizen. In their analysis of advocacy and empowerment in community mental health services Rose and Black do not discuss the identity of service users as citizens. However, their emphasis on the significance of participation in the process of production as well as the consumption of services is an important starting point for an analysis of different types of relationship between providers and users. While these various relationships can all be characterised as representing a shift away from the passivity of the client or patient, the degree and nature of activities to which service recipients are being encouraged to move are very varied and have different consequences for those concerned with service provision. And the somewhat ambiguous relationship between family carers and statutory services with its consequences for relationships within families constitutes another dimension to be considered within this shift.

There are four questions which can be posed to structure this discussion:

• How far do contemporary interpretations of community care presuppose the active involvement of service users within the service providing and receiving relationship? And are family care providers primarily 'recipients' or 'providers' within this triad?
• What are the implications of seeing users and family carers as resources for service planning, development, management and evaluation, i.e. as *co-producers* of services rather than simply as recipients of them?
• What does it mean to see users and carers as citizens with rights to participate within the political community and to whom services are accountable? Are there tensions between user-citizens and citizens in general?
• What is the relationship between community care and the social, economic and political rights of disabled and older citizens?

In this chapter I will address the first two of those questions. I will consider the relationship between services and citizens to whom they are accountable, and that between community care and the rights of citizenship in Chapter 8.

The active involvement of users and carers within the service providing and receiving relationship

Community care is intended to replace the batch processing model of institutional care. It emphasises that services should be based on an analysis of individual need, rather than expecting people to be slotted into existing services. A greater responsiveness to individual need is considered to be one way in which community care can be a more empowering service option than institutional care has been. But individual need is itself a product of the person's relationships with significant others in their lives, as well as with social structures and systems which may exclude and oppress the person because of their status as 'service user' or 'disabled person'. A community care assessment which ignores the significance of such inter-relatedness is in danger of pathologising individual weakness in spite of seeming to prioritise individual responsiveness. Assessments which follow a pre-defined format intended to allocate the individual to pre-determined dependency categories in order to indicate the level and type of service to which they are 'entitled' represent a more sophisticated attempt at need analysis than assessment for eligibility for specific services. However, they are still constructed around provider assumptions about appropriate interventions. The 'package of care' which follows is as much a prescription of a service as medication is a prescription following a medical diagnosis.

Carers involved in panels established as part of the research evaluation of the Birmingham Community Care Special Action Project (Barnes and Wistow, 1993) were very sceptical about the assessment procedures introduced as a key part of the community care reforms. They were sceptical not only because they thought there was not a lot of point in assessing need if services were not available to meet those needs, but also because of the way in which they thought assessments were likely to be carried out. They knew that a full exploration and understanding of an individual's needs is unlikely to be possible from a one-off interview conducted by someone previously unknown and therefore with whom a relationship of trust has not been established. And their previous experiences of professionals who were either unwilling to tell them about the range of options open to them, or were indeed ignorant of those options, had not given them confidence that the people conducting assessments would have an appropriate combination of professional skills, together with an understanding of and sympathy for the problem solving skills of carers and those they care for.

Marsh and Fisher (1992) worked with different service providers in social services departments to develop working practices based on partnerships between workers and service users. While workers were committed in principle to the notion of partnership, Marsh and Fisher found that social workers in particular were concerned that enabling users to self-define the problems that they wanted help with was 'de-skilling'. This was based on a view that social work expertise lay in defining problems for the user. Empowering users to take a more active part in the assessment process was perceived as disempowering workers.

Following the passage of the NHS and Community Care Act considerable effort went into designing assessment forms, agreeing eligibility criteria and determining who would undertake assessments. Rather less effort went into training intended to develop partnership skills in those making assessments. Involvement in assessment and developing strategies for working on problems is not just a question of responding to a series of pre-defined questions on the assessment schedule. It involves negotiations; the ability to work with effective problem solving strategies which have been developed by the people already involved; the ability to recognise when those strategies have themselves become a problem and how that can be addressed. It involves drawing on the insights which service users and their carers have developed into their needs, individually and jointly, and then working out how they can be enabled to meet them, again both individually and jointly. Fundamentally it involves recognising that assessment is not just a question of applying professional knowledge, but also of learning from the knowledge of those they are assessing, becoming '*experts in the problem-solving process rather than experts in problem-solving as such*' as Marsh and Fisher (*ibid.*) describe it. If carers and users are to experience the new procedures as empowering at the individual level, then as much attention must be given to the development of partnership skills among those working at the front line as was given to the development of criteria, procedures and structures for the implementation of assessment and care management.

Beyond this, it requires what Freire (1968) has described as the transformation of people who have been constructed as objects into subjects capable of acting on circumstances in the world which contribute to their oppression and exclusion. Part of the dialogue which needs to take place between the worker and service user should be focussed on enabling the worker to learn from the service user about the circumstances which constrain their lives and which are not objectively part of their 'condition': poverty; the physical inaccessibility of the environment; stigma; or loneliness deriving from enforced isolation. Rose and Black (1985) describe this dialogue taking place as workers accompany service users going about their daily lives: attending day care centres or treatment programmes, or visiting their homes or lodgings, for example. The aim is to understand the social reality of the lives of those whom workers define by reference to their status as service users, but whose lives are shaped by circumstances beyond the design of services and service systems. For an assessment to lead to a response which can empower users in their whole lives requires workers to learn from users about the reality of those wider lives. And this cannot happen as a result of a one-off encounter when the 'assessment' takes place.

As the self-organisation of users has become more firmly established, user trainers have emerged who contribute to professional training programmes within universities as well as to in-service training within health and social services agencies. Training has a crucial role to play in enabling the development of the new types of practice implied by involving service users and family carers as active participants in the service relationship. The involvement of users as trainers is perhaps the most explicit statement there can be that users have knowledge and expertise without which it is not possible for paid service providers to practise effectively.

The above discussion assumes that there is still an active role for professional workers in statutory agencies in undertaking assessments as well as in providing services. The nature of their practice will need to undergo a substantial change, but nevertheless they retain an 'expert' role. But there is another model in which that expert role is subject to a perhaps more fundamental challenge. At the time of writing (early 1996) a bill was about to be introduced into parliament which would make it legal for local authorities to provide direct financial payments to disabled people to enable them to purchase their own services. Some authorities had already introduced schemes in which a third party, often a voluntary organisation, acted as an agency through which such payments could be directed. Such schemes enable disabled people to select and purchase their own aids and equipment without requiring assessment by an occupational therapist, and to employ their own care assistants and thus determine the content, timing and nature of personal care provided. They are no longer dependent on professional assessment of their care needs nor subject to the rota systems worked by care assistants and community nurses employed by statutory social and health care agencies.

This model of the active consumer implies a substantially different relationship between the disabled person and the statutory agency which is the source of the money than is involved in a negotiated partnership between service user and, say, their care manager. Are such schemes likely to increase the competitive individualism among users concerned only about their private relationship with their employee care assistant or their equipment supplier? Is there a potential for increasing the disadvantage of those least able to negotiate the role of employer and most at risk from exploitation from unscrupulous employees? And is this model applicable to those whose support needs are not related to personal care and equipment, but to the meeting of emotional and inter-personal needs?

Where such schemes are being developed, disabled people's groups are often involved in providing advice to those wanting to access them. One example of this is in Derbyshire where Derbyshire Centre for Integrated Living (jointly managed by the Derbyshire Coalition of

Disabled People and the local authority) employs care assistants and supports individual disabled people who enter into contractual relationships with them. Such models of support and mediation may limit both the danger that only those with substantial personal resources are able to make use of them, and that any sense of collective interest in the nature and quality of services will be lost. Nevertheless, the conclusion that only cash transactions will enable service users to exercise sufficient control over the services they receive at an individual level would imply a faith in market forces which is not well founded in evidence of the performance of the market in many contexts. Nor is such an option ever likely to be realistic for many of those with complex emotional and interpersonal needs for whom trust rather than control may be the more important value.

The greater openness implied in negotiated assessments involving paid worker, family carer and care receiver should clarify the role of the family carer within this relationship. They may be both recipients themselves, and providers of services. For example, carers may need advice and counselling about ways in which they can sustain their own work and leisure interests in a situation in which time and energy for these are in short supply. Those who watch in distress as a wife's personality starts to disintegrate with the onset of dementia, or whose emotional resources are stretched by supporting a partner experiencing severe anxiety or depression are likely to need support in their own right and should be able to receive this at no detriment to the person they care for. If both carer and user are agreed that their preference is for personal care tasks to be performed by the carer, then that wish should be respected without resulting in the withdrawal of other forms of support. Alternatively, if disabled people are able to attain greater control over personal care (tending) provided by paid carers, then lay carers may be able to 'revert' to their roles as wives, daughters, or partners in the knowledge that they are not leaving their relative unsupported. It is within a negotiated process of assessment that the issue of choice involving both users and carers should become a reality. That choice should reflect the particular circumstances of the relationships involved and enable appropriate decisions to be made about the varying roles to be played by user, lay carer and paid carers.

Users and carers as resources for service planning, management and evaluation.

Empowerment at an individual level is influenced not just by the way in which needs are assessed and the extent to which users and carers are able to control the subsequent delivery of services, but also by the extent to which those who use services are empowered to influence decisions about service planning and management. Typically service planning has involved the collection of information from a variety of sources:

- statistical data describing the relevant population;
- models such as the Department of Health's 'Balance of Care' model which sought to assist decision making about the appropriate balance between residential and domiciliary care services, as well as between local authority, health service and independent sector providers;
- information contained in professional literature and data bases describing examples of good practice from elsewhere;
- information deriving from the experience of professionals within the organisation; and
- information and advice from external consultants to provide a broader perspective than that available within the particular locality.

All these are useful sources of information for planning, but the types of knowledge on which they draw are very different from the experiential knowledge of those who have experienced the frustrations and benefits of receiving services, as well as the experience of being old, of experiencing mental distress and the stigma that attaches to that, of being disabled by an environment designed only for those who are able-bodied, or of tending and providing emotional support to a chronically ill relative seven days a week. Such knowledge also needs to be tapped for service planning as well as individual assessment. In contributing the knowledge and understanding which comes from these sources, both people who use services and family carers can become co-producers of services as a whole, in addition to becoming more effective individual consumers. So how might such knowledge be accessed in order to contribute to a sense of empowerment in influencing services more generally?

As we have seen, the 1990 NHS and Community Care Act placed a duty on social services departments to consult with service users and their carers in the production of community care plans. As experience of consultation developed, it became clearer that the whole process of planning needed to be rethought if users and carers were to make an effective contribution to the planning process as a whole, rather than simply to the production of a document in which plans for service development were set out for public consumption. Different mechanisms would be needed to enable people in different circumstances to contribute and to define as well as respond to agency agendas.

In Birmingham consultations with carers demonstrated that public consultation could be a useful mechanism for identifying issues to be placed on the agenda and for enabling people to feel that their contribution was valued (Barnes and Wistow, 1992c and d). However, a process which relies on individuals identifying themselves with the group targeted for consultation, and which depends on people feeling able to meet with providers on their territory and on their terms will exclude those already likely to be most isolated and marginalised. For example, the Birmingham consultations failed to make contact with many black carers and with those who had only recently taken on the caring role. Subsequently the head of the Carers' Unit made contact with different ethnic minority groups, including carers in the Chinese community, by gaining entry through workers or community members who were known and trusted within that community and meeting with them on their own ground.

One group unable to respond to open invitations to attend consultations, focus groups or other meetings intended to access user views are frail older people who are unable to leave the house without assistance. In Scotland the Fife User Panel Project (see Chapter 3) demonstrated that this does not mean that such people are unable or unwilling to participate in collective discussions as a means of con-tributing to community care planning (Barnes and Bennett-Emslie, 1996). Community development and groupwork skills were applied to enable frail older people to build collective awareness of shared experiences and collective approaches to problem solving where these had not previously had the opportuntity to develop. This enhanced the capacity of members of the panels to contribute to service planning and evaluation. They not only identified problems with existing services, but identified criteria for good quality services and made proposals for service developments.

If the production of 'the plan' is only an intermittent output in what should be seen as a continuous process of community care planning, there is a need for mechanisms to enable continuing involvement in monitoring, review and more detailed planning as this moves into the implementation phase. The experience of working with panels of carers in Birmingham provided one example of how this might happen (Barnes and Wistow, 1994c). Over a period of twelve months two panels of carers met to monitor outcomes from the consultation process. As well as monitoring action taken by officers in response to issues raised during the consultations, they were also able to take a more pro-active role in defining quality criteria to be used in judging the effectiveness of outcomes; they defined the issues on which action was required in more detail in order to assist decision making about what action was appropriate; and some became active participants in working groups established to progress action. Elsewhere, service users have become involved in defining criteria for service contract specifications and in monitoring provider compliance (Harrison, 1993); some have become lay members of social services inspection teams; while others have entered into long-term relationships with providers in jointly managed service enterprises (Davis and Mullender, 1993).

Such relationships are not without their difficulties, and are based on very different assumptions about appropriate roles for service users than are implied by one-off consultation exercises. Continuing involvement increases the capacity of users and carers to make an active contribution to problem solving, rather than simply to identify strengths and weaknesses of existing systems which is all that is possible through one off consultation, consumer research projects or through complaints procedures. It creates change in the participants as well as in the decision-making process as they become more knowledgeable, more experienced and more confident of what they have to offer. Rather than being consumers of what others are offering, they become active participants in determining the services available to themselves and to others in similar circumstances.

Perhaps for that reason such models of involvement run the risk of provoking provider accusations that participants are no longer 'representative' of the acquiescent majority of service users (Barnes, Cormie and Crichton, 1994). Those who engage in long-term relationships of co-production with service purchasers and providers are not a random sample of users selected according to the rules of statistical sampling, with an option of opting out by refusal to respond, but no option to opt in by choosing to participate. They are people who have made a commitment to work with statutory services with the objective of securing improvement in those services. They will always be a minority of service users, but this does not invalidate the experience they bring to such participation, nor the outcome of their involvement for themselves and others. Their increasing capacity to contribute to the production of services should be welcomed and, indeed, should be an explicit objective of such involvement, rather than a factor which invalidates their contribution. The challenge for officials within statutory health and social care agencies is to find ways of engaging with different groups, many of whom have little experience of involvement, and who are vulnerable to exploitation. It may be necessary to create separate opportunities for women users of services and for different ethnic minority groups to enable them to articulate their particular experiences and needs (see e.g. Asafu-Adjaye *et al.*, 1993; Downer and Ferns, 1993). It will certainly be necessary to use language and methods of communication appropriate to those unused to professional jargon and to those who find words difficult. The aim should be to develop a range of models through which it is possible for all those who want to contribute in this way to do so.

But such models also pose their own dilemmas for users themselves. In asking people to contribute to these organisational processes there is a danger that heavy demands are being made on people whose lives are already complex and demanding. Users and carers are often asked to contribute their time, knowledge and energies without payment, alongside people who are carrying out a job for which they are getting paid. While the objective may be empowerment, the experience can be one of exploitation or inequality. The long-term outcomes of involvement are uncertain and if people are to experience such processes as in any way empowering, they must receive shorter-term benefits to make it worth their while. Those who ask users and carers to become involved in such activities must ensure that the process itself is rewarding or empowering – they must give something in return for the knowledge that users and carers contribute; and they must not accuse participants of being unrepresentative because they have become more articulate and more personally empowered as a result of this process.

Involvement in mechanisms intended to contribute to service planning and development may also bear an opportunity cost for users in terms of limiting resources for other types of activity. For user groups whose objectives extend beyond the transformation of health and social care service systems, the time spent in negotiation over issues such as the location of new mental health centres, or the specifications for respite care contracts, will be at the expense of time spent in raising public awareness; campaigning against the extension of the controlling powers of mental health legislation; or supporting individuals in their battles with the social security system in order to obtain the basic resources to feed and house themselves. One result of the re-organisation of health and social care services following the 1990 Act has been a proliferation of planning and consultation mechanisms, with the consequent danger that users and user groups may spend all their energies responding to agendas not of their making and have few resources left to support their members and to build the movement according to their own agendas (Barnes *et al.*, 1996a).

People's sense of empowerment will also be affected by the extent to which what they have to say is taken seriously. There was evidence in Birmingham that some issues got 'lost' between the carer consultation meetings and the action agenda defined to respond to the consultations (Barnes and Wistow, 1992c). It is not clear why some issues appeared to have been filtered out, but it may be that they were seen to be too difficult to deal with, or they did not 'fit' with professional views about future directions for services. Nor was the important issue of differences between what *carers* had to say about services and what those they cared for had to say, really addressed within the context of the Birmingham project. Evidence from professional responses to mental health user councils indicated that some psychiatrists had no intention of seeing these councils as anything other than a therapeutic opportunity for people to 'get things off their chests' (Barnes and Wistow, 1994a). Elsewhere, research has suggested that health and social care officials distinguish between user groups according to factors such as the perceived efficiency of their organisation when attributing legitimacy to the views expressed and the people expressing them (Barnes *et al.*, 1996). Unequal power relationships enable officials to exercise discretion over who they are prepared to listen to as well as what they are prepared to hear.

It would be unrealistic to expect that user input will not have to compete with other voices and other pressures and constraints on decision making. Nor am I arguing for responsibilities for decision making to be handed over to users. Enabling people who have previously been excluded from such processes to enter into dialogue about services will complicate, not simplify the debates which take place within them. Users' views are not homogeneous and may be expressed in ways which service managers and professionals find difficult to accept. Differences between different stakeholders will need to be made explicit, including any differences in the perspectives of users and carers, and will need to be negotiated. Obscuring differences will not contribute to empowerment, but dealing with those differences will call for complex negotiating skills on the part of all those involved.

New relationships

In the course of the discussion so far a number of different types of relationship between users and community care services have been suggested. I have considered ways in which users may be enabled to become more effective consumers as well as co-producers of services. I now turn to consider what this means from the perspective of purchasers and providers of services and to consider prerequisites for the building of new relationships.

Informing relationships

An effective consumer requires good information in order to make choices about which service to select. At one level providing better information to people needing to use services can be seen as a funda-mental necessity for the establishment of any type of relationship. There is overwhelming evidence from many studies of both service users and family carers that people do not know what services are available and therefore are unable to engage with them. Restricting the availability of information about services can be a mechanism for rationing scarce resources. It is certainly a means through which providers can retain control. Not only are they the gatekeepers, but to unlock the gate the potential user needs to know the right question to ask to seek access.

The ability to exercise the very basic choice to 'enter' the health or social services is dependent on knowledge that there is a service available which might meet identified needs. Access to any service depends on knowing that it exists, that it is relevant to the needs being experienced, and that one is entitled to use it. But effective consumers are also those who can make informed choices. Choice *between* services depends on having such information about different options, and on having additional information about significant differences between services in terms of their essential characteristics, such as the range of activities available within a day centre, or the different methods of therapy that staff in a community mental health team are trained to provide. If simply finding out that something is available has been experienced as a battle, then few users of community care services are likely to have the energies to seek information about alternatives. And, unless they are already experienced users of such services, such information may not mean much: how possible is it to distinguish between cognitive and behavioural therapies without having experienced them?

Another issue relating to information to enable choice concerns information about the effectiveness of services. Debates and dispute over the measurement of performance of public services suggest that exercising choice based on information about the comparable performance of public services is far from straightforward. Information about the performance of many public services often raises more questions than it answers (Stewart and Walsh, 1994). Not only is performance difficult to define, measure and compare, but professional, political and lay notions of success differ and performance measurement systems will rarely enable users to consider alternative measures based on different criteria. Performance indicators may be highly technical and difficult to understand by any but those involved in their production.

Choosing between services on the basis of evidence of the effectiveness of their performance will rarely be a priority for users of community care services (Barnes and Prior, 1995). However, the provision of better information to actual or potential users of services should be a priority for all service providers, and may enable people to become more effective consumers as information becomes more freely available. Information provision should not be understood solely as the production of more and better leaflets for people to pick up in the waiting room, it should also involve professionals being prepared to share their knowledge face to face in terms that are understandable to lay people. Yet the one-way provision of information still leaves service purchasers and providers in the role of experts informing the public to enable them to make their own 'purchasing' decisions as consumers within the health and social care market place. Such relationships are not directly reciprocal and contain limited opportunity for learning on both sides.

Relationships of learning and trust

Acknowledgement of users as knowledgeable about their own lives and experiences and of carers as knowledgeable about the efficacy of different ways of providing support, as well as of the impact of disability or age on interpersonal relationships, requires that learning must be a three-way process. Through dialogue between user, family carer and professional service worker understanding can grow and problem-solving strategies be developed. If an 'informing' relationship stresses the responsibility of the service provider to give information, a 'learning' relationship emphasises their responsibility to receive and make sense of information from the user.

The dialogue through which learning can take place depends on a reciprocal relationship of trust and the assumed competence of all involved within it. Trust between users, carers and providers is necessary for learning to take place. Barnes and Prior have suggested that trust between individuals requires six distinct elements:

- *Acceptance* of the validity of the other's experiences, knowledge and interpretations (but acceptance does not automatically entail *belief* in the other's viewpoint)
- *Confidence* that the other has the capacity to make appropriate judgements about how to act in varying circumstances
- *Respect* for the role of the other as an active contributor to the relationship
- *Honesty* towards the other in a willingness to share all relevant information about the relationship
- *Reciprocity of duty,* recognising that each partner in the relationship has responsibilities toward the other
- *Reciprocity of interest,* recognising that each partner has their own goals which they will want to pursue through the relationship.

(Barnes and Prior, 1996)

While community care policy is founded on a trust in the capacity of family carers to provide a major source of support to older people and other users of community care services, that trust is not always evident in a willingness on the part of individual service providers to learn from their experience of providing support. Nor is there much evidence that disabled people, those with mental health problems or learning difficulties are trusted to be able to determine their own needs. Without the development of such trust, learning will be difficult to achieve.

There are a number of factors which affect the extent to which reciprocal trusting relationships can be developed. For the user, willingness and capacity to trust officials will be mediated by factors such as:

- Previous experience of that particular service, or public services in general. One negative indicator will be experience of interventions made against the will of the person concerned. In some circum-stances (such as compulsory hospital admission under the Mental

Health Act) such interventions are legally sanctioned. In those circumstances what is vital if trust is to be re-established is that there is an open discussion about the reason for that decision and the opportunity to explore what would be necessary to avoid such an event happening again.

• The experience of exclusion or oppression resulting from poverty, disability or discrimination. Service providers need not only to recognise the significance of these experiences in affecting the capacity of the person concerned to trust anyone 'in authority', but also to ensure that the experience of receiving services does not contribute further to such oppression. (Dominelli and McLeod, 1989; Hugman, 1991)

• The impact of experiences such as sexual abuse which can impair the basic capacity to trust. Abusive relationships can leave women (and men) not only with little self-esteem, but little willingness or capacity to trust others. They may act in ways which seem to deliberately confirm their belief that others are not to be trusted˙ and to undermine the willingness of others to trust them. Yet trust is vital to effective interventions in such situations. (Barnes and Maple, 1992; Casement, 1985)

The ability of individual providers to adopt an open approach necessary to the establishment of trust between themselves and service users will also be affected by their experiences as employees within the agency in which they work. If they are not trusted by their managers, and if their managers are not prepared to learn from their experience as front-line service providers, how are they to trust and learn from service users? Issues such as their sense of security of employment; their ability to control or influence the way in which they work; and the extent to which their skills and knowledge are valued within and beyond the organisation, will all affect their capacity to develop learning relationships with users and family carers (Carpenter, 1994).

Learning must also take place at an organisational level. Stewart (1986) discussed the danger of organisations only learning what they already know. He suggested that organisations can counter this tendency by allowing an element of 'disorganization'. He also described the way in which learning depends on information coming into the authority and the need to deliberately construct ways to ensure that information of different types can flow into the organisation. For example, waiting lists for a service say something about the level of demand for a service that is available. They say nothing about what underlies the demand or the potential demand for services which could be, but which are not available.

Organisational learning implies that the conditions of trust outlined above must apply between users and the service system as well as between users and individual providers within the system (see Barnes and Prior, 1996 for a development of this point). Dialogue is vital for the establishment of trust and for learning to flow from this. Dialogue requires an opportunity to speak – for 'voice' – and to be listened to. Both speaking and listening are skilled activities and people (both users and workers) require to be supported as they develop such skills. But a relationship of learning involves acting on what is learnt, as well as simply 'finding out'. It is about change and movement, not the administration of stasis. Hence it requires the empowerment of workers to enable them to act on what they have learnt within an organisation which supports 'disorganisation' and change. If risk and reflexivity are central characteristics of contemporary society (Beck, 1992), welfare organisations need to develop reflexive capacity to support risk and innovation.

Health and social care agencies can also learn from user groups. I have described the way in which some groups of users have used their personal experiences to develop alternative models to explain such experiences and to provide the basis for alternative ways of meeting need. The social model of disability is the most obvious example of this. The promotion of alternative forms of knowledge is an important way in which the exclusion of subordinate groups can be overcome:

One of the characteristics of 'social movements', of which service user groups are an example, is the development of forms of knowledge and skill which challenge the professional or official knowledge of formal organizations. It is the dominance of formal or 'expert' knowledge, and the assumption of its superiority, which functions as one of the means of excluding lay people from exercising an effective voice in their relationships with service providers. A key component of public trust and hence one of the bases for the development of learning relationships must be the willingness of providers to accept the collective understanding and knowledge generated by user groups as a legitimate basis for dialogue and negotiation.

(Barnes and Prior, 1996)

Relationships of partnership

If relationships of learning are based on a belief that not all the expertise and knowledge required exists within the organisation itself, relationships of partnership are based on a belief that the best way to harness the expertise and knowledge which exists among users and family carers as well as among workers in health and social care agencies is to find ways of working together.

Partnership is an extension of dialogue. The emphasis is not so much on communication as on co-working. The flow of information from workers to users and carers, and in the other direction, takes place during the course of a working relationship which is intended to focus on a particular task or tasks which will produce an outcome satisfactory to both groups. This is likely to involve some renego-tiation of the nature of the task itself. There was an example of this in the Birmingham project discussed elsewhere in this book. A family carer and a disabled woman joined a working group consisting of planners, architects, policy makers and social services managers to work on developing a transport and mobility strategy for the city. One immediate effect was that short-term practical action targets, such as increasing the number of dropped kerbs in out of town centre shopping streets, were added to the longer-term strategic objectives initially set by the officer members of the group. Both sides of the partnership learn more about the nature of 'problems' and how they can be solved through the process of working together. Each may have different roles and responsibilities, but both have the ability to shape the encounter.

The example of the Derbyshire Centre for Integrated Living (DCIL) quoted above provides another model of partnership. DCIL itself (and other similar centres in other parts of the UK and the USA) is an example of the way in which the social model of disability has led to the establishment of new forms of service. In this instance local authority officials were prepared to learn from disabled people that the development of a new residential unit would not be the best way of meeting the needs of younger disabled people in the area (Davis and Mullender, 1993). Instead they developed DCIL in partnership with the Derbyshire Coalition of Disabled People (DCDP). The Centre is managed by a board comprising an equal number of council representatives and representatives from DCDP.

Some user groups have expressed uncertainty about the notion of partnership because of an implied equality which they do not experience in practice. It would certainly be wrong to characterise the relationships between DCDP and Derbyshire County Council as unproblematic. At the same time, few user groups seek to usurp the responsibilities of public authorities for service provision. There will continue to be inequalities between users and officials in the responsibilities each have for the management and governance of local services. At the level of specific participation and partnership initiatives there will continue to be a need for roles such as that of chair, facilitator, enabler, or group worker, roles which will sometimes be occupied by service users and sometimes by paid workers from within statutory agencies. New institutional forms which enable decision making to be opened up may not lead to a direct transfer of power within an existing structure, rather they transform the structure and the terms on which debate is conducted within this. I consider this latter point in more detail in the final chapter.

Individual or collective relationships

The initiatives to involve or empower service users which have been considered during the course of this book have been based both on changing the nature of the relationship between individual service providers and recipients, and the development of relationships between new constituencies of users and carers who have sought to empower themselves through collective organisation. Some officials within statutory health and social care agencies have sought to differentiate between the legitimacy of developing more responsive relationships with individual service users, and being influenced by 'pressure groups' of service users which are perceived as having considerably less legitimacy (Harrison and Mort, 1996).

The identity of the welfare consumer is one of an individual in competition with others for a share of scarce resources. The competitiveness inherent in consumerism can be seen as tending to erode trust and limit the potential for the identification of collective interest and action (Barnes and Prior, forthcoming). In contrast, the potential for an alternative and more constructive approach is evident in the development of the organisations of users and carers discussed in Chapters 4 and 5. These organisations build trust between users and develop their capacity for collective action in their own interests and the interest of users more generally. They build the capacity of individual users to assert their own needs, to represent the needs of others and thus help to redress the power imbalance between users and providers. As they develop partnership relationships with providers and others, they have the capacity to contribute to the development of trust between users and providers through a recognition of the value of the different knowledge each brings to that partnership.

A further stage must be the development of trusting relationships between user and carer groups. Parker (1993) concludes her study of spouse carers by observing: 'Seeing both sides also shows clearly that disabled people, and those who provide them with help and support on an unpaid basis have, or should have, a *common* agenda for change, albeit that certain elements of that agenda might be different for different groups of disabled people and their carers' (p. 126). Tactically, alliances between user and carer groups have the potential for enhancing the influence which it is possible to exert on policy makers and service providers as well as reducing the possibility of groups being played off against each other. But also, if the objective is a community care policy and practice which responds to the interdependencies and reciprocity of relationships between disabled people and their families, friends and lovers, then user and carer groups need to explore their experiences together rather than compete for influence in opposition to each other.

An overwhelming conclusion from this exploration and analysis of action within welfare services and among users of those services is that new relationships cannot effectively be developed without opportunities for self-organisation among service users. Developing individual partnership practice is a necessary but not sufficient condition for increasing the empowerment of users of community care services and for family carers. But this is not to suggest that all users and carers have to become actively involved in user organisations. Such organisations campaign and act not solely on behalf of their members, but on behalf of all disabled people, older people, people with learning difficulties or mental health problems. And their influence and significance extends beyond the service systems of the welfare state to affect the conditions in which people can become active participants in determining how they can live their lives as a whole.

At the same time as users have been organising themselves and developing their own change agendas, many public policy makers have also rediscovered the value of community participation. Craig and Mayo (1995) identify the tensions inherent in moves to link community empowerment with a reduction in public sector budgets. If the objective of releasing people's potential to take more control over their lives is pursued without adequately resourcing the community organisations through which such empowerment·can come about, the outcome will be exploitation rather than empowerment. The user movements discussed in Chapter 3 all experience the stresses and frustrations of trying to develop support for their members and influence on the public provision of welfare with minimal resources. If, as Marilyn Taylor (1995) observes, public policy for community regeneration is to require not only consultation with communities, but the development of alliances within networks which cross sectors and different community groups, then funding must recognise the role being played by such groups. Mai Wann (1995) suggests 'arm's length' funding mechanisms for this which would be designed to limit the potential for public funding to become public control.

There is evidence that some user groups have been brought into being or encouraged by the pressure on statutory services to consult with users. Nevertheless there are tensions between the objectives of groups and those working within the formal service system. Users involved in joint projects with statutory purchasers and providers still often feel they are there as a result of token gestures and that the unequal power and resources of each group mean that their position is vulnerable. More cynically, some officials within the statutory sector appear happy to play the 'user card' when it suits them, but to find reasons for excluding users from consultative and decision-making forums when this is likely to prompt 'unacceptable' challenges (Mort and Harrison, 1996).

But the legitimacy of user input is now widely accepted and the self-organisation of users is now too widely developed for it to be possible for this to be completely ignored. And their significance extends beyond their immediate impact on any particular service organisation. It also has significance for our understanding of the three concepts underpinning community care policy and practice which form the title of this book. It is to this that I now turn in the final chapter.

CHAPTER 8

Citizens within a community

What ought to be the objective of community care? I want to suggest a single answer to what is a bold and wide ranging question: the objective of community care should be to enable those previously excluded from community to participate within it. This claim derives its theoretical justification from Doyal and Gough's work *A Theory of Human Need* (Doyal and Gough, 1991). They argue that participation within social life is necessary not only to avoid harm, but more fundamentally to 'be human', since identities are formed through interaction with others and all human goals can only be achieved through interaction with others (p. 50). Thus universal needs are those which relate to the conditions required to enable social participation; the needs themselves are universal, although the 'intermediate satisfiers' through which those needs may be met will vary according to cultural and historical conditions.

The ultimate objective of services provided as a result of community care policies should thus be to ensure that the 'satisfiers' which all people require to meet 'intermediate needs', include and do not marginalise older people, those with physical or sensory impairments, learning difficulties, or mental health problems. Doyal and Gough define these intermediate needs as: adequate nutritional food and water; adequate protective housing; a non-hazardous work environment; a non-hazardous physical environment; security in childhood; significant primary relationships; economic security; physical security; education; and safe birth control and child rearing. There may be instances where addititional means of satisfying need are necessary, but the ultimate objective of enabling social participation without serious harm should be the same for all people.

Unless individuals are capable of participating in some form of life without arbitrary and serious limitations being placed on what they attempt to accomplish, their potential for private and public success will remain unfulfilled – whatever the detail of their actual choices.

(Doyal and Gough, *ibid.*, p. 50)

But the analysis has to be taken a step further. If the objective is the participation of those previously excluded from community, this implies that those communities themselves become transformed. Participation or 'inclusion' results in change in that in which excluded people become participants. In some ways this can be considered to relate to the higher level universal goal which Doyal and Gough define as 'liberation' rather than participation. The provision of basic services may enable disabled people, those with mental health problems or older people to participate to the extent that they are able to move within communities without coming to harm, but if the aim is to go beyond minimal needs satisfaction to a point at which people are able to exercise their moral responsibilities as citizens with duties as well as rights, then a transformation is required to enable the fulfilment of those responsibilities.

It is this which forms the subject matter for this final chapter. Here I return to the notions of community and citizenship considered earlier in the book in order to suggest how our understandings of both concepts must be developed if they are to be inclusive of those people who are the subjects of community care policy.

It is important to be aware of the macro-context within which community care policy is being implemented. Structural exclusions affect all those subject to the policy – poverty is a shared experience of many older people, many of those who experience mental health problems, as well as those with learning difficulties and physical or sensory impairments. Those discharged from long-stay hospitals often find themselves discharged to communities in which people living in poverty feel *themselves* to be marginalised and excluded from citizenship. Those communities can feel they have little capacity to include new people whose personal resources are at a low ebb. Some of the alternative models which I discuss below seek to respond directly to this situation. While a detailed consideration of the policy action required to address such structural inequalities is beyond the scope of this book, it is clear that the successful implementation of an inclusive policy for community care requires action in economic and social policy arenas not usually considered within the context of community care.

Community and communities

Including people with identities which are not considered 'normal' within social life must be a positive objective of community care policy. A broad objective of many of the user groups discussed in Chapter 3 is to promote understanding that experiences of mental distress, disability, learning difficulties and ageing, constitute part of what it means to be human. They seek to achieve this by public awareness campaigns and also by practical projects aimed to support people's inclusion within the localities in which they live. One example of this is the Derbyshire Centre for Integrated Living (DCIL) discussed in the previous chapter. DCIL focusses its attention on the provision of services and support in response to seven basic needs to be met if disabled people are to live integrated lives within local communities: information, peer counselling, housing, personal assistance, technical aids, access and transport (Davis, 1983).

Another model is that offered by 'Ecoworks', an initiative initially developed under the umbrella of the Nottingham Advocacy Group, which supports the self-organisation of people with mental health problems. Ecoworks was inspired by Atlantis in Berlin, a social work rehabilitation agency for young people with mental health problems. Atlantis provides training in environmental technology for the young people referred for rehabilitation. Both Atlantis and Ecoworks are based on a holistic analysis of the way in which economic and social organisation creates a mentally 'unhealthy' environment. Ecoworks promotes the development of small-scale, local initiatives which can enable people experiencing emotional distress, and other unemployed people in the locality, to take on work which not only contributes to their own personal empowerment, but also to the achievement of ecological objectives. Specific initiatives include a permaculture project (*perma*nent agri*culture*) based in local allotments, and a project to supply more efficient energy to local hostels. The thinking behind Ecoworks and the project itself has been developed by Brian Davey (1994).

To the extent that such initiatives emphasise small-scale, local developments, they reinforce the significance of community as locality as the source of both opportunities and support for disabled people or people with mental health problems. But whereas community care policy makers equate community with family when discussing the provision of social support, these schemes draw on support within the community which comes not only, or even primarily, from the family. It is more likely to be other disabled people, or other people with mental health problems, drawing on their collective experiences and proposing the action required to overcome the barriers and exclusions they face, who provide the support networks which enable community participation. Two dynamics are operating here: on the one hand new 'communities of identity' are being formed which may be of more significance than identification as a member of a community defined by locality. On the other hand, such communities of identity are contributing to the diversity of identities which may be included within the population of any particular locality. Such initiatives demonstrate the importance of communal relationships, but imply different origins of those relationships from those assumed by policy makers.

Much of the appeal of the communitarian ethic derives from an aversion to the emphasis on the atomistic individual which became a powerful strand of new right thinking in the 1980s. But in re-emphasising the importance of connectedness, the populist communitarianism as defined by Etzioni (1995), places the family at the centre of the moral 'spirit of community', and does not adequately address the way in which communities (localities) can exclude those whose identities and affiliations derive from other types of collectivity. It is necessary to look elsewhere for ways of understanding the relationship between developments taking place among those who use community care services, and for notions of community more appropriate to the twenty-first century.

One approach is that offered by Iris Marion Young (1995). She argues 'that the ideal of community fails to offer an appropriate alternative vision of a democratic polity. This ideal expresses a desire for fusion of subjects with one another which in practice oppresses those with whom the group does not identify. The ideal of community denies and represses social difference, the fact that the polity cannot be thought of as a unity in which all participants share a common experience and common values' (*ibid.*, p. 251) As an alternative she offers an ideal of what she calls 'city life' in which group difference is affirmed. An important part of Young's argument is the way in which the ideal of community 'privileges face-to-face relations'. She argues that it is unrealistic to base a model of the good society on small units in which social interaction is based on face-to-face relationships. Such a view, she argues, is Utopian and would involve dismantling the entire structure of urban society. By implication, she would be unlikely to find in either the decentralising strategies of welfare bureaucracies, or the local initiatives of projects such as Ecoworks, a complete solution to the problem of alienated, commodified relations. Her view of city life is one in which many different groups, sub-cultures and communities co-exist side by side, all dependent on a vast infrastructure and thus bound together by this common need, but without 'dissolving into unity or commonness' (p. 264). She suggests that city life both enables and encourages difference to flourish: 'In the ideal of city life freedom leads to group differentiation, to the formation of affinity groups, but this social and spatial differentiation of groups is without exclusion' (p. 265) In this context social justice 'requires the realisation of a politics of difference' (p. 268).

While Young focusses on the way in which different cultural or identity groups may live alongside each other without seeking an elusive and unwelcome homogeneity, Martha Ackelsberg (1983), Janice Raymond (1986) and Marilyn Friedman (1989) address the nature of the bond which might draw identity groups together. Ackelsberg considers the extent to which 'friends' might perform the nurturing functions which families have been considered to perform. The question she addresses is: 'How can feminists continue to affirm the values of nurturance without affirming, at the same time, the subordination of women within the institution [the family] that can, under certain circumstances, provide that nurturance?' (1983, p. 343). She argues that families in fact have not been the only source of nurturance within most social systems – relationships between women have always been of considerable significance as a source of material support, by sharing scarce commodities, as well as sharing the labour of child care and providing emotional support. For men, too, male friendships have always been significant: 'It seems no accident that early associations of working men, which provided the basis for unions, were called "friendly societies" ' (p. 344). Beyond nurturance, Ackelsberg also notes that many writers have argued that friendship is as important as family relationships to the maintenance of a political–social community. But the importance of friendship, Ackelsberg claims, is that it can challenge the dichotomy between the personal and the political: 'While generally treated as falling within the "private" sphere, friendships can be intensely political. They can form – and have formed – the basis for radical political association' (p. 351).

Raymond (1986) describes historical examples of circumstances in which organisations of women have been sustained by friendship bonds which are more then 'mere' ties of personal affection. For women in convents in the Middle Ages, and among the Chinese 'Marriage Resisters', female friendship offered a source of empowerment which enabled resistance to dominant social norms, and opportunities to develop abilities and knowledge denied to them within mainstream society. Raymond claims: 'While it is true that certain kinds of political activity are and have to be possible between persons who are not friends, both politics and friendship are restored to a deeper meaning when they are brought together – that is, when political activity proceeds from a shared affection, vision, and spirit and when friendship has a more expansive political effect' (*ibid.*, p. 8).

Marilyn Friedman (1989) also discusses the significance of friendship in her critique of communitarianism. This critique focusses on the legitimacy of the moral authority communities can be seen to possess: 'To evaluate the moral identities conferred by communities on their members, we need a theory of communities, of their inter-relationships, of the structures of power, dominance and oppression within and among them' (p. 280). Friedman points to the fact that, for adults, the communities with which they engage are 'communities of choice' rather than the community in which they find themselves as children. Friends are the people with whom one chooses to share activities and confidences and thus friendship is grounded in shared values and interests. Like Ackelsberg and Raymond, Friedman sees friendship as a source of political action, especially for those excluded from conventional community: 'Friendship is more likely than many other close personal relationships to provide social support for people who are idiosyncratic, whose unconventional values and deviant lifestyles make them victims of intolerance from family members and others who are unwillingly related to them. In this regard, friendship has socially disruptive possibilities, for out of the unconventional living which it helps to sustain there often arise influential forces for social change' (p. 286–7).

The notion of 'communities of choice' is also a key element within

Paul Hirst's work on associationalism (Hirst, 1994). Hirst distinguishes between communities of choice and communities of fate. He argues that voluntary membership of associations creates the circumstances in which individual freedom can be enhanced more effectively than is possible by purely private, individual action. Since such associations are based on entirely voluntary association, individuals have an unquestioned right of exit from them – they cannot 'compel loyalty' in the way that states can. In order to win and keep members there is a necessity to build co-operation and trust, However, while Hirst cites Friendly Societies as examples of welfare based on associationalist principles, he does not develop an analysis of friendship as a potential source of such co-operation.

What might these analyses contribute to an understanding of the way in which the self-organisation of users of community care services might serve to enhance our notion of community itself? Firstly, there is the significance of difference. It has sometimes been suggested that the discharge of people with learning difficulties and those with mental health problems from long stay hospitals into the community has resulted in the creation of 'ghettoes' within which those people continue to interact only with those with whom they lived in the hospitals and thus remain segregated from, while living in, community (e.g. Prior, 1993). That is certainly a problem if it means that they continue to live in poverty, subject to oppression and discrimination. But Iris Marion Young's analysis would suggest that it is neither realistic nor desirable to seek to 'dissolve' all groups so that they lose their different identities. Such a perspective is clearly evident among deaf communities who refuse to give up their language (British Sign Language) in order to integrate with the oral community (Corker, 1996). It is also evident in the cultural projects of other disability groups and in the rejection of the imposition of notions of normality in relation to physical bodies (Davis, 1995). By no means all of the groups discussed in this book would want to live their lives only within communities defined by the identities they share as disabled people, mental health service users, older people, or people with learning difficulties. But nor is it helpful to devalue the diversity such groups contribute to 'city life . . . a being together of strangers, diverse and overlapping neighbours' (Young, 1995, p. 268). The aim of many such groups is better expressed by reference to the recognition and acceptance of their difference, than to integration based on enforced 'normality'.

The bond of friendship is also evident in the self-organisation of users of community care services. The suggestion that friendship is of particular importance to those regarded as in some way deviant is supported by evidence from a study of self-organisation among mental health service users (Barnes and Shardlow, 1996). For those with stigmatised identities, being with others who share an understanding of that experience is an important source of support. Related to this is the sense of 'vulnerability that people with mental health problems experience – one can never be sure that you will not become ill again. That shared awareness also contributes to the supportive, nurturing relationship which Ackelsberg associates with friendship. People with learning difficulties also attach considerable significance to friendship. It is one of the things which they value from attending day centres which might be regarded as segregating, but which are an important source of friendships. It is also an unstated bond under-pinning self-organisation such as Project Two in Nebraska, USA, described by Paul Williams and Bonnie Schoultz (1984).

Through friendship, non-oppressive care can be provided. User organisations provide and are sustained by such relationships. 'Making friends' was identified as a benefit by more than three quarters of the older people involved in the Fife User Panels project and nearly all the panel members thought that 'Sharing experiences with others' and 'Learning more about other people's lives' were important benefits of involvement (Barnes and Bennett-Emslie, 1996). The value attached to interpersonal relationships within user groups by those we interviewed in research into disabled people's groups and groups of mental health service users belies the assertion that notions of 'care' should be entirely replaced by the attainment of rights (Barnes and Shardlow, 1996, Barnes *et al.*, 1996). While a commitment to social justice was a powerful motivating force for many of those participating in such groups and this directs energies outwards to seek change in services and legislation, 'caring about' each other within the groups was also vital to maintaining the commitment of many members. Individual advocacy can be a means through which rights are asserted, but in many cases the informal advocacy group members provided to each other was based on an acceptance and care for the other as much as on any notion of rights.

Nevertheless, the friendship relationships which sustain user self-organisation can also be the source of political action, as both Ackelsberg and Friedman suggest has been the case within the women's movement. This can come about through the modelling of alternative forms of social relationships, and through the personal empowerment which comes from developing skills and understanding within a safe and supportive environment. I develop this point below.

At the same time, and for some people who are not comfortable with the idea of being part of a community of identity, user groups can serve the rather more instrumental purposes which Hirst (1994) suggests are the basis of voluntary associations. He claims two positive outcomes for associations:

The first is that by banding together individuals attain some purpose or govern some activity defined by them as important to their interests, and do so in a way that they could not unless they associated. Thus the superior social governance associationalists see being achieved through the extensive control of major activities by voluntary bodies can be expressed in terms of the benefit it brings to individuals. The second is that in the process of banding together individuals develop themselves; they are further individuated by associating with others.

(ibid., p. 50)

This developmental potential, and the potential for political action, emphasise the role which can be played by user and carer groups in developing community capacity. Building capacity among groups that have been excluded or subordinated is an important pre-requisite for social change (Dominelli, 1990; Craig and Mayo, 1995; Mayo, 1994). As we have seen, user and carer groups are concerned not so much with social change in terms of redistribution of resources (although they do seek the resources which enable the social participation of their members and others), as with opening up decision-making processes and thus achieving change in the way in which issues are being thought about and discussed. They aim to demonstrate that professionals and paid officials within the welfare services do not have a monopoly on the knowledge necessary to the provision of effective community care. The significance of building community capacity is recognised within regeneration initiatives and new forms of networks and partnerships between local government and community groups are seen as vital to achieving social and economic regeneration at a local level (Department of the Environment, 1995; Skelcher *et al.*, 1996). Groups of users of community care services have the potential to contribute to these broader objectives to ensure that locality based participation initiatives include the full diversity of groups within the area.

User movements – the link between community and citizenship?

Collective organisation within user groups is an end as well as a means. Motivation to participate comes from shared experiences of poor treatment within services and discrimination outside, resulting in a desire to challenge such treatment not only for themselves, but to use that experience to support others and challenge on their behalf. The development of an awareness of shared identities is an important spur to collective action (Barnes and Shardlow, 1996; Rose and Kiger, 1995). This reflects Anne Phillips's description of what she describes as 'the new pluralism':

The new pluralism homes in on identity rather than interest groups: not those gathered together around some temporary unifying concern – to defend their neighbourhood against a major road development, to lobby their representative against some proposed new law – but those linked by a common culture, a common experience, a common language. These links are often intensely felt, and more importantly, are often felt as opposition and exclusion. Identity groups frequently secure their identity precisely around their opposition to some 'other', focussing on a past experience of being excluded, and sometimes formulating a present determination to exclude.

(Phillips, 1993, pp. 146–7)

A growing distrust of traditional political organisation and strategies has led to the formation of new social movements which have sought social and cultural change through direct action, such as the action to prevent road building taken by many environmental groups; through modelling alternative forms of welfare, for example, the women's refuge movement (Lovenduski and Randall, 1993); and through cultural and political projects such as many of those pursued by lesbians and gay men (e.g. Johnston, 1973). Pluralist political action has been criticised as leading to the proliferation of competing interest groups with little opportunity for the solidarity claimed for class-based political organisation. However, new social movements have demonstrated the spurious solidarity underpinning class politics and have enabled those excluded from such organisation to become empowered within social groups which reflect the differences which exist within contemporary society. They bring new voices into political dialogue, challenging dominant values and causing dominant groups to re-assess their own perspectives (Phillips, 1993).

User movements have many of the characteristics and share many of the objectives of other new social movements (Oliver, 1990; Rogers and Pilgrim, 1991; Shakespeare, 1993). Through collective action derived from their shared experiences as users of services, as disabled people or as older people, those who use community care services can be considered to express their own citizenship and to contribute to the enhancement of citizenship of others. They do this in a number of ways.

Civil and social rights

Many disabled people's groups are at the forefront of action to achieve legislation which would extend the protection from discrimination against women and black people to disabled people. Even among those groups in which the discourse of civil rights is not prominent, notions of fair treatment, social justice and social rights in terms of access to health and social care and to mainstream community resources (such as transport) provide an important motivation for action. Disabled activists recognise that the experience of women and black people demonstrates that legislation is an insufficient condition for the achievement of civil rights (Barnes and Oliver, 1995). Nevertheless, the argument for 'rights not charity' is a powerful expression of the objective of inclusive citizenship.

'The Government is firmly committed to a policy of community care which enables such people to achieve their full potential'

(Secretaries of State, 1989, p. 3). Community care is not just about receiving services from health and social care agencies. If community care is to be a truly empowering option, then it must enable people to be empowered beyond their role as service users. If previously marginalised and excluded people are to become part of local communities then that has implications not only for services, but also for social, economic and political institutions more broadly.

This will require change on a number of fronts. As the American experience demonstrates, the passage of anti-discrimination legislation is a starting point rather than a final outcome. The implementation of disability rights in the USA led to a series of legislative changes, court actions and institutional and policy changes throughout the public and private sectors (Percy, 1989). The implementation of a community care policy which recognises rights to participation within communal life as well as needs for services to support this implies that, in the UK context, responsibilities for community care rest with the whole local authority. In addition to social services departments, architects and planning departments, engineers and those involved in economic development, housing, education, leisure and recreation all have a role to play. So too do employers, private landlords and those providing leisure and other services within the commercial sector. Working across agency boundaries can be as difficult as developing new ways of working with service users (Barnes and Wistow, 1995b), but is a necessary aspect of transforming community *care* into community participation. It was suggested by one senior local government officer working in Birmingham at the time of the Community Care Special Action Project that:

While it may not be appropriate at this stage to think in terms of a unified community care department, there is certainly scope for thinking about the advantages of a single local authority budget for community care provision administered by a new distinct committee, with responsibility for ensuring the achievement of corporate community care policy objectives.

(Prior, 1990)

At the level of policy, community participation involves action in the context of transport policy, community safety policy, equal opportunities policies, education policy and others, as well as in the arena more usually defined by community care policy.

Accountability

As citizens, service users have a right to express their views about services in general, not only about the individual care package which they may be receiving. They should be able to participate in determining priorities and should receive information not only about the availability of services, but also about their performance. A relationship of accountability implies an important shift in the balance of power between service users and providers. Relationships between public services and citizens are not the same as those between the producer of merchandise and his customers: 'Action in the public domain rests upon public consent, for without consent collective choice is deprived of legitimate authority' (Ranson and Stewart, 1994, p. 221). Through their presence within the different forums in which they meet with community care purchasers and providers service users can hold these public officials to account.

The accountability of public services, both to their users and to citizens generally, has been identified as having become increasingly problematic as services have moved out of the control of elected bodies and accountability has become equated with performance review (Burton and Duncan, 1996; Ranson and Stewart, 1994). At the same time, the 'democratic deficit' has also been evident in low turn-outs in local government elections and it is recognised that increasing accountability will involve more than reversing the trend towards appointment rather than election to public bodies (Stewart, 1996). Ranson and Stewart argue that traditional models of representative democracy are no longer sufficient to achieve accountability in a way which can contribute to a learning society, because they offer few opportunities for discourse. The dialogue which some user groups have started to enter into with service purchasers and providers provides a model of the communication process which Ranson and Stewart argue should be the basis of accountability:

Those held to account are drawn to communicate why they have been doing what they have been doing and how they have gone about it. Accountability is a court of judgement which distributes praise and blame, but it must in the public domain institutionalise a discourse about purposes, practice and performance.

(1994, p. 233)

Giving account and being held to account can often be an uncomfortable experience for professionals who see accountability as something to be given to professional peers, rather than to either managers, politicians or the users of their services. Professional defensiveness has been evident in many initiatives which have sought to empower service users, in particular those involving users of mental health services. Nevertheless, users do see opportunities for holding public servants to account emerging from the increasing contact they have with purchasers and providers (Barnes *et al.*, 1996). Increased dialogue in the course of individual advocacy or participation in planning forums provides opportunities for answers to be sought about the use of resources, the reasons for particular service decisions, and the justification for the application of forms of treatment. The development of trust and the learning relationships which can be established in such fora provide a context in which it is possible to break down such defensiveness and institutionalise accountability as a continuing process of dialogue.

Analysis of practical initiatives through which health authorities sought to respond to the call to listen to 'Local Voices' (NHSME, 1992) concluded that there remained a substantial democratic deficit within health services (Cooper *et al.*, 1995). Cooper and her colleagues advocated not only initiatives such as citizen's juries as a means of overcoming this deficit, but also suggested that there should be experiments to enable local authorities, as the only democratically elected authorities at local level, to become health purchasers. Citizens' juries have been suggested as one model which local authorities themselves could adopt to develop debate and enable more direct accountability on specific issues (Stewart, 1996). Prior, Stewart and Walsh (1995) also suggest that local government has a role in acting as the representative of local citizens by monitoring the activities of agencies managed by unelected bodies (such as NHS Trusts) and presenting this information to citizens so that they can engage in debate about them.

Citizens' juries, deliberative opinion polls (Fishkin, 1991), standing citizens' panels and other methods of enhancing participation in the democratic process all have potential for enhancing accountability to citizens as a whole, rather than directly to users of community care services. The interest of local citizens in community care is broader than that of those who currently use services. As citizens who may become elderly, disabled or experience mental distress, or who may care for someone in this position, we all have an interest in the availability of high-quality services and we are all potential users of those services. Yet conflicts of interest between current users and other citizens are evident in, for example, campaigns to prevent group homes for people with learning difficulties being opened in certain residential areas, and more generally in the willingness or otherwise of local citizens to pay for high-quality services through local and national taxation. The empowerment of current users will be influenced by the ability of service providers to engage with other local citizens to gain their commitment to the implementation of effective community care policies through the delivery of publicly funded services.

Renewing Democracy

Ranson and Stewart (1994) go on to locate the significance of discursive accountability within the framework offered by Habermas's notion of 'communicative rationality' (Habermas, 1984). Theories of communicative democracy would suggest that by taking part in dialogues which contribute to decision making about the nature of services provided through local governance, disabled people and other users of community care services are contributing to a process of transformation of democratic and decision making processes themselves. In Chapter 3 I quoted Iris Young: 'By giving voice to formerly silenced or devalued needs and experiences, group representation forces participants in discussion to take a reflective distance on their assumptions and think beyond their own interests' (Young, quoted in Phillips, 1993, p. 158). Similar points about the transformative potential of the involvement of formerly excluded groups within governmental processes are made by Hilary Wainwright (1994).

User involvement can lead not only to different outcomes in terms of service decision making, but also can effect change in the way in which professionals and managers think about problems and issues. The evidence suggests that such a transformation is enormously hard to achieve, but the presence of groups often regarded as 'incompetent' (Barnes and Prior, forthcoming) within forums in which their authority is recognised is an important step forward.

There are both epistemological and political dimensions to this. Experiential knowledge is being recognised as having an authority to place alongside the expert knowledge of policy makers. It has long been recognised that policy making cannot be understood as a rational process deriving solely (or even primarily) from the disinterested application of objective knowledge. Lane (1993) reviews different models of public policy making and concludes that no one model is adequate to explain the way in which policy is both made and implemented in all circumstances. Nevertheless the current emphasis on 'evidence based policy making' in the NHS is but one example of the way in which reference to scientific evidence is seen as providing legitimacy for policy decisions. But science itself has been subject to critique that the supposedly objective insights deriving from scientific methodology are the result of primarily white, male, western perspectives, and that different standpoints are necessary to achieve 'strong objectivity' within the physical as well as the social sciences (Harding, 1991). The standpoints of those who receive services and who have experienced the process of ageing, disablement or mental distress provide a necessarily different perspective from those available to young, able-bodied policy makers, who have never had experience of being on the receiving end of the services they produce.

In his critique of 'instrumental rationality' within political institutions and the policy process, Dryzek (1990) claims that it destroys egalitarian aspects of human association and is fundamentally undemocratic. He claims: 'Administrators, marketing consultants, police, social workers, counselors, physicians, lawyers and clinical psychologists are in the vanguard of this invasion of processes that were once constructed and conducted by ordinary people' (p. 5). This analysis has similarities with that offered by Ehrenreich and English (1979) of the way in which the knowledge and skills which women applied to health care were taken over by medical professionals.

Dryzek does not reject rationality out of hand, but, drawing on the work of Habermas, argues that it be 'democratised'. He sees in new social movements a source of renewal contributing to the development of what he calls 'discursive democracy'. His analysis represents one way in which a link can be made between the epistemological question of the legitimacy and authority of the knowledge available to users and users groups, and the political question of the institutional forms within which such knowledge can contribute to policy making.

Hirst's (1994) response to this institutional question is to argue for a welfare state based on associationalist principles. While welfare would continue to be publicly funded, it would be provided by voluntary self-governing organisations providing whatever range of services its members chose. However, Jordan and Jones (1995) argue that self-governing voluntary organisations would not provide a panacea to the problems of the welfare state as currently constituted. While some of the user groups discussed in Chapter 3 would welcome the transfer of some resources from state services to support their activities and services, few are currently arguing for a wholesale restructuring of the welfare state on the lines suggested by Hirst. Rather their objectives are transformations *within* publicly provided services, as well as support for user self-organisation to extend their capacity to play a part in decision making.

The nature and practice of citizenship

User groups also enable those involved in them to fulfil the obligations of citizenship by participating in collective purposes (Phillips, 1991; Prior, Stewart and Walsh, 1995). Not only do the groups themselves fulfil a self-help function, providing opportunities for personal growth and development which are valuable in themselves, they increase the confidence and self-esteem of participants so that they develop a sense that change is possible through collective action; they allow people to develop skills which can enable participation in other spheres; and they provide an opportunity through which people can participate in decision making as co-producers of services. The experience of negotiation and decision making *within* groups can provide an 'education for citizenship' as excluded people learn the skills necessary for collective decision making (Williams and Schoultz, 1984; Gastil, 1993).

Another important aspect of citizenship which is highlighted by the experiences of users of community care services and of family carers is that concerning the sphere within citizenship is expressed. I have referred earlier to the classical notion of the citizen as public actor. Indeed citizenship was taken to refer solely to the public sphere in which citizens 'did their bit' for the state. The status of citizenship was both defined by the right to participate in decision making within the political community (most clearly by the right to vote), and earned by contributions to the state in the form of taxes. Thus women have only been included as citizens within the twentieth century after winning the right to vote, and throughout much of the twentieth century have effectively been 'secondary' citizens, dependent on contributions from their husbands' pay packets to secure the social and welfare rights attached to citizenship. The dilemma for feminists concerned to address the exclusion of women from full citizenship status has been whether to seek the right to equal participation with men within the public sphere, including the right to fight and die for their country as soldiers, or whether to assert the different contribution which is made by women and which should earn equivalent status (Lister, 1995; Pateman, 1992). Similar issues and dilemmas can be considered in respect of those excluded from full citizenship by virtue of disability or age.

For many younger disabled people, exclusion from employment has been an important target for action intended to enable them to participate as full citizens. Employment is seen as confirming adult identity as well as providing the material resources to enable further participation (Leonard, 1984). The exclusion of disabled people from employment both infantilises and marginalises them. As well as action on the part of disabled people themselves, action taken from within welfare services has sought to support the employment of those with learning difficulties, mental health problems, and physical or sensory impairments (e.g. Barnes and Wistow, 1995b; Nehring *et al.*, 1993). While such action is a necessary part of the project which seeks to overcome the construction of disabled people and others as welfare dependants, it is not a sufficient condition for the achievement of citizenship for users of community care services.

The prioritisation of paid employment over all other roles as a means through which citizenship can be expressed and experienced denies the value of other types of contributions and itself excludes those for whom work is not, or is no longer, an option. The position of older people is particularly significant in this respect. Many older people want to continue working beyond the age at which they are expected to retire gracefully, and the stereotyping of old age as a period of passivity and decline is neither accurate nor helpful to the many older people who undertake new and active roles after retirement age. But those whose frailty means that they need substantial support from health and social care services should not, therefore, be consigned to the category of ex-citizens. The Fife project (see Chapter 3) has demonstrated the way in which very frail older people can contribute to projects designed to improve and enhance health and social care services and Thornton and Tozer (1995) have identified other projects which similarly enable frail older people to contribute to service planning. Knowledge based on the experience of growing older can contribute a perspective not available to younger people and is a means through which frail older people can participate in collective public purposes without engaging in paid employment. Such knowledge has been more readily recognised in cultures other than that of Western Europe and the USA, but is being introduced through initiatives such as those discussed above and other initiatives such as those described by Friedan (1993) and Onyx and Benton (1995).

Similarly, the earlier discussion of the range of roles which people with learning difficulties can play within families and in supporting friends and neighbours, provides another example of the way in which 'private' roles might be considered to offer a route to citizenship. Both Patemen and Lister argue for a new understanding and practice of citizenship in which a fairer distribution of care responsibilities between women and men is one part of the equation, and in which the other is a recognition of the value of such contributions to the well-being of the community, expressed through state support for caring responsibilities. Lister (1995) also addresses the challenge from disabled people to the language and ideology of caring and argues for a synthesis between the ethic of care and the ethic of justice: 'Such a synthesis is necessary if our understanding of citizenship is to be enriched by an ethic of care on the one hand and if the practice of care is to be underwritten by the social rights associated with citizenship on the other' (p. 25). I would argue that to achieve such a synthesis we need to recognise the value of roles undertaken within the private sphere which can be a source of individual fulfilment and can also contribute to collective well-being. Those roles may be undertaken within organised user groups or within family or friendship groups. If those roles are taken on by choice, and exercised within relationships of respect and equality, then they can provide as great opportunities for the development of autonomy as can more public roles – and potentially greater opportunities than are available through many of the poorly paid jobs undertaken by disabled people.

There is another way in which the position of older people provides a particular perspective on citizenship. Roche (1992) discusses the temporal dimension of social citizenship and the significance of inter-generational relations within this. He argues the limitations of a rights-based approach to citizenship and emphasises the significance of citizenship obligation, not least because an emphasis on individual rights fails to recognise duties to future generations. The retreat of the NHS from the provision of continuing care services for older people is a particular example of a reluctance on the part of current workers to contribute to meeting the social rights of older people. The argument that continuing care should be financed through private insurance and through the sale of personal assets rather than through the tax revenue which finances other aspects of health care within the National Health Service, represents a broken contract between the state and older citizens. At the time of writing it was uncertain what position the various political parties would take on the issue of the funding of long-term care in the impending general election. But it was clear that this issue had provided a focus for a re-affirmation of social rights:

The government has thrown down the gauntlet and shown its intention to deliberately constrict and charge for care in the community. We are now undoubtedly at a watershed with regard to all health care provision. This path must be resisted and opposed. Care must be a right based on need, not a privilege based on a person's ability to pay.

(Goldenberg, quoted in Courtney and Walker, 1996)

This issue fundamentally delineates the state's perspective on the issue of rights to care. It represents an attempt to draw a clear line between two intersecting forms of care – social care and health care – and to define one as a social right of citizens to be met by the state, and the other as the responsibility of individuals and their families to meet through private resources. In so doing there is the danger of reversing the move to 'de-medicalise' needs as it is in individuals' interests for their needs to be defined as health rather than social care needs. This is one area in which bringing together the role of local authorities as 'social care' purchasers with that of 'health care' purchasers might ease the anomalies caused by the different structures through which health and social care services are currently commissioned.

Conclusion

The consensus on community care policy is starting to appear a fragile one as scandals indicating a lack of care within communities have come to replace scandals about abuses of care within institutions. Inquiry reports point to failures of practice and co-ordination within and between health and social care agencies. A welcome for the principles of community care has been replaced, in some quarters, by cynicism at government failure to adequately resource the implementation of those principles. Perhaps part of the problem relates to a failure to understand the nature of 'community' and 'care'. Part also relates to the dominance of the de-institutionalisation origins of the policy over its community development origins. And further difficulties have resulted from a reluctance on the part of both practitioners and policy makers to recognise the dual identity of users of services who are also citizens with contributions to make to services, and both rights and needs to participate within society as a whole.

As I have demonstrated, important developments are evident, coming from within services and from the self-organisation of users and carers. The significance of these developments for an understanding of care and communities, as well as for the relevance of rights and citizenship, is as important as the practical outcomes being achieved at local levels. These lessons need to be learned if the promise of the policy is to be fully achieved.

One implication of this is that the concept of community care needs to be extended to include community participation. Community care is intended to overturn the separation of disabled or 'deviant' people from 'normal' people. If this is to be successful then it has to involve rather more than the production of individualised care packages, based on professional assessments of need. It has to involve enabling people to participate in decision making processes about services, and in social, economic and political life more broadly. The concept of 'care' is an inadequate one to describe what it is that needs to be delivered in order to enable people to live their lives within communities, but, in contrast with some disability activists, I do not agree that it should be replaced solely with an assertion of rights.

Community participation relates to the way in which disabled people, older people and those with learning difficulties or mental health problems, can contribute to the collective well-being of society. It also refers to the participation of family carers in supporting that contribution and in themselves contributing an understanding of the knowledge, skills and qualities required for effective caring relationships. In both instances those contributions will often be enhanced by collective organisation, and support for those organisations should thus be a public responsibility. At the same time, the participation of user and carer groups can enhance the capacity of public services to provide empowering and accountable services to local citizens. While user and carer input may threaten existing practices, it has the potential to strengthen support and commitment for public services.

One benefit of this analysis for beleaguered health and social services agencies is that all public services have a role in enabling community participation. Those authorities which have responded imaginatively to the possibilities of community care have seen how a wider range of resources can be drawn on to deliver services. To achieve this involves a preparedness to loosen one's grip on the part of professionals. But the potential benefits extend beyond those accruing to individual users of services. If, for example, the use of long-term anti-depressant medication can be reduced as a result of support for people to participate in adult education classes through which they can gain both self-esteem and usable skills, then the public good is well served.

Consumerism cannot be the only solution to shifting the balance between producer and consumer interests within community care services. But a concept of citizenship as a practice through which diverse groups can be enabled to contribute to collective purposes can suggest a way forward. We are all potential beneficiaries of the transformation which can be achieved.

REFERENCES

Abrams, M. and O'Brien, J. (1981). *Political Attitudes and Ageing in Britain.* Mitcham, Surrey: Age Concern England.

Abrams, P., Abrams, S., Humphrey, R. and Snaith, R. (1989). *Neighbourhood Care and Social Policy.* London: Department of Health/HMSO.

Ackelsberg, M. A. (1983). ' "Sisters" or "Comrades"? The politics of friends and families', in I. Diamond (ed.), *Families, Politics and Public Policies. A Feminist Dialogue on Women and the State.* New York and London: Longman.

Age Concern (1993). *Recognising Our Voices.* Age Concern.

Age Concern Scotland (1994). *New Ways of Working. Fife User Panels Project.* Edinburgh: Age Concern Scotland.

Alcock, P. (1989). 'Why citizenship and welfare rights offer new hope for new welfare in Britain', *Critical Social Policy,* **26** (Autumn), pp. 32–43.

Amans, D. and Darbyshire, C. (1989). 'A Voice of Our Own', in A. Brechin and J. Walmsley (eds), *Making Connections: Reflecting on the Lives and Experiences of People with Learning Difficulties.* London: Hodder & Stoughton.

Arber, S. and Gilbert, N. (1989). 'Men: the forgotten carers', *Sociology,* **23**, pp. 111–18.

Asafu-Adjaye, B., Manchego-Pellane, M. A. and Whall-Roberts, D. (1993). 'Support for disabled elderly people from ethnic minority groups', in P. Beresford and T. Harding (eds), *A Challenge to Change. Practical Experiences of Building User-led Services.* London: National Institute for Social Work.

Atkin, K. (1991). 'Health, illness, disability and black minorities: a speculative critique of present day discourse', *Disability, Handicap and Society,* **6**(1), pp. 37–47.

Atkinson, D. and Williams F. (eds) (1990). *Know Me As I Am.* London: Open University Press.

Audit Commission (1986). *Making a Reality of Community Care.* London: HMSO.

Banton, R., Clifford P., Frosh S., Lousada, J. and Rosenthall, J. (1985). *The Politics of Mental Health.* Basingstoke: Macmillan.

Barclay Report (1982). *Social Workers: Their Role and Tasks (Report of a Working Party under the Chairmanship of Mr P. M. Barclay).* London: Bedford Square Press.

Barnes, C. (1991). *Disabled People in Britain and Discrimination. A Case for Anti-Discrimination Legislation.* London: Hurst/Calgary.

Barnes, C. and Oliver, M. (1995). 'Disability Rights: rhetoric and reality in the UK', *Disability and Society,* **10**(1), pp. 111–16.

Barnes, M. (1981). 'Acres Hill Day Nursery – the first six months', *Clearing House for Local Authority Social Services Reseach* (6), pp. 75–107.

Barnes, M. (1982). 'Shiregreen Family Centre – the first six months', *Clearing House for Local Authority Social Services Research* (7), pp. 1–74.

Barnes, M. (1987). 'Editorial', *Social Services Research* (2).

Barnes, M. (1993). *Developing Partnerships Between Carers and Managers. A project conducted as part of the NHSME Developing Managers for Community Care Programme.* Leeds: Nuffield Institute for Health, University of Leeds.

Barnes, M. (1996a). 'Citizens in detention: the role of the Mental Health Act Commission in protecting the rights of detained patients, *Local Government Studies,* **22**(3), pp. 28–46.

Barnes, M. (1996b). 'Empowerment and families', in G. Grant and P. Ramcharan (eds), *Empowerment in Everyday Life: Learning Disability.* London: Jessica Kingsley.

Barnes, M. (1996c). 'User movements and the local governance of welfare'. Paper given at the Social Policy Association Conference, Sheffield, 17 July.

Barnes, M. and Bennett-Emslie, G. (1995). *'If they would listen . . .' An Evaluation of the Fife User Panels Project.* Edinburgh: Age Concern Scotland.

Barnes, M. and Cormie, J. (1995). 'On the Panel', *Health Service Journal* (March 2nd), pp. 30–1.

Barnes, M., Cormie, J. and Crichton, M. (1994). *Seeking Representative Views from Frail Older People.* Edinburgh: Age Concern Scotland.

Barnes, M., Harrison, S., Mort, M., Shardlow, P. and Wistow, G. (1996a). *Consumerism and Citizenship amongst Users of Health and Social Care Services.* Final report to ESRC of Award No. L311253025.

Barnes, M., Harrison, S., Mort, M., Shardlow, P. and Wistow, G. (1996b). 'Users, officials and citizens in health and social care', *Local Government Policy Making,* **22**(4), pp. 9–17.

Barnes, M. and Maple, N. (1992). *Women and Mental Health: Challenging the Stereotypes.* Birmingham: Venture Press.

Barnes, M. and Miller, N. (1988). 'Performance measurement in the personal social services', *Research, Policy and Planning* (6)2.

Barnes, M. and Prior, D. (1995). 'Spoilt for Choice: How consumerism can disempower public service users?' *Public Money and Management,* **15**(3), pp. 53–8.

Barnes, M. and Prior, D. (1996). 'From private choice to public trust: a new social basis for welfare', *Public Money and Management,* **16**.

Barnes, M. and Prior, D. (forthcoming). 'Trust and the competence of the welfare consumer', in S. Bagguley and A. Coulsen (eds), *Trust in the Public Domain.*

Barnes, M., Prior, D. and Thomas, N. (1990). 'Social services', in N. Deakin and A. Wright (eds), *Consuming Public Services.* London: Routledge.

Barnes, M. and Shardlow, P. (1996). 'Identity crisis? Mental health user groups and the ''problem'' of identity', in C. Barnes and G. Mercer (eds.), *Accounting for Illness and Disability: Exploring the Divide.* Leeds: Disability Press.

Barnes, M. and Walker, A. (1996). 'Consumerism versus empowerment: a principled approach to the involvement of older service users' *Policy and Politics*, **24**(4).

Barnes, M. and Wilson, T. (1986). 'The impact of social services research', *Research, Policy and Planning*, **4** (1 and 2), pp. 19–24.

Barnes, M. and Wistow, G. (1991). *Changing Relationships in Community Care*. Leeds: Nuffield Institute for Health, University of Leeds.

Barnes, M. and Wistow, G. (1992a). *Finding a Voice of Our Own. Initiatives Designed to Hear from Users of Mental Health Services*. Leeds: Nuffield Institute for Health, University of Leeds.

Barnes, M. and Wistow, G. (1992b). *Coming in from the Wilderness? Carers' Views of the Consultations and their Outcomes*. Research evaluation of the Birmingham Community Care Special Action Project No. 2. Leeds: Nuffield Institute for Health, University of Leeds.

Barnes, M. and Wistow, G. (1992c). 'Consulting with carers: what do they think?', *Social Services Research* (no. 1), pp. 9–30.

Barnes, M. and Wistow, G. (1992d). 'Sustaining innovation in community care', *Local Government Policy Making* **18**(4), pp. 3–10.

Barnes, M. and Wistow, G. (1992e). *Developments in Day Time Opportunities*. Leeds: Nuffield Institute for Health, University of Leeds.

Barnes, M. and Wistow, G. (1993). *Gaining Influence, Gaining Support: Working with Carers in Research and Practice*. Leeds: Nuffield Institute for Health, University of Leeds.

Barnes, M. and Wistow, G. (1994a). 'Learning to hear voices: listening to users of mental health services', *Journal of Mental Health* (2).

Barnes, M. and Wistow, G. (1994b). 'Achieving a strategy for user involvement in community care', *Health and Social Care in the Community* (2), pp. 347–56.

Barnes, M. and Wistow, G. (1994c) 'Involving carers in planning and review', in A. Connor and S. Black (eds), *Performance Review and Quality in Social Care*. London: Jessica Kingsley.

Barnes, M. and Wistow, G. (1995a) *User Oriented Community Care: An Overview of Findings from an Evaluation of the Birmingham Community Care Special Action Project*. Leeds: Nuffield Institute for Health, University of Leeds.

Barnes, M. and Wistow, G. (1995b). 'Moving towards employment: corporate responsibilities for community care', *Social Services Research* (1), pp. 36–47.

Barton, L. (1993). 'The struggle for citizenship: the case of disabled people', *Disability, Handicap and Society*, **8**(3), pp. 235–48.

Bauman, Z. (1991). *Modernity and Ambivalence*. Cambridge: Polity Press.

Bayley, M. J. (1973). *Mental Handicap and Community Care*. London: Routledge & Kegan Paul.

BCODP (n.d.). *Information Pack*. Belper, Derbyshire: British Council of Organisations of Disabled People.

Beck, U. (1992). *Risk Society: Towards a New Modernity*. London: Sage.

Beeforth, M., Conlan, E. and Graley, R. (1994). *Have We Got Views For You. User Evaluation of Case Management.* London: The Sainsbury Centre for Mental Health.

Beeforth, M., Gell, C., Read, J. and Wallcraft, J. (1994). *Guidelines for a Local Charter for Users of Mental Health Services.* London: NHS Executive, Mental Health Task Force User Group.

Beresford, P. (1992). 'Researching citizen involvement: a collaborative or colonizing enterprise?' in M. Barnes and G. Wistow (eds), *Researching User Involvement.* Leeds: Nuffield Institute for Health, University of Leeds.

Beresford, P. and Croft, S. (1986). *Whose Welfare? Private Care or Public Service.* Brighton: Lewis Cohen Urban Studies Centre, Brighton Polytechnic.

Beresford, P. and Croft, S. (1993). *Citizen Involvement: A Practical Guide for Change.* Basingstoke: Macmillan.

Birchall, J. (1988). *Building Communities the Co-Operative Way.* London: Routledge & Kegan Paul.

Bock, G. and James, S. (eds) (1992). *Beyond Equality and Difference.* London: Routledge.

Booth, T. (1988). *Developing Policy Research.* Aldershot: Gower.

Booth, T. and Booth W. (1994). *Parenting Under Pressure. Mothers and Fathers with Learning Difficulties.* Buckingham: Open University Press.

Bowl, R. and Barnes, M. (1990). 'Race, racism and mental health social work: implications for local authority policy and training', *Research, Policy and Planning,* **8**(2), pp. 12–18.

Braithwaite, V. A. (1990). *Bound to Care.* Sydney: Allen & Unwin.

Brandon, D. and Towe, N. (1989). *Free to Choose. An Introduction to Service Brokerage.* London: Good Impressions Publishers.

Brechin, A. and Walmsley, J. (eds) (1989). *Making Connections: Reflecting on the Lives and Experiences of People with Learning Difficulties.* London: Hodder & Stoughton.

Bulmer, M. (1987). *The Social Basis of Community Care.* London: Allen & Unwin.

Burton, P. and Duncan, S. (1996). 'Democracy and accountability in public bodies: new agendas in British governance', *Policy and Politics,* **24**(1), pp. 5–16.

Butt, H. and Palmer, B. (1985). *Value for Money in the Public Sector.* Oxford: Basil Blackwell.

Campaign for the Mentally Handicapped (1973). *Listen.* London: CMH.

Carpenter, M. (1994). *Normality is Hard Work. Trade Unions and the Politics of Community Care.* London: Lawrence & Wishart.

Casement, P. J. (1985). *On Learning from the Patient.* London: Tavistock.

Chamberlin, J. (1988). *On our Own. Patient Controlled Alternatives to the Mental Health System.* London: MIND.

Clarke, J., Cochrane, A. and McLaughlin, E. (eds) (1994). *Managing Social Policy.* London: Sage.

CMH (1986). *Self Advocacy Pack.* London: The Campaign for People with Mental Handicaps.

Cockburn, C. (1977). *The Local State*. London: Pluto Press.

Community Psychiatric Nurses Association (1987). *The Patient's Case. Views from Experience: Living Inside and Out of a Psychiatric Hospital*. Rossendale: Lancashire, CPNA.

Connelly, N. (1990). *Raising Voices: Social Services Departments and People with Disabilities*. London: Policy Studies Institute.

Consumer Involvement Sub-Group (1991). *Consumer Involvement and the All Wales Strategy*. Cardiff: The Welsh Office.

Cooper, L., Coote, A., Davies A. and Jackson, C. (1995). *Voices Off: Tackling the Democratic Deficit in Health*. London: Institute for Public Policy Research.

Corker, M. (1993). 'Integration and deaf people; the policy and power of enabling environments', in J. Swain, V. Finkelstein, S. French and M. Oliver (eds), *Disabling Barriers – Enabling Environments*. London: Sage.

Corker, M. (1996). 'A hearing difficulty as impairment', in G. Hales (ed.), *Beyond Disability. Towards an Enabling Society*. London: Sage.

Courtney, M. and Walker, M. (1996). *Stand and Deliver: Making Pensioners Pay for Care*. Birmingham: NHS Support Federation/West Midlands Health Research Unit.

Craig, G. and Mayo, M. (eds) (1995). *Community Empowerment. A Reader in Participation and Development*. London: Zed Books.

Croft, S. and Beresford P. (1990). *From Paternalism to Participation. Involving People in Social Services*. Open Services Project/Joseph Rowntree Foundation.

Dalley, G. (1988). *Ideologies of Caring*. Basingstoke: Macmillan.

Darton, K., Gorman, J. and Sayce, L. (1994). *Eve Fights Back. The Successes of MIND's Stress on Women Campaign*. London: MIND.

Davey, B. (1994). *Empowerment through Holistic Development: A Framework for Egalitarianism in the Ecological Age*. Nottingham: Nottingham Advocacy Group/Ecoworks.

Davis, A. (1992). 'Who needs User Research?' in M. Barnes and G. Wistow (eds), *Researching User Involvement*. Leeds: Nuffield Institute for Health, University of Leeds.

Davis, K. (1983). *Consumer Participation in Service Design, Delivery and Control*. Clay Cross: Derbyshire Coalition of Disabled People.

Davis, K. (1993). 'On the movement', in J. Swain, V. Finkelstein, S. French and M. Oliver (eds), *Disabling Barriers – Enabling Environments*. London: Sage.

Davis, K. and Mullender, A. (1993). *Ten Turbulent Years. A Review of the Work of the Derbyshire Coalition of Disabled People*. Nottingham: DCDP/Centre for Social Action, University of Nottingham.

Davis, L. J. (1995). *Enforcing Normalcy. Disability, Deafness and the Body*. London, New York: Verso.

Deakin, N. (1987). *The Politics of Welfare*. London: Methuen.

Deakin, N. and Wright, A. (eds) (1990). *Consuming Public Services*. London: Routledge.

Department of Health (1990). *Care in the Community: Making it Happen*. London: DoH.

Department of Health and Social Security (1971). *Better Services for the Mentally Handicapped.* London: HMSO.

Department of Health and Social Security (1975). *Better Services for the Mentally Ill.* London: HMSO.

Department of the Environment (1995). *Involving Communities in Urban and Rural Regeneration. A Guide for Practitioners.* London: Department of the Environment.

Dominelli, L. (1990). *Women and Community Action.* Birmingham: Venture Press.

Dominelli, L. and McLeod, E. (1989). *Feminist Social Work.* Basingstoke: Macmillan.

Downer, J. and Ferns, P. (1993). 'Self-advocacy by Black people with learning difficulties', in P. Beresford and T. Harding (eds), *A Challenge to Change. Practical Experiences of Building User-led Services.* London: National Institute for Social Work.

Doyal, L. and Gough, I. (1991). *A Theory of Human Need.* Basingstoke: Macmillan.

Doyle, N. and Harding, T. (1992). 'Community care: applying procedural fairness', in A. Coote (ed.), *The Welfare of Citizens.* London: Rivers Oram Press.

Dryzek, J. S. (1990). *Discursive Democracy. Politics, Policy and Political Science.* Cambridge: Cambridge University Press.

Duff, G. (1994). 'The RHA/Kings Fund Carers Project', in *Carers Initiatives in Yorkshire 'Ideas into Action'.* Leeds: Nuffield Institute for Health, Community Care Division.

Dyer, L. (1985). *Wrong End of the Telescope.* London: MIND.

Ehrenreich, B. and English, D. (1979). *For Her Own Good. 150 Years of the Experts Advice to Women.* London: Pluto Press.

Ellis, K. (1993). *Squaring the Circle. User and Carer Participation in Needs Assessment.* York: Joseph Rowntree Foundation.

Ellis, K. (1995). 'Are women becoming a burden? Independence, dependency and community care', *Social Services Research* (2), pp. 1–10.

Elman, C. (1995). 'An age-based mobilisation: the emergence of old age in American politics', *Ageing and Society,* **15**(3), pp. 299–324.

Etzioni, A. (1995). *The Spirit of Community, Rights, Responsibilities and the Communitarian Agenda.* London: Fontana.

Finch, J. and Groves, D. (1985). 'Community care and the family: a case for equal opportunities?' in C. Ungerson (ed.), *Women and Social Policy: A Reader.* Basingstoke: Macmillan.

Finch, J. and Mason, J. (1993). *Negotiating Family Responsibilities.* London: Routledge.

Finkelstein, V. (1980). *Attitudes and Disabled People: Issues for Discussion.* New York: World Rehabilitation Fund.

Fisher, M. (ed.). (1983). *Speaking of Clients.* Sheffield: University of Sheffield, Joint Unit for Social Services Research/Community Care.

Fisher, M. (1994). 'Man-made care: community care and older male carers', *British Journal of Social Work,* **24**, pp. 659–90.

Fishkin, J. S. (1991). *Democracy and Deliberation*. New Haven and London: Yale University Press.

Flynn, M. and Ward, L. (1991). ' "We can change the future": self and citizen advocacy', in S. S. Segal and V. P. Varma (eds), *Prospects for People with Learning Difficulties*. London: David Fulton Publishers.

Flynn, N. (1993). *Public Sector Management*. Hemel Hempstead: Harvester Wheatsheaf.

Freire, P. (1968). *Pedagogy of the Oppressed*. New York: The Seabury Press.

Friedan, B. (1993). *The Fountain of Age*. New York: Cape.

Friedman, M. (1989). 'Feminism and modern friendship: dislocating the community', *Ethics*, **99**, pp. 275–90.

Gastil, J. (1993). *Democracy in Small Groups. Participation, Decision Making and Communication*. Philadelphia: New Society Publishers.

Gell, C. (1987). 'Learning to lobby. The growth of patients' council in Nottingham', in I. Barker and E. Peck (eds), *Power in Strange Places. User Empowerment in Mental Health Services*. London: Good Practices in Mental Health.

Giddens, A. (1991). *Modernity and Self-Identity*. Cambridge: Polity Press.

Glendinning, C. (1992). *The Costs of Informal Care: Looking Inside the Household*. London: HMSO.

Glendon, M. A. (1991). *Rights Talk. The Impoverishment of Political Discourse*. New York: Free Press.

Goffman, E. (1961). *Asylums: Essays on the Social Situation of Mental Patients and Other Inmates*. New York: Anchor.

Goode, D. A. (1979). 'The world of the congenitally deaf-blind: towards the grounds for achieving human understanding', in H. Schvarte and J. Jacobs (eds), *Qualitative Sociology: a Method to Madness*. New York: The Free Press.

Goss, S. and Miller, C. (1995). *From Margin to Mainstream*. York: Joseph Rowntree Foundation.

GPMH/ERCWFMH (1994). *Good Practices in Mental Health Services for Women*. London: Good Practices in Mental Health/ European Regional Council of the World Federation for Mental Health.

Graham, H. (1991). 'The concept of caring in feminist research: the case of domestic service', *Sociology* (25), pp. 61–78.

Graley, R., Nettle, M. and Wallcraft, J. (eds) (1994). *Building on Experience. A Training Pack for Mental Health Service Users Working as Trainers, Speakers and Workshop Facilitators*. London: NHS Executive, Mental Health Task Force User Group.

Grant, G. (1992). 'Researching user and carer involvement in mental handicap services', in M. Barnes and G. Wistow (eds), *Researching User Involvement*. Leeds: Nuffield Institute for Health, University of Leeds.

Grant, G. and Nolan, M. (1993). 'Informal carers: sources and concomitants of satisfaction', *Health and Social Care in the Community*, **1**(3), pp. 147–59.

Griffiths, R. (1988). *Community Care: Agenda for Action*. London: HMSO.

Habermas, J. (1984). *The Theory of Communicative Action; vol. 1: Reason and the Rationalization of Society*. London: Heineman.

Hadley, R. and Hatch, S. (1981). *Social Welfare and the Failure of the State.* London: George Allen & Unwin.

Hampshire CIL (1986). *Source Book Towards Independent Living.* Bordon, Hampshire: HCIL.

Harding, S. (1991). *Whose Science? Whose Knowledge? Thinking from Women's Lives.* Milton Keynes: Open University Press.

Harris, C. (1988). 'Nicholson Street: implications for planners and the provision of services in a small inner city redevelopment in Hull', *Social Services Research* (4), pp. 1–11.

Harrison, L. (1993). 'Newcastle's Mental Health Services Consumer Group: a case study of user involvement', in L. Gaster, L. Harrison, L. Martin, R. Means and P. Thistlethwaite (eds), *Working Together for Better Community Care.* Bristol: School for Advanced Urban Studies, University of Bristol.

Harrison, S. and Mort, M. (1996). 'Constructing user group legitimacy: a case study of officials in mental health care', in *Political Studies Association Annual Conference*, Glasgow:

Hasler, F. (1993). 'Developments in the disabled people's movement', in J. Swain, V. Finkelstein, S. French and M. Oliver (eds), *Disabling Barriers – Enabling Environments.* London: Sage.

Hepplewhite, R. (1988). 'Introduction', in *Common Concerns. International Conference on User Involvement in Mental Health Services.* University of Sussex, Brighton: East Sussex County Council, Brighton Health Authority, MIND.

Hirst, P. (1994). *Associative Democracy. New Forms of Economic and Social Governance.* Cambridge: Polity.

Hodge, P. (1970). 'The future of community development,' in W. A. Robson and B. Crick (eds), *The Future of the Social Services.* Harmondsworth: Penguin.

Hoyes, L., Lart, R., Means, R. and Taylor, M. (1994). *Community Care in Transition.* York: Joseph Rowntree Foundation.

Hugman, R. (1991). *Power in Caring Professions.* Basingstoke: Macmillan.

Humphreys, S. (1987). 'Participation in practice', *Social Policy and Administration, 21*(1), pp. 28–39.

Ivers, V. (1994). *Citizen Advocacy in Action: Working with Older People.* Stoke-on-Trent: Beth Johnson Foundation, in association with the European Commission.

Jenner, A. (1988). 'A psychiatrist's apologia', in *Common Concerns. International Conference on User Involvement in Mental Health Services.* University of Sussex, Brighton: East Sussex County Council, Brighton Health Authority, MIND.

Johnston, J. (1973). *Lesbian Nation.* New York: Simon & Schuster.

Jordan, B. and Jones, M. (1995). 'Association and exclusion in the organisation of social care', *Social Work and Social Sciences Review, 6*(1), pp. 5–18.

Jowell, T. (1989). 'More care for the carers', *The Guardian* (20 September), p. 27.

Jowell, T. and Wistow, G. (1989). 'Give them a voice', *Insight* (28 February), pp. 22–3.

Kaase, M. (1990). 'Social movements and political innovation', in R. J. Dalton and M. Kuechler (eds), *Challenging the Political Order. New Social and Political Movements*. Cambridge: Polity Press.

Kaplan, A. G. and Surrey, J. L. (1986). 'The relational self in women: developmental theory and public policy', in L. E. Walker (ed.), *Women and Mental Health Policy*. Beverley Hills and London: Sage.

Keat, R., Whiteley, N. and Abercrombie, N. (eds) (1994). *The Authority of the Consumer*. London: Routledge.

Kempker, K. (1995). 'Users and survivors', *The European Newsletter of Users and Ex-Users in Mental Health*, January, pp. 2–3.

King's Fund (1980). *An Ordinary Life*. London: King's Fund Centre.

Kohner, N. (1993). *A Stronger Voice. The Achievements of the Carers' Movement 1963–93*. London: Carers' National Association.

Kurt Lewin Institut (n.d). *Seniors Help Decide. Handbook for Senior Citizen Interest Support*. Amsterdam: Kurt Lewin Institut, Free University of Amsterdam.

Land, H. (1985). 'The introduction of family allowances: an act of historic justice?' in C. Ungerson (ed.), *Women and Social Policy. A Reader*. Basingstoke: Macmillan.

Lane, J.-E. (1993). *The Public Sector. Concepts, Models and Approaches*. London: Sage.

Law Commission (1991). *Mentally Incapacitated Adults and Decision-Making: An Overview*. London: HMSO.

Law Commission (1995). *Mental Incapacity*. London: HMSO.

LeGrand, J. and Bartlett, W. (eds) (1993). *Quasi-Markets and Social Policy*. Basingstoke: Macmillan.

Leonard, P. (1984). *Personality and Ideology*. Basingstoke: Macmillan.

Lewando-Hundt, G. and Grant, L. (1987). 'Studies of Black Elders – an exercise in window dressing or the groundwork for widening provision', *Social Services Research* (5/6), pp. 1–9.

Lister, R. (1995). 'Dilemmas in engendering citizenship', *Economy and Society*, **24**(1), pp. 1–36.

Lovenduski, J. and Randall, V. (1993). *Contemporary Feminist Politics*. Oxford: Oxford University Press.

McGrath, M. (1989). 'Consumer participation in service planning – the AWS Experience', *Journal of Social Policy*, **18**(1), pp. 67–89.

McKenzie, H. (1995). 'Empowering older persons through organizations: a case study', in D. Thursz, C. Nusberg and J. Prather (eds), *Empowering Older People*. London: Cassell.

McMurphy's (1995). *Mental Health is the Issue. The New McMurphy Review*. Sheffield: McMurphy's.

Marsh, P. and Fisher, M. (1992). *Good Intentions: Developing Partnership in Social Services*. York: Joseph Rowntree Foundation.

Mayer, J. E. and Timms, N. (1970). *The Client Speaks*. London: Routledge & Kegan Paul.

Mayo, M. (1994). *Communities and Caring. The Mixed Economy of Welfare*. Basingstoke: Macmillan.

Means, R. and Smith, R. (1994). *Community Care. Policy and Practice.* Basingstoke: Macmillan.

Melucci, A. (1985). 'The symbolic challenge of contemporary movements', *Social Research,* **52**(4), pp. 789–816.

Minister for Disabled People (1995). *Ending Discrimination against Disabled People.* London: HMSO.

Morris, J. (ed.) (1989). *Able Lives: Women's Experience of Paralysis.* London: The Women's Press.

Morris, J. (1993). 'Gender and disability', in J. Swain, V. Finkelstein, S. French and M. Oliver (eds), *Disabling Barriers – Enabling Environments.* London: Sage.

Morris, J. (1993). *Independent Lives. Community Care and Disabled People.* Basingstoke: Macmillan.

Morris, J. and Lindow, V. (1993). *User Participation in Community Care.* Leeds: NHSME Community Care Support Force.

Morrison, E. and Finkelstein, V. (1993). 'Broken arts and cultural repair: the role of culture in the empowerment of disabled people', in J. Swain, V. Finkelstein, S. French and M. Oliver (eds), *Disabling Barriers – Enabling Environments.* London: Sage.

Mort, M. and Harrison, S. (1996). 'User Involvement as a Technology of Legitimation: representation, participation and incorporation'. Paper presented at joint sessions of European Consortium for Political Research, Oslo, 4 April.

NBMHA (n.d.). *Tuning in to the Voice of the Consumer.* Birmingham: National Black Mental Health Association.

Nehring, J., Hill, R. and Poole, L. (1993). *Work, Empowerment and Community. Opportunities for People with Long-term Mental Health Problems. An RDP Study of Four New Work Projects.* London: Research and Development in Psychiatry.

Newman, J. and Clarke, J. (1994). 'Going about our business? The new managerialization of public services', in J. Clarke, A. Cochrane and E. McLaughlin (eds), *Managing Social Policy.* London: Sage.

NHS Training Directorate (1993). *Developing Managers for Community Care.* Bristol: NHSTD.

NHS Training Directorate (1993). *Involving Users and Carers in Inter-Agency Management Development.* Bristol: NHSTD.

NHSME (1992). *Local Voices. The Views of Local People in Purchasing for Health.* London: Department of Health.

North, N. (1993). 'Empowerment in Welfare Markets', *Health and Social Care in the Community,* **1**(3), 129–38.

Nozick, R. (1974). *Anarchy, State and Utopia.* Oxford: Blackwell.

O'Brien, J. (1986). 'A guide to personal futures planning', in G. T. Bellamy and S. Wilcox (eds), *A Comprehensive Guide to the Activities Catalogue: An Alternative Curriculum for Youth and Adults with Severe Disabilities.* Baltimore, Maryland: Paul H Brookes.

O'Brien, J. (1987). *Learning from Citizen Advocacy Programs.* Atlanta: Georgia Advocacy Office.

Oliver, M. (1990). *The Politics of Disablement*. Basingstoke: Macmillan.

Oliver, M. (1996). *Understanding Disability: From Theory to Practice*. Basingstoke: Macmillan.

Onyx, J. and Benton, P. (1995). 'Empowerment and ageing: towards honoured places for crones and sages', in G. Craig and M. Mayo (eds), *Community Empowerment. A Reader in Participation and Development*. London: Zed Books.

Osborn, A. (1992). *Taking Part in Community Care Planning*. Leeds/Edinburgh: Nuffield Institute for Health/Age Concern Scotland.

Parker, G. (1990). *With Due Care and Attention: A Review of Research on Informal Care*. London: Family Policy Studies Centre.

Parker, G. (1993). *With This Body. Caring and Disability in Marriage*. Buckingham: Open University Press.

Parker, R. (1981). 'Tending and social policy', in E. M. Goldberg and S. Hatch (eds), *A New Look at the Personal Social Services*. London: Policy Studies Institute.

Pateman, C. (1992). 'Equality, difference, subordination: the politics of motherhood and women's citizenship', in G. Bock and S. James (eds), *Beyond Equality and Difference. Citizenship, Feminist Politics, Female Subjectivity*. London: Routledge.

People First (n.d.). *People First Information Pack*. London: People First.

Percy, S. L. (1989). *Disability, Civil Rights and Public Policy*. Tuscaloosa: University of Alabama Press.

Phillips, A. (1991). 'Citizenship and feminist theory', in G. Andrews (ed.), *Citizenship*. London: Lawrence & Wishart.

Phillips, A. (1993). *Democracy and Difference*. Cambridge: Polity.

Plant, R. (1992). 'Citizenship, rights and welfare', in A. Coote (ed.), *The Welfare of Citizens*. London: Rivers Oram Press.

Pollitt, C. (1990). *Managerialism and the Public Services*. Oxford: Basil Blackwell.

Pollitt, C. (1994). 'The Citizens' Charter: a preliminary analysis', *Public Money and Management,* April–June, pp. 9–14.

Prime Minister (1991). *The Citizen's Charter*. London: HMSO.

Prior, D. (1990). 'Deciding how to care', *Local Government Chronicle* (20 April), p. 21.

Prior, D. (1995). 'Citizen's Charters', in J. Stewart and G. Stoker (eds), *Local Government in the 1990s*. Basingstoke: Macmillan.

Prior, D., Jowell, T. and Lawrence, R. (1989). 'Carer consultations: towards a strategy for consumer-led change', *Local Government Policy Making,* **16**(2), pp. 17–25.

Prior, D., Stewart, J. and Walsh, K. (1993). *Is the Citizens' Charter a Charter for Citizens?* Luton: Local Government Management Board.

Prior, D., Stewart, J. and Walsh, K. (1995). *Citizenship: Rights, Community and Participation*. London: Pitman.

Prior, L. (1993). *The Social Organisation of Mental Illness*. London: Sage.

Qureshi, H. and Walker, A. (1989). *The Caring Relationship: Elderly People and their Families*. Basingstoke: Macmillan.

Ramcharan, P. and Grant, G. (1993). *Individual Planning and Citizen Advocacy in the State of Victoria, Australia: Report of a Brief Study Visit.* Bangor: Centre for Social Policy Research and Development, University of Wales.

Ramon, S. (ed.) (1991). *Beyond Community Care. Normalisation and Integration Work.* Basingstoke: Macmillan.

Ramon, S. (ed.). (1992). *Psychiatric Hospital Closure. Myths and Realities.* London: Chapman & Hall.

Ranson, S. and Stewart, J. (1994). *Management for the Public Domain.* Basingstoke: Macmillan.

Raymond, J. (1986). *A Passion for Friends. Towards a Philosophy of Female Affection.* London: The Women's Press.

Read, J. and Wallcraft, J. (1992). *Guidelines for Empowering Users of Mental Health Services.* London: COHSE/MIND.

Roche, M. (1992). *Rethinking Citizenship. Welfare, Ideology and Change in Modern Society.* Cambridge: Polity.

Rogers, A. and Pilgrim, D. (1991). ' "Pulling down churches": Accounting for the British Mental Health Users' Movement', *Sociology of Health and Illness,* 13(2), pp. 129–48.

Rose, P. and Kiger, G. (1995). 'Intergroup relations: political action and identity in the deaf community', *Disability and Society,* 10(4), pp. 521–8.

Rose, S. M. and Black, B. L. (1985). *Advocacy and Empowerment. Mental Health Care in the Community.* Boston: Routledge & Kegan Paul.

Royal College of Psychiatrists (1993). *Community Supervision Orders.* London: RCP.

Ryan, J. and Thomas, F. (1980). *The Politics of Mental Handicap.* Harmondsworth: Penguin.

Sainsbury, E. (1983). 'Client studies and social policy', in M. Fisher (ed.), *Speaking of Clients.* Sheffield: University of Sheffield: Joint Unit for Social Services Research/Community Care.

Scott, A. (1990). *Ideology and the New Social Movements.* London: Unwin Hyman.

Secretaries of State for Health, Social Security, Wales and Scotland (1989). *Caring for People: Community Care in the Next Decade and Beyond.* London: HMSO.

Seebohm, F. (1968). *Report of the Committee on Local Authority and Allied Personal Social Services.* London: HMSO.

Shakespeare, T. (1993). 'Disabled people's self-organisation: a new social movement?', *Disability, Handicap and Society,* 8(3), pp. 249–64.

Siim, B. (1994). 'Engendering democracy: social citizenship and political participation for women in Scandinavia', *Social Politics,* 1(3), pp. 286–305.

Simpkin, M. (1979). *Trapped Within Welfare. Surviving Social Work.* London: Macmillan.

Skelcher, C., McCabe, A., Lowndes, V. and Nanton, P. (1996). *Community Networks in Urban Regeneration.* Bristol: The Policy Press.

Smith, P. and Thomas, N. (1993). 'Contracts and competition in public services', in *Association of Directors of Social Services Annual Conference.* Birmingham: University of Birmingham.

Smith, R. and West, G. (1985). 'The effects of mental illness on the family: social work practitioner's view', in G. Horobin (ed.), *Responding to Mental Illness*. Aberdeen/London: Kogan Page.

SSI (1992). *Implementing Caring for People: Assessment Circular*. London: Department of Health.

Stewart, J. (1986). *The New Management of Local Government*. London: Allen & Unwin.

Stewart, J. (1996). 'Innovation in democratic practice in local government', *Policy and Politics*, **24**(1), pp. 29–41.

Stewart, J., Kendall, E. and Coote, A. (eds) (1994). *Citizens' Juries*. London: Institute for Public Policy Research.

Stewart, J. and Stoker G. (1994). *The Future of Local Government*. Basingstoke: Macmillan.

Stewart, J. and Walsh, K. (1994). 'Performance measurement: when performance can never be finally defined', *Public Money and Management*, **14**(2), pp. 45–50.

Stuart, O. (1993). 'Double oppression: an appropriate starting point? in J. Swain, V. Finkelstein, S. French, and M. Oliver (eds), *Disabling Barriers – Enabling Environments*. London: Sage.

Swain, J., Finkelstein, F., French, S. and Oliver, M. (eds) (1993). *Disabling Barriers – Enabling Environments*. London: Sage.

Sykes, W., Collins, M., Hunter, D. J., Popay, J. and Williams, G. (1992). *Listening to Local Voices. A Guide to Research Methods*. Leeds/Salford: Nuffield Institute for Health/Public Health Research and Resource Centre.

Taylor, M. (1995). 'Community work and the state: the changing context of UK practice' in G. Craig and M. Mayo (eds), *Community Empowerment. A Reader in Participation and Development*. London: Zed Books.

The Labour Party (1995). *Renewing the NHS. Labour's Agenda for a Healthier Britain*. London: The Labour Party.

Thomas, C. (1993). 'De-constructing concepts of care', *Sociology*, **27**(4), pp. 649–69.

Thompson, C. and Hirst, M. (1994). 'Packages of need: a typology of dependency', *Research, Policy and Planning*, **12**(3), pp. 11–17.

Thornton, P. and Tozer, R. (1995). *Having a Say in Change: Older People and Community Care*. York: Joseph Rowntree Foundation.

Thornton, P. and Tozer, R. (1995). 'Involving Older People in Planning and Evaluating Community Care: A Review of Initiatives'. York: Social Policy Research Unit, University of York.

Titmuss, R. (1973). *Commitment to Welfare*. London: George Allen & Unwin.

Took, M. (n.d). *Mental Illness and the Services People Need*. Southampton: NSF Southern Region.

Touraine, A. (1985). 'An introduction to the study of social movements', *Social Research*, **52**(4), pp. 749–87.

Townsend, P. (1963). *The Family Life of Old People*. Harmondsworth: Penguin.

Twigg, J (1989). 'Models of carers: how do social care agencies conceptualise their relationship with informal carers?', *Journal of Social Policy*, **18**(1), pp. 53–66.

Twigg, J. and Atkin, K. (1994). *Carers Perceived. Policy and Practice in Informal Care*. Buckingham: Open University Press.

Twigg, J., Atkin, K. and Perring, C. (1990). *Carers and Services: a Review of Research*. London: HMSO.

Ungerson, C. (1987). *Policy is Personal. Sex, Gender and Informal Care*. London: Tavistock.

Waerness, K. (1987). 'On the rationality of caring', in A. S. Sassoon (ed.), *Women and the State*. London: Hutchinson.

Wainwright, H. (1994). *Arguments for a New Left. Answering the Free Market Right*. Oxford: Blackwell.

Walker, A. (1987). 'Enlarging the caring capacity of the community: informal support networks and the welfare state', *International Journal of Health Services*, **17**(3), pp. 369–86.

Walker, A. (1994). *Half a Century of Promises*. London: Counsel and Care.

Walker, A. (1996). 'From acquiesence to dissent? A political sociology of population ageing in the UK, in V. Minichiello, N. Chappell, A. Walker and H. Kending (eds), *Sociology of Ageing*. International Sociological Association.

Walker, A., Walker, C. and Ryan, T. (1996). 'Older people with learning difficulties: a case of double jeopardy', *Ageing and Society*, **16**, pp. 125–50.

Walmsley, J. (1993). 'Contradictions in caring: reciprocity and interdependence', *Disability, Handicap and Society*, **8**(2), pp. 129–41.

Walsh, K. (1995). *Public Services and Market Mechanisms*. Basingstoke: Macmillan.

Wann, M. (1995). *Building Social Capital. Self-Help in a Twenty-first Century Welfare State*. London: Institute for Public Policy Research.

Warner, A. (1987). 'The quality of life for elderly people living in Birmingham's residential homes', *Social Services Research* (3), pp. 11–25.

Warren, L. (1990). ' "We're home helps because we care": the experience of home helps caring for elderly people', in P. Abbott and G. Payne (eds), *New Directions in the Sociology of Health*. London: The Falmer Press.

Welsh Office (1983). *All Wales Strategy for the Development of Services for Mentally Handicapped People*. Cardiff: Welsh Office.

Wenger, C. (1991). 'A network typology: from theory to practice', *Journal of Ageing Studies*, **5**(2), pp. 147–62.

West Midlands Mental Handicap Forum (1987). *Philosophy and Principles of a Local Comprehensive Service for People with a Mental Handicap*. Worcester: British Institute of Mental Handicap.

Whittaker, A., Gardner, S. and Kershaw, J. (1990). *Service Evaluation by People with Learning Difficulties*. London: The King's Fund Centre.

Williams, P. (1978). *Our Mutual Handicap*. London: The Campaign for Mentally Handicapped People.

Williams, P. and Schoultz, B. (1984). *We Can Speak for Ourselves*. Bloomington: Indiana University Press.

Williams, F. (1993). 'Women and community', in J. Bornat, C. Pereira, D. Pilgrim and F. Williams (eds), *Community Care: a Reader*. Basingstoke: Macmillan.

Williams, R. (1976). *Keywords*. London: Croom Helm.

Wilson, E. (1977). *Women and the Welfare State*. London: Tavistock.

Wistow, G. and Barnes, M. (1993). 'User involvement in community care: origins, purposes and applications', *Public Administration*, **71**(3), pp. 279–99.

Wistow, G and Barnes, M. (1995). 'Central Nottinghamshire, England: a case study of managed innovation in mental health', in R. Schulz and J. R. Greenley (eds), *Innovating in Community Mental Health. International Perspectives*. Westport, Connecticut: Praeger.

Wistow, G., Knapp, M., Hardy, B. and Allen, C. (1994). *Social Care in a Mixed Economy*. Buckingham: Open University Press.

Wolfensberger, W. (1972). *The Principle of Normalization in Human Services*. Toronto: National Institute on Mental Retardation.

Wolfensberger, W. (1983). 'Social role valorization: a proposed new term for the principle of normalization', *Mental Retardation*, **21**(6), pp. 234–9.

Wood, R. (1991). 'Care of disabled people', in G. Dalley (ed.), *Disability and Social Policy*. London: Policy Studies Institute.

Young, I. M. (1990). *Justice and the Politics of Difference*. Princeton, N.J.: Princeton University Press.

Young, I. M. (1995). 'City life and difference', in P. Kasinitz (ed.), *Metropolis: Centre and Symbol of Our Times*. Basingstoke: Macmillan.

Young, M. and Wilmott, P. (1962). *Family and Kinship in East London*. Harmondsworth: Penguin.

SUBJECT INDEX

NAME INDEX